Sex Roles, Population and Development in West Africa

Sex Roles, Population and Development in West Africa

Policy-Related Studies on Work and Demographic Issues

Edited by
Christine Oppong

Heinemann · PORTSMOUTH (N.H.)
James Currey · LONDON

James Currey Ltd
54b Thornhill Square, Islington
London N1 1BE

Heinemann Educational Books, Inc
70 Court Street, Portsmouth
New Hampshire 03801

A study prepared for the International Labour Office (ILO) within the framework
of the World Employment Programme with the financial support of the United
Nations Fund for Population Activities (UNFPA)

British Library Cataloguing in Publication Data

Sex Roles, population and development in
    West Africa: policy-related studies
    on work and demographic issues.
    1. Africa, West—Population
    I. Oppong, Christine
    304.6'0966   HB3665.5
    ISBN 0-85255-400-1

Library of Congress Cataloging-in-Publication Data

Sex roles, population and development in West Africa: policy-related studies on
work and demographic issues/edited by Christine Oppong.
    p. cm.
    Bibliography: p.
    Includes index.
    ISBN 0-435-08022-9
1. Africa, West—Population policy—Case studies. 2. Women—Employment—
Africa, West—Case studies. 3. Women in development—Africa, West—Case
studies. 4. Manpower policy—Africa, West—Case studies. 5. Fertility, Human—
Africa, West—Case studies. 6. Birth control—Africa, West—Case studies.
I. Oppong, Christine.
HB3665.5.A3S49 1988
304.6'0966—dc19   87-27386
                                                                        CIP

Typeset in 10/11pt Times by Colset Private Limited, Singapore
Printed and bound in Great Britain

Contents

Part I: Women's Work

Part II: Fertility, Parenthood and Development: Yoruba Experiences

Part III: Population Policies, Family Planning and Family Life Education: Ghanaian Lessons

Part IV: Government Plans and Development Policies

List of Tables

List of Figures

Preface

This volume has been produced within the scope of a widely ranging set of studies emanating from a programme on women's roles and demographic change carried out in the Employment and Development Department of the International Labour Office and financed by the United Nations Fund for Population Activities (UNFPA).

The technical co-operation and research activities of the International Labour Office in the field of Population, Family Welfare and Development Planning in Africa and other regions of the world followed upon the world-wide debate in the mid-sixties on population and development issues. The establishment of UNFPA helped to make ILO action in this field possible. The ILO's Population programme comprises policy-related research and technical co-operation on population and employment issues including human resources and development planning and population education and family welfare. Since 1977 there has been a regional team extending the headquarters' work in Africa.

The basic objectives of the African Population and Labour Policies programme are to contribute towards the evolution of comprehensive national development planning in the countries of Africa by integrating population and related human resources factors and issues into socio-economic planning and to encourage the acceptance of a broader and more comprehensive concept of labour welfare, of which family welfare and planning are an integral part.

The population of the continent as a whole and of West Africa in particular has been growing rapidly due to continuing high fertility and a lowering of mortality rates in several countries. This has created a situation of high youth dependency, with half or sometimes more than half the population dependent minors, which puts a great strain on attempts to provide adequate child health and educational facilities and appropriate vocational training and employment opportunities for the youth. Rural–urban migration continues to increase in face of the wide disparities in facilities and opportunities between rural and urban areas, thus underlining the pressing need for accelerated rural development and increased opportunities for urban employment.

Change is occurring at a rapid rate on all sides, political, economic and social, but in the context of the continuation of many ethnic institutions and traditions. Planning is hampered by the dearth of data, including basic census counts.

This volume takes up a number of issues regarding economic development and population growth and planning from the point of view of gender, examining among other issues the extent to which women's roles have been documented and considered and noting the potential effects of possible neglect of these roles on economic and population policy design. Empirical examples are taken from several countries which provide case studies relevant to the region.

The data used are of many kinds, including census statistics, household surveys, studies of individuals and groups, collected through focused interviewing and participant observation, and studies of historical and contemporary texts. The writers of the essays come from several disciplines including agricultural economics, demography, economics, engineering, linguistics, social anthropology and sociology. The readership for which this book is intended includes researchers, planners, policy-makers, and students of population and development issues. Indeed, it should be of interest to all those concerned with a better understanding and improved design of policies and programmes regarding women's roles in the world of work and to anyone in the field of population issues.

Several of the studies included here demonstrate that whatever decisions and plans are made at the national or community level it is at the level of the individual and the family that crucial decisions concerning production, fertility and mortality occur. Knowledge of how such decisions are made, and the nature of the pressures to innovate, as well as cultural and economic constraints are therefore necessary prerequisites for the design of successful population and development programmes.

Other volumes in the series of which this forms a part which focus on women's roles, particularly in the workplace, and demographic issues include Anker and Hein (ed.), *Sex inequalities in urban employment in the Third World* (1986) and Bodrova and Anker (ed.), *Working women in socialist countries: The fertility connection* (1985).

This work appears at a time when the attention of the world has been focused on the review and appraisal of the achievements of the United Nations Decade for Women: Equality, Development and Peace. The Report of the World Conference held in Nairobi, Kenya, in July 1985 and the Forward Looking Strategies for the Advancement of Women stressed that the relationships between development and the advancement of women under specific socio-cultural conditions should be studied locally, to permit the effective formation of policies, programmes and projects designed for stable and equitable growth. The report also stated that the findings of such studies should be used to develop social awareness of the need for effective participation of women in development and to create realistic images of women in society.

The general approach and the specific recommendations of the Forward Looking Strategies were reported to the International Organisations Committee of the Governing Body of the International Labour Office during its 232nd Session held in February/March 1986. In this report it was noted that the interest and concern generated by the Strategies—particularly in so far as they affect employment-related issues—are bound to have an impact on ILO activities in the years to come. At the same time the objectives and policy measures are already reflected in the Resolution on Equal Opportunities and Equal Treatment for Men and Women in Employment adopted at the 71st Session of the International Labour Conference in 1985.

Kailas C. Doctor

Editor's Acknowledgement

The successful completion of this volume owes much to many people, including the patient contributors whose essays underwent several transformations over time; the colleagues and others who read and commented on various versions of chapters, including Aderanti Adepoju, Zubeida Ahmad, Richard Anker, Eddie Lee, Franklyn Lisk, Gerry Rodgers and René Wéry and last but not least Caryle Farley who gallantly processed successive editions.

Christine Oppong

Contributors

Laurence A. Adeokun is senior lecturer in the Department of Demography and Social Statistics, University of Ife, Nigeria. He has published widely on population issues in Nigeria.

Felix Odei Akuffo undertook research on the topic covered here under the auspices of the Institute of African Studies, University of Ghana, Legon. He subsequently became a university administrator.

Wolf Bleek, an anthropologist lecturing at the University of Amsterdam, has published several books and many papers on marriage and family life in southern Ghana. He has also more recently carried out field work in Cameroon on medical issues.

Florence Abena Dolphyne is associate professor at the University of Ghana, Legon, and Head of the Department of Linguistics. She was formerly also Chairperson of the Ghana National Council on Women and Development.

Catherine di Domenico is a senior lecturer in the Department of Sociology of the University of Ibadan, Nigeria who has been involved in several studies of working women and their problems.

Ita I. Ekanem, formerly a senior lecturer at the Department of Demography and Social Statistics, University of Ife, is a population affairs officer in the United Nations Economic Commission for Africa, Addis Ababa. A demographer by profession, he has written extensively on the demography of West Africa.

Eleanor R. Fapohunda is an economist formerly lecturing at the University of Lagos and has published several papers on aspects of the Nigerian economy and women's roles.

Ghazi M. Farooq is a senior population economist in the Employment Planning and Population Branch of the Employment and Development Department, ILO, Geneva. He has written and edited several papers and volumes on the economics of fertility, labour policy, population and development and related topics.

Patricia Ladipo lectures in the Department of Agricultural Extension of the University of Ife and has been involved in a range of practically oriented field projects and publications.

Franklyn Lisk, formerly a senior economist in the Employment Planning and Population Branch of the Employment and Development Department of the ILO and now Regional Adviser in the Caribbean, has written extensively on aspects of economic development in Africa.

Christine Oppong edited the volume. She is a senior anthropologist in the Employment Planning and Population Branch, Employment and Development Department, ILO, Geneva. She has written and edited several volumes and essays on aspects of socio-demographic change in West Africa.

Oyetunji Orubuloye is a demographer at the Obafemi Awolowo University, Ondo State, Nigeria. He has published a number of papers based upon his field research among the Yoruba.

Renée Pittin is a sociologist who formerly lectured in the Sociology Department of Ahmadu Bello University, Zaria, Nigeria. She has done extensive research in northern Nigeria and published a number of papers.

Yvette Stevens is an engineer who was employed as a Village Technology Expert at the International Labour Office and is now working with the UN High Commission for Refugees. She is internationally known for her work in the areas of technological change and rural women, energy, and new technologies and income-generating activities.

René Wéry is a senior economist in the Employment Planning and Population Branch of the Employment and Development Department, ILO, Geneva. He has written widely on economic-demographic issues including pioneering and innovative modelling work.

Introduction

This volume uses West African data from varied cultural contexts in four countries, Ghana, Mali, Nigeria and Sierra Leone, to address a number of recurrent research and policy issues relating to sexual division of labour, demographic change and economic development which are of immediate and worldwide concern. Indeed their importance and current salience was continually stressed during the statements made and discussions held at both the International Conference on Population in Mexico City in August 1984 and the World Conference to Review and Appraise the Achievements of the United Nations Decade for Women: Equality, Development and Peace in Nairobi in July 1985.

Mexico: Population and Development

The Mexico City Declaration emphasised that population issues have been increasingly recognised as a fundamental element in development planning and that to be realistic development policies, plans and programmes must reflect the inextricable links between population, resources, environment and development.[1] Furthermore, the Declaration stressed that improving the status of women and enhancing their roles is an important goal in itself and will also influence family life and size in a positive way. It clearly stated that institutional, economic and cultural barriers should be removed and effective action taken to assist women to attain full equality with men in the social, political and economic life of their communities. In order to achieve this aim the Declaration noted that it will be necessary for men and women to share jointly responsibilities in areas such as family life, child-care and family planning. It called upon governments to formulate and implement policies to enhance the status and roles of women.

Nairobi: Women and Development

As the Plenary discussions in Nairobi indicated, an important achievement of the past decade has been the growing realisation by national and international bodies concerned with development planning and large-scale resource allocation, of the importance of women's activities in agricultural development and small-scale production in countries of the developing world. The extent of their work burdens, shouldered simultaneously with the often continuous processes of child-bearing, breastfeeding and child-care was in fact already well known at the local level and within their own regions and was often well documented in anthropological monographs for several decades. Yet national labour force surveys and consequently economists' models, planners' designs and agricultural programmes based upon these figures had continually ignored women's contributions. Such neglect of relevant knowledge not only harmed women, often serving to marginalise their activities, but also hindered seriously the growth of agricultural output in many countries. In some cases large-scale waste of resources ensued and in Africa serious aggravation of the agricultural crisis. Fortunately, the focus of attention given to women by the UN Decade for Women as well as the new findings of the numerous detailed studies of domestic and agricultural production carried out during the decade[2] helped information about their productive activities to become common knowledge.

This raising of awareness of the crucial part played by women in the production, processing and distribution of goods, which in some cases led to their subsequent consideration in economic plans, was a necessary precondition for the achievement of the decade's development goals. This raising of consciousness has put women and their concerns on many national and international agenda: their often unrecorded work, their frequently unpaid production and services, and consequently their needs for education, training and resources to carry out their manifold tasks.

One of the most outstanding achievements of the decade has been the widespread reform of the laws, including those affecting employment opportunities and conditions of work including equal pay acts and maternity leave provisions, as well as the ratifications of International Labour Conventions including Convention 111 on Discrimination in Employment and the growing number of countries ratifying the UN Convention on the Elimination of All Forms of Discrimination Against Women (see table 1). However, new laws do not change attitudes of prejudice and discrimination nor deliver justice and in many cases a wide gap exists between legal achievements and the actual position of women. Maternity leave provisions and protective legislation may not necessarily be respected by employers. Indeed most women work in the informal legally unprotected sector.

An important outcome of the Decade has been the setting up of various national and international machineries to promote equality and the participation of women in employment and development. A number of these have been set up in West Africa (see Appendix I). Such institutions have played critical parts in creating awareness, collecting, analysing and disseminating information, designing and implementing programmes and serving as catalysts among government departments to spur development of appropriate policies and projects.

The forces perpetuating discrimination against women, however, and supporting the continuity of unequal patterns of sexual division of labour and responsibilities, as well as introducing new forms of inequalities, are increasingly realised as being complex and pervasive, making it quite clear that there are no simple or easy solutions. Ancient cultural values and social practices as well as their greater burden of household work, subsistence labour and child-bearing and rearing were noted to maintain and perpetuate women's unequal and subordinate position in social systems. Even in those countries which have made revolutionary efforts to promote equality, women still do not share equally in power and decision-making at all levels and sexual segregation of some kind in labour forces is still apparent.

Another obstacle to progress highlighted in Nairobi was the persistent lack of information about women's economic activities and the pervasiveness of sexist stereotypes. For in spite of the massive focus on women during the decade, the many studies carried out and the attempts to make women visible in labour processes, the lack of information about women is still acutely felt in many countries, including even in some instances the lack of breakdown of statistics by sex. At the same time studies of stereotyping in media messages and official educational texts have brought to light the prejudices and false ideas about women and the roles they play.

Table 1   Ratification of selected International Labour Conventions affecting children and women workers by West African states and of the United Nations Convention on the Elimination of All Forms of Discrimination Against Women

Country	International Labour Convention No.							United Nations Convention on Discrimination
	3	100	102	111	118	122	138	
Benin		x		x				
Burkina Faso	x	x		x				
Cameroon	x	x				x		
Cape Verde		x		x				x
Gabon	x	x		x				
The Gambia								
Ghana		x		x				
Guinea	x	x		x	x	x		
Guinea-Bissau		x		x				
Côte d'Ivoire	x	x		x				
Liberia		x		x				x
Mali	x			x				
Mauritania	x		x	x	x	x		
Niger		x		x			x	
Nigeria		x						
Senegal		x	x	x		x		
Sierra Leone		x		x				
Togo		x		x			x	x

Notes No. 3:   Maternity Protection;
No. 100:   Equal Remuneration;
No. 102:   Social Security (Minimum Standards);
No. 111:   Discrimination (Employment and Occupation);
No. 118:   Equality of Treatment (Social Security);
No. 122:   Employment Policy;
No. 138:   Minimum Age.

This 'invisibility' of women and reliance on false stereotypes of female roles and femininity has resulted in widespread lack of attention to women in macro-planning exercises in the past. African delegates in Nairobi noted the widespread failure of planning agencies to incorporate women on an equal basis with men into macro-economic planning both as decision-makers and as foci of concern and the fact that women are frequently treated as peripheral and marginal.

The fact that illiteracy and lack of training are still obstacles to women's advancement was noted and that the numbers of illiterate women continue to grow and the gaps in literacy between women and men in Africa continue to widen, in spite of the fact that in many countries the proportion and numbers of literate women has increased.

Moreover, a number of countries noted that they had a high drop-out rate of girls in the higher levels of education often because of unplanned births. The problems of teenage girls' education and vocational training and employment opportunities being affected by unplanned pregnancies and early marriage was noted as a serious issue by several African countries, including Central African

Republic, Congo, Gabon, Sierra Leone and Togo. In view of the pervasive and growing nature of such problems, the need for training in responsible parenthood and sexual values was stressed in addition to career training, since without the former the latter may be put in jeopardy.

Voluntary access to family planning and dissemination of information and the capacity to make reproductive decisions was noted by many countries, including Burundi and Kenya, to be a critical service to women. The problem of repeated pregnancies in quick succession was observed and the importance of making available information on child spacing to protect mothers' health and ensure the well-being of children (Senegal and Central African Republic, etc.). Connections between too rapid population growth and unemployment were made and between women's higher education, employment, later marriage and lower fertility. The need was stressed for women to be able to plan their sexual and reproductive lives so as to be able to benefit from available vocational training and employment opportunities (e.g. Gabon). The problem of maternal/occupational role conflicts and the need to alleviate them if women are to be treated equally with men in labour markets was also emphasised.

There was in Nairobi a message with potentially pervasive impact for the organisation of population and development activities in the coming decade. It was stressed time after time that women and their work can no longer be considered as marginal, special or minority group issues. It has now become common knowledge, as the World Bank spokesperson admitted, that women's contributions to national economies are not of minor significance but central to economic as well as social development; that women workers, whether their activities are yet recorded in official labour statistics or not, must be taken into account in all national planning exercises; that frequently, though formerly ignored, they form the backbone of agricultural labour forces; that often their unpaid and undervalued work in house, community and farm is essential for the subsistence and well-being of their dependent families; that they alone are increasingly responsible for the maintenance and well-being of a large proportion of the world's children; that they often work far longer hours per day than their men folk, as well as carrying, bearing, nursing and caring for their children and processing the food consumed and finding the necessary fuel.

The message was that national governments and international agencies can continue to ignore these facts at their peril. The economic crises of many countries today are realised as having been aggravated by the neglect in development plans of major producers of food and services—women. Marginal welfare-oriented special programmes are not enough.

Global Issues

The various essays in this volume continue these global debates and underscore the fact that due consideration must be given to the diverse and changing roles of women and men, and equality of opportunities and treatment must be promoted if population policies and plans for national development and individual family well-being are to succeed. They also stress the need for more conceptually rigorous documentation and understanding of social processes on which to base such policies and plans.

A variety of people from different walks of life form the subject of the essays. They include pregnant teenagers who drop out of school without usable skills;

female farmers who have inadequate access to extension services, etc.; 'house-wives' whose work in house, farm and market is not recognised in censuses, surveys and development plans; women perceived as 'wives' whose independent and auto-nomous needs for training, housing, credit, contraceptives, co-operative formation, new technologies, etc., are often overlooked, and, at the same time, men whose important activities as parents and househusbands have often been ignored.

Discussion of women's activities, expectations and needs draws attention to the practical issues of the provision of required vocational training, family life and family planning education programme facilities, agricultural extension and credit, urban crèches, etc. It also draws attention to the need to document more carefully women's as well as men's work inside and outside the home. At the same time it emphasises a number of conceptual issues which require confrontation by researchers, census takers and survey-makers, such as the diverse and changing nature of marriage, parenthood and the domestic group in different societies, and the types of activities and expectations attached to the roles of spouse, parent, kin and household member (Oppong (ed.), 1983a).

The Region

The total population of the wider geographical region within the context of which these essays are set is 155 million or more, of whom half or slightly more are female and of whom more than half are Nigerians. Culturally, climatically, economically and politically the region is diverse, comprising 18 states. In demographic terms there is less diversity, the whole region being characterised by high fertility and high mortality.

During the decade of the 1970s, censuses were carried out in most countries of West Africa. Relatively low population density (19 persons per square kilometre), high crude birth rates (ranging from 28 to 51 per thousand) and high death rates (ranging from 9 to 28) are all characteristic of the region. The fertility profile is described as monotonically high, with an average crude birth rate of 49 making it the world's most prolific area. Nine of the 18 countries, including Nigeria, Ghana and Mali, have total fertility rates of 6.7 or higher. Annual natural increase averages about 3.1 per cent, leading to a doubling of the population in 23 years. Recent population projections predict that by the year 2000 the population will be 266 million, over 40 per cent of which will be under 15 years. By the year 2020, it is predicted that the population will be 455 million.

Nigeria and Ghana are among the most densely populated areas, with the highest growth rates (3.3 and 3.2 per cent respectively), and our case studies come mainly from these rapidly expanding populations.

The crude death rate for the region is 18 and the infant mortality rate 139, the highest for any region, and life expectancy at birth is only 47 years. A review of existing data on mortality and life expectancy (Ware, 1983) indicates that mortality is generally a little higher for males than females among young and old alike. In Muslim northern Nigeria, however, men appear to have the advantage in longevity and data from Liberia, and Burkina Faso also indicate that men live longer. For women in the reproductive years, 20–30 per cent of all deaths are associated with pregnancy or childbirth.

Educational opportunities in West African countries have been very limited until recently, and for girls they still continue to be more limited than for boys, the percentage of literates who are female ranging from 11 per cent in Liberia to 39 per cent in Ghana. In all countries the illiterate form the majority. Ghana is the only country where the literate population approaches a majority, and the only country where more than a third of the literates are women and girls. The past decade saw an increase in attempts to provide universal primary education, notably in Nigeria.

Not only are girls kept at home to act as baby-minders and home helps and to work in market and farm, they are also kept away from school for fear that they will become pregnant, a serious problem as we shall see in Chapter 9, for unknown numbers of girls drop out of schools annually for this reason. In the higher levels of the educational system there are fewer girls. At the same time there are significant differences in the subjects studied by girls and boys—in particular, girls are scarcely found in agricultural courses, yet women in many areas constitute an important part of the farming population.

The whole area is predominantly rural with only an estimated 22 per cent of the population in urban areas. For the past 20 years, however, most of the capital cities of the region have been growing at a rate of 10 per cent or more per year, which has lead to problems of urban planning. And now four countries—Ghana, Côte d'Ivoire, Liberia and Senegal—have more than a third of their populace living in urban areas.

Agriculture remains the main source of livelihood, employment and production for export, the percentage of the labour force in agriculture varying from 56 per cent in Ghana to 96 per cent in Niger. In each country a greater proportion of the female labour force is involved in agriculture than of the male labour force, leading to Boserup's (1970, p. 17) classification of the region as a female farming system, even though it is estimated that unpaid female workers on family farms are under-enumerated in censuses and surveys. Indeed, in the continent as a whole, three-quarters of the female labour force is recorded as being involved in agriculture, constituting over a third of the total recorded agricultural labour force. In 1970, in fact, in almost half of the countries of the continent, nine out of ten women considered economically active were working in agriculture.

Analyses of existing labour force statistics for African countries have demonstrated diversity in the recorded levels of female labour force participation by country and age group; they also indicate changes which have taken place over the past few decades and which are projected for the future (ILO, 1978b). In many countries, trade is the second most important area of employment after agriculture. In Ghana women are more heavily concentrated in this sector than in any other West African country outnumbering men by two to one.

Service and industrial sector employment account for relatively few workers. The latter includes both the small category of modern factory workers and the traditional sector of mainly self-employed or unpaid family workers as well as people working in small enterprises. The latter two categories, designated 'the informal sector', provide many employment opportunities because they are labour intensive (e.g. see Joshi et al., 1976 on the Côte d'Ivoire). Women are densely concentrated in this sector, less than 5 per cent being in wage employment. Indeed, in several countries a large proportion of women are enumerated as family workers (e.g. Liberia 75 per cent in 1962; Sierra Leone 82 per cent in 1963). The majority of men are recorded as being employers or workers on their own account; less than 30 per cent are in wage employment and a minority are family workers.

While men are generally recorded as being active in the labour force from 20 to 65 and over, women are recorded as being overall less economically active than men, while different countries show variations in women's work experience over the life cycle. In Burkina Faso and Mali the peak of participation occurs at 45–54; in Ghana and Nigeria it occurs at a later age. In Niger and Mauritania only a small minority of women are recorded as working in each age group.

Overall attempts to portray the work of the population are beset with a number of basic problems, however. Such statistical data as do exist for the region are limited and fragmented and often impossible to compare because of variations in definitions or different survey procedures (Fapohunda, 1983). In particular, the figures for women's labour force participation are affected by census or sample survey enumeration procedures, since women's production and trade within the home or even outside it may not be counted. Few, if any, women do nothing to support themselves and their dependent children. As women tend to have lower educational levels than men, when in wage employment they are generally in lower status, lower-income occupations in the modern sector. Patterns of occupation vary widely in different countries and even within single countries the labour force participation rates may vary widely in different urban centres, as for instance in Ibadan, Lagos, Zaria, Onitsha and Kaduna in Nigeria, as Fapohunda (1983) has described. The lack of adequate labour force data remains a widespread and serious problem.

Data Bases and Development Planning

Several of these essays demonstrate ways in which planners, policy-makers and researchers often make assumptions regarding occupational and familial roles which are culture bound and so inappropriate to the African context. These misconceptions also compound the problems of inadequate documentation and thus contribute to the weakness of the data bases upon which development plans and programmes are based. Part I is therefore concerned with data bases for employment and manpower planning and the extent to which women may be invisible in available statistics.

Many writers in the past on the position of African women in development processes have called attention to the serious failure to take into account women's productive contributions to the economy, and consequent omission in the design of development plans and policies. Thus, the study of plans propagated by planners trained in Euro-American traditions in the developing world has shown pervasive misconceptions about women's existing activities and responsibilities, resources and goals. Rogers (1979) discussed at length, with telling examples, how Western male ideology relating to gender distinctions, the division of labour, and perceptions of other cultures has been used to support myths about the 'natural' place of women in the home. Such misperceptions, and the kinds of data collected to support them have formed a basis for development plans, which in some cases have had discriminatory effects upon women with a consequent detrimental impact upon their subsistence farming and other activities. The need for critical examination of the concepts of work and household and their implications for research, analysis and development planning has thus been stressed (Nelson, 1981, p. 2).

Beneriá (1981) has indicated how the shortcomings of available data for the purpose of evaluating women's work are rooted in the conceptual categories which are used. Tracing the development for international comparisons of the concept 'labour force', she notes the link between the concept and the national product, which includes essentially only goods and services exchanged in the market. But non-market production remains very prevalent in the developing world. The issue of recording thus remains most problematic in areas where the market has not penetrated widely.

Many efforts to deal with the problems have been made, and are still being made, by international and national agencies which collect and analyse labour force statistics, and this is leading to increased sophistication in data collection and labour force estimations. The underestimation of active workers in the so-called informal sector, especially female workers, remains a significant stumbling block, however. Benería has spelt out the major problems such as the definition of an unpaid family worker, a critical issue being the separation of 'unpaid family work' and 'domestic work'. These issues are taken up in Part I of this volume.

Fertility and Development

In Part II the theme is fertility and development. The case studies are taken from the large Yoruba populace of western Nigeria and the clear underlying message is that the impacts upon fertility of large-scale developments affecting employment, such as urban growth, industrialisation, the introduction of schools can only be understood if parenthood and its context of kinship and marriage are taken into account.

In spite of the vast amount of research on the determinants of fertility carried out in the past decade, still comparatively little is known about it or how to change it (United Nations, 1981, p. 76). Moreover, most of the existing research has been based mainly upon statistical correlations and multiple regression techniques. Using these methods many separate variables have been associated with high or low fertility levels, including education, women's labour force participation, urban or rural residence, use of contraception, etc.

In the case of education it is recognised that neither the extent of the association between education and fertility, nor the conditions under which it has an effect, nor the way in which it exerts effects, are clearly known. Indeed, there are cases as here among the Yoruba, in which education to primary level is seen to have a positive effect on fertility in comparison with no education. Moreover, the fact that education is inversely associated with fertility may have little relevance to practical policies (United Nations, 1981). It has thus been stressed that there is a need to understand the mechanisms through which education may have an effect upon fertility directly, indirectly, and in an interactive fashion and particularly the way in which it may form part of a change in the direction of flows of benefits between the generations (Caldwell, 1980).

Increasing disenchantment with the examination of direct links between survey data on education levels and fertility outcomes, in terms of understanding the interaction between the two, has been paralleled by an increasing emphasis upon and interest in the impact of education upon changing relationships between kin, parents and children, husbands and wives, as well as upon personal aspirations, values and concepts of self (see Oppong and Abu, 1984). Among the multiple potential effects on family relationships reckoned to be important are the reduction in economic benefits and status accruing to parents from children's labour and income and the increase to parents in the costs of child-care. For some, children are changing into protected dependants rather than responsible, productive supports to their elders. In addition, the relative equality of husband and wife, and the division of labour and resources and communication patterns between them, are noted to be significant, as are the increased potential for individual autonomy and control and the increase in opportunities for innovative behaviour (Oppong, 1983a). There are several compelling sets of evidence from Ghana which point to the necessity to consider carefully the nature of parental roles, the degree of overlap between biological and social parenthood, the extent to which responsibilities may be avoided or transferred, the extent to which benefits are shared—all of which are likely to have a profound impact upon decision-making regarding birth control, an issue to which we move in Part III (see, for example, Oppong and Bleek, 1982; Oppong, 1985a).

In the case of women's work the same kinds of positive and negative effects have been observed in statistical analyses. Several considerations need to be taken into account, including the degree of separation of work from home, the availability of household members to share household work and child-care, the extent to which children can accompany their mothers to their workplaces, and indeed assist them and the extent to which children may care for each other (Standing, 1983). At the level of the individual parent, many hypotheses focus upon the potential effects of relative costs and benefits of having children, role strain and the opportunity costs or role conflicts (Oppong, 1983a).

It is clear from many West African accounts that fertility patterns, and how they are or are not changing, can never be understood without reference to the contexts of parenthood, kinship and marriage within which they occur. And one point is central: it is parenthood not marriage that is the cornerstone of the family in West Africa. And West African family relations cannot be understood in isolation from the total social systems in which they are situated and without consideration of the values that prevail in the society at large (Fortes, 1978, pp. 17–18).

Population Policies and Programmes

Part III examines aspects of population policies, family planning programmes and family life education in the region. Recent UNFPA Population Needs Assessment missions to West African countries have often emphasised the pressing need for improved demographic data collection and analysis as a prerequisite for planning of any kind, including employment, training, education and health (e.g. UNFPA, 1984, p. 2). Some countries of the region have been found to suffer from an almost total lack of demographic information on which to base planning. In such cases national planning has to take place in a vacuum of ignorance.

An increase in knowledge may spur on the process of policy formulation. For example in Senegal official concern about population growth developed only after the 1976 census had shown that it was much more rapid than expected, and this concern was expressed in the Fifth Development Plan. There, as in many other countries, however, the basic obstacle to the formulation of a population policy is the lack of evidence on demographic trends and on the relationship between these and development factors. For many governments the first and overriding consideration in population policy is the lowering of levels of mortality and morbidity, especially infant mortality. Only six country governments officially perceive their fertility levels as too high. These are Cameroon, The Gambia, Ghana, Liberia, Senegal and Sierra Leone. Only two governments, those of The Gambia and Ghana, actually have policies to reduce fertility.

A fully developed population policy—involving legislative measures, administrative programmes and other governmental action, and intended to alter or modify population trends in the interest of national well-being—is found in only one country of the region, Ghana.[3] A comprehensive policy statement was published by Ghana in 1969. Central to it was the establishment of the Ghana National Family Planning Programme in 1970, the objectives of which included the reduction of the population growth rate. An educational campaign was also set up with emphasis on mass media and interpersonal communication. The major focus of the programme was married women.

The government of Sierra Leone, conscious that the rapid expansion of its population might be a constraint on economic and social development, referred in its Five Year Plan for 1974–79 to some of the population-related problems to be confronted, including unemployment, increasing school age populations, migration and pressure on health and housing (UNFPA, 1984). Evidence of official concern was also provided by the establishment in 1978 of a population section in the Ministry of Development and Economic Planning and the creation in 1982 of the National Population Commission to co-ordinate all population related planning and policy making.

In 1985 a high-level workshop was held in Nigeria on a plan of action for a population and development programme. This workshop reviewed the Nigerian population data and projections and their potential effects on health and welfare and the pursuit of economic and social goals. The recommendations of the workshop were submitted to government for approval and action. (See also pp. 72–6.)

Family planning programmes are reported to be a common feature of almost all West African countries, whether or not they have a population policy. The relative failure of most of these programmes has been attributed to poor communications as well as insufficient funding, restrictive laws and illiteracy and the fact that the large family size ideals still prevail (Arowolo, 1982). Table 2 shows that ten countries in the region are members of the International Planned Parenthood Federation (IPPF) or other family planning association. As far as contraceptive services are concerned, six governments give active support, five give some support, four are interested, two give no support and in Gabon there are restrictions on availability.

In French-speaking countries the law on contraception has remained the French law of July 1920 under which the publicity and sale of contraceptives are not allowed, while induced abortion is forbidden except to save the mother's life. In some places this has given rise to a discrepancy between law and practice and the growth of a black market in contraceptives. In many cases obtaining contraceptives is mainly a financial question as they are available in private pharmacies at a price. Mali is one French-speaking country which has liberalised its laws on contraceptives and permits family planning services at several clinics.

English-speaking nations in Africa seem to have a more tolerant attitude towards contraceptive practice. In a number of English-speaking countries there is in fact considerable government support. In 1979 The Gambia adopted a policy approving the provision of family planning services in the context of mother and child health services (MCH), and Chapter 18 of the Five Year Plan then in existence already included the statement that MCH should include planned parenthood. In Liberia the government has supported MCH and family planning programmes, and such services have been expanded since 1973. The Nigerian government also expects to develop a nationwide family planning programme.

Table 2 Fertility and family planning

Country	Population in millions (mid-1984)	Annual population growth rate (per cent) 1980-85	Number of children per woman (1980-85)	Government perception of fertility level*	Government policy to influence fertility**	Government position on contraceptive services***	Availability of contraceptive services and supplies
Benin	4.0	3.1	6.7	a	g	i	Some services through government MCH centres and FPA
Burkina Faso	7.9	2.7	6.5	a	d	k	Contraceptives through FPA and pharmacies
Cameroon	9.3	2.5	5.7	b	g	h	Contraceptives at a government clinic, some mission hospitals and pharmacies
Cape Verde	0.3	1.6	2.6	a	g	h	FP to be developed as part of MCH
Gabon	0.6	1.5	4.7	c	f	k	Some contraceptives at pharmacies
The Gambia	0.7	2.6	6.4	b	e	j	Through government health services and FPA
Ghana	13.3	3.3	6.7	a	e	j	Through government programme, FPA and other organisations
Guinea	5.6	2.7	6.2	c	f	h	Plans to introduce FP within MCH
Guinea-Bissau	0.6	1.8	5.4	a	g	h	Plans for a pilot MCH/FP programme
Côte d'Ivoire	9.1	3.2	6.7	a	g	k	At private clinics and pharmacies
Liberia	2.3	3.6	6.9	b	g	j	Through government programme; some FPA services through government clinics

Table 2   Continued

Country	Population in millions (mid-1984)	Annual population growth rate (per cent) 1980–85	Number of children per woman (1980–85)	Government perception of fertility level*	Government policy to influence fertility**	Government position on contraceptive services***	Availability of contraceptive services and supplies
Mali	7.8	2.8	6.7	a	d	j	FP being integrated with MCH; some government and FPA services
Mauritania	1.8	2.9	6.9	a	d	k	Some contraceptives at pharmacies
Niger	6.0	3.0	7.1	a	d	h	No services
Nigeria	93.0	3.4	6.9	a	g	j	FP being integrated in health services; some services through government, FPA and other organisations
Senegal	6.3	2.7	6.5	b	e	j	FP being integrated with MCH; some government services
Sierra Leone	3.9	2.8	6.1	b	g	i	Pilot MCH/FP clinics; some FPA services with government support
Togo	3.0	3.1	6.5	a	d	i	FP being integrated with MCH; some government and FPA services

* a — acceptable; b — too high; c — too low.
** d — to maintain; e — to reduce; f — to raise; g — no intervention.
*** h — interest; i — some support; j — active support; k — no support.

Source IPPF, People, 1984.

However, concern for infant mortality is an important hindrance to parents' and policy-makers' acceptance either of smaller family size norms or of the use of contraception. For example, Ketkar (1979–80), using household survey data from Sierra Leone, linked child mortality rates to fertility rates in different communities, and argued that reduction in child mortality is a sound method of reducing fertility.

Indeed, using macro-global evidence, the level of infant mortality has been demonstrated to be the most important predictor of contraceptive policy in the developing world. On the other hand there is compelling evidence of widespread unmet need for modern birth control measures. One index is the prevalence of abortion. A survey has shown that African gynaecologists are in agreement that complications from abortions are one of the most frequent causes of hospitalisation among women of reproductive age (Corvalen, 1978). In some countries this phenomenon is noted to be particularly common among unmarried students. Another index is the growing problem in some West African cities of abandoned children. The purpose of much contraceptive activity is not of course to limit family size within marriage, but rather to avoid extramarital births or to space births within marriage.

The Conference of African Parliamentarians on Population and Development in 1981 devoted a considerable amount of its time to the question of population education, which in Africa has usually emphasised cultural diversity, education for development, environmental issues, and family life education for girls (UNESCO, 1971). During the past decade a number of national population education programmes were started in schools in the African region. An important aspect of such educational programmes is that when they include family life and sex education they can introduce and encourage concepts of responsible parenthood and/or smaller family values to both males and females, before reproductive activities have in fact begun, rather than concentrating upon married women, who may already have borne more children than they can readily cope with. Such education for adolescents is particularly important in countries in which half of the population comprises children and youth and a large proportion of these are in formal education and training systems. Indeed, the latter provide an ideal setting for such educational programmes. Again, as is frequently remarked and demonstrated, the massive urban migrations of recent years have led to a diminution of the authority and control of parents, kin and community. There is consequently an increasing potential and need for influence by the schools and mass media.

In Sierra Leone a national programme was started in 1977, administered by the Institute of Education of the University of Sierra Leone. The content of this programme emphasises population trends and the effects of these and is incorporated into social studies curricula for grades 8–10. Teachers are trained in summer workshops. In Ghana a programme began to be developed in 1972, with the Ghana Home Science Association and the Ministry of Education. Here the emphasis was on family planning and family life education which was incorporated into home economics in several schools. Family planning concepts were also incorporated into the home economics curriculum for teacher training.[4]

Some women's bureaux in the region are active in the field of population education and are currently seeking assistance in this field. The National Union of Malian women has held seminars on family health and sex education and organised mass communication campaigns to educate women about family planning, child spacing and maternal and child health. The Union has also often shown concern about the growing incidence of abortion which is suspected to be occurring, and the poor health of mothers and children as a result of repeated births. Classes on family health and sex education have accordingly been organised at women's centres (UNFPA, 1978b). Ghana took the step of carrying out a survey in schools and colleges, including both students and teachers, to provide basic information for the design of family life education curricula in the seventies. In Nigeria systematic population education outside the formal education system was formerly only given by the Planned Parenthood Federation of Nigeria, which was a private organisation with severely limited scope. Such education was given to women during ante- and postnatal medical treatment (UNFPA, 1980, p. 99). Recently an agreement has been entered with UNESCO for large-scale population activities in educational establishments and the Nigerian Educational Research Council has been involved in the design of suitable curricula.

One of the aspects of reproduction that is critical for women's educational and employment status, as well as for their ultimate fertility levels, is the age at which they become mothers. Several governments in the region have recently expressed grave concern about the numbers of teenage pregnancies occurring and their effects both upon health and upon women's education and training opportunities (see UNFPA, 1978b regarding Mali and the Sierra Leone mission report, UNFPA, 1984, p. 3). In Togo in particular the government has recently taken severe legislative steps to ensure that anyone who makes a student pregnant and thus causes her studies to be interrupted, will be punished. Family planning policy-makers, health personnel and service providers in both developed and developing countries are seriously considering what is to be done about this problem.[5]

In the developing world much adolescent pregnancy occurs within marriage but at the same time the disruption of traditional family systems through rural–urban migration may be associated with an increasing number of illegitimate early births (Darabi et al., 1979). Fertility rates for girls aged 15–19 reach over 200 per thousand in twelve countries of the region and in all 15 or more per cent of births occur to mothers in their teens (see table 3).

Studies in several African countries have demonstrated that early pregnancy is closely associated with high rates of abortion, stillbirth, infant and maternal mortality and morbidity and high levels of school drop-out rates among teenage girls (Gyepi-Garbrah, 1985).

Adolescent pregnancy outside marriage is an increasingly serious problem in many countries and urbanisation is an important concomitant of adolescent vulnerability.[6] Yet teenagers are seldom included in programme planning, and there is a lack of relevant data or current research.[7]

In Nigeria over a decade ago pregnancy and abortion among unmarried school-girls were already noted to be increasing (see Akingba, 1974), and to a catastrophic extent in urban areas (Pauls, 1974). More recently a study of schoolgirls with pregnancy-related problems showed that 'lack of experience in family life and knowledge about contraceptive methods, coupled with poor parental control, are the major factors that put the young adolescent at risk of unwanted pregnancy' (Oronsaye et al., 1982).

An IPPF survey has estimated that in developing countries less than half of those aged 15–19 have access to family planning information and services, but in many developing countries there has been no recognition that adolescents need access to family planning services (Chui and UNFPA, 1978). In the seventies WHO and

Table 3   Teenage mothers in West Africa

Country	Fertility rate among girls 15–19	Percentage contribution of girls 15–19 to total fertility rate	Secondary school enrolment female/male
Benin	206.3	15.4	10/26
Burkina Faso	218.3	16.8	2/4
Cameroon	184.6	16.3	13/25
Cape Verde	78.6	14.9	
Gabon	145.9	15.6	
The Gambia	214.8	16.8	8/19
Ghana	206.3	15.4	27/44
Guinea	198.1	16.0	9/23
Guinea-Bissau	175.4	16.3	7/33
Côte d'Ivoire	206.3	15.4	9/25
Liberia	207.6	15.0	11/29
Mali	206.1	15.4	5/13
Mauritania	231.9	16.8	4/16
Niger	238.7	16.8	
Nigeria	212.6	15.4	
Senegal	218.3	16.8	8/16
Sierra Leone	199.9	16.3	7/16
Togo	204.2	15.7	16/46

Source IPPF, *Youth in Society*, 1985, People Wallchart.

IPPF initiated a cross-cultural survey on family life education and services for adolescents. Thirteen country studies were undertaken, including two in West Africa—in Ghana and Senegal. These studies showed among other things that the demographic effects include large family size and short intervals between generations as well as higher infant and maternal mortality. A number of studies pointed to the effects of increasingly early ages at menarche, a trend likely to continue and become more widespread.

Children born out of wedlock whose fathers take no responsibility for them are also more likely to have deprived childhoods and low levels of education and training and some studies suggest that they themselves are more likely to repeat the cycle of early pregnancy.

Another important aspect, which some of the health specialists and family planning educationists fail to emphasise sufficiently, is the effect on the education and training, and therefore the employment and income prospects, of the young mothers, who may also, as a result of male neglect of parental responsibilities be compelled to maintain two or more people alone. A significant diminution of mothers' opportunities for education, employment and thus financial security and economic well-being has been demonstrated in a number of studies.[8] This should be a matter for regional and global concern, given that a substantial proportion of women in many countries have their first births before they reach seventeen (Pebley et al., 1982). Certainly all West African countries are characterised by the lower secondary school enrolment of girls than boys (see table 3).

The most important factor amenable to policy intervention is the lack of teenage access to contraception and abortion services as well as family life education (Presser, 1974; McGrath, 1979). Effective provision of contraceptive services to teenagers is reported to be difficult, however. Among the barriers are the attitudes of policy-makers, service producers and others.[9]

Here case studies relevant to these concerns are taken from one country, Ghana. The policy-relevant points are that family planning and educational programmes might usefully pay more attention to the young and to potential fathers, who have hitherto been somewhat neglected, as well as recognising the relative autonomy and responsibility of mothers. Again attention is drawn to the fact that women's training and employment opportunities are critically linked to the timing of their first birth and entry into maternal responsibilities and constraints.

Government Plans and Projects

In the last section, Part IV, three selected examples of government plans and projects are described from Ghana, Nigeria and Sierra Leone. Planning, for countries in which the household mode of production remains pervasive for large sectors of the population, obviously requires improved understanding and recognition of the ways in which domestic economies operate. Paramount among these considerations are the divisions of labour, resources, skills, power and opportunities between women and men and the ways in which these are changing.

This volume thus deals with issues central to the national planning exercises of a range of countries in which family-based agricultural production, food processing, marketing and commodity production continue into the 1980s, but in which, at the same time, radical changes are taking place entailing widespread social and spatial mobility of populations, and in which ecological pressures and revolutionary politics are making it imperative that innovative solutions should be found to problems of economic development and the promotion of enhanced health and well-being of rapidly expanding populations.

The Lagos Plan of Action

In the Lagos Plan of Action in 1981, which set out strategies for economic development in Africa for 1980–2000, the Organisation of African Unity firmly stressed the importance of giving special attention to women in the analyses of situations and in measures taken in each sector of activities. Among the areas of action highlighted as needing priority attention in 1980–85 were organisational machinery; education, training and employment; communications and mass media; health, nutrition and family life; research, data collection and analysis; and legislative and administrative matters.

With regard to employment the Plan emphasised the need to promote recognition and documentation of women's contributions to agriculture, especially in terms of food supply and the need for continuous research to accomplish this. It also stressed the need for national plans to recognise women's contribution and skills, and the need to prepare labour and welfare legislation codes adapted to African conditions and women's multiple responsibilities in both urban and rural settings. In the case of health, nutrition and family life, research training and institution-building were noted to be pressing requirements. In addition attention was drawn to the need to encourage analysis and exchange of country experiences through examination of case studies. It was partly with this last goal in view that the present volume of case studies was compiled.

Notes

1 See Mexico City Declaration on Population and Development adopted by the International Conference on Population, Mexico City, 14 August 1984.

2 An example of such studies is provided by the monographs in the Women, Work and Development series published by the International Labour Office since 1982. See also *Rural development and women in Africa*, Proceedings of an ILO Tripartite African Regional Seminar held in Dakar, Senegal, June 1981 (Geneva, ILO, 1984).

3 Gwatkin (1975) mentions two but is contradicted by Arowolo (1982).

4 Other countries in sub-Saharan Africa in which such programmes have been started include Kenya (1972), Somalia (1981) and Mauritius (1970). In addition, relevant training and seminars have been held in the Côte d'Ivoire (1977 and 1980), Nigeria (1981), Sierra Leone (1977–82), Burkina Faso (1976), Somalia (1981–82), Sudan (1980–83), Tunisia (1974–82), Morocco (1981–83). All these activities have been supported by the United Nations Fund for Population Activities.

5 See, for example, IPPF, *Medical Bulletin*, Vol. 9, No. 2, April 1984, 'Meeting the needs of young people'.

6 See WHO (1980) report of a meeting on adolescent sexuality and reproductive health—studies were undertaken in 16 countries.

7 An annotated bibliography of some of the literature of the last decade has documented the situation and problems in a number of countries. Jandl-Jager (1982) highlights both the extent of the problems and the inadequacy of the materials relating to the developing world, in particular, Africa. Few entries were based on African data. Studies mentioned included Gachuchi (1974) on Kenya; Ezimokhai et al. (1981) on Nigeria; Government of Ghana (1979) on Ghana.

8 For example, see Hofferth and Moore, 1979; Koo et al., 1981; and Stewart, 1982.

9 See Eldstrom, 1981 and evidence on successful programme intervention in Jamaica in McNeil, et al., 1983.

Part I

Women's Work

. . . the subsistence activities usually omitted in the statistics of production and incomes are largely women's work (Boserup, 1970, p. 163).

The question of determining who are members of the active labour force is important to an understanding of women's integration into development. If women's work is not considered as employment, women are likely to be overlooked and excluded from projects and programmes of planners who base their planning on these statistics (UNECA, 1975).

As studies of women's labour force participation have proliferated, the inadequacies of available statistics in capturing the degree of their participation in economic life has become progressively more obvious (Benería, 1981, p. 10).

Labour Force Data

Quantitative data sets, surveys, censuses and bodies of statistics form the bases upon which governments draw up their 'manpower' and development plans. The attempt to improve national statistical services in the Third World has thus been an important aspect of the economic work of the United Nations and its agencies for three decades or more and international recommendations on employment and related statistics both provide guidelines for the development of national statistics and help to improve international comparability of such statistics. These efforts date back to the Second International Conference of Labour Statisticians in 1925. Most employment statistics have been notorious, however, for their omission of informal sector activities and home-based production—the areas of activity in which the women of the developing world tend to concentrate most. This is particularly the case inWest Africa, as we have already noted. Criticism of the inadequacies of this type of data has been growing during the past decade,[1] and a number of attempts have been made recently to try to improve the situation. Changes in international definitions of work were made by the International Conference of Labour Statisticians in 1982. Relevant recommendations were also made by the Expert Group on Improving Statistics and Indicators on the Situation of Women convened in 1983 by the United Nations Statistical Office, Department of Economic and Social Affairs, in co-operation with the United Nations International Research and Training Institute for the Advancement of Women.

At the 1982 Conference of Labour Statisticians it was stated that, as a result of the ideas and social forces current in the United Nations Decade for Women, there was a need to re-examine existing concepts and methods so as to improve the conceptualisation and measurement of the participation of women in economic activities both inside and outside the home (ILO, 1982c). There was also a need to expand the information base so as to provide separate statistics reflecting more accurately the specific employment issues and problems relating to women. Accordingly new recommendations were put forward for the definition of labour force activity.

With regard to global statistics since 1980 (ILO, *Yearbook of labour statistics*) and 1981 (ILO, *Bulletin of labour statistics*), statistics for women have at last been presented separately from those for men. These give total and economically active population, employment, unemployment, hours of work, and wages. This new breakdown of data facilitates comparative examination for a much larger number of countries of new developments concerning women's employment and their working conditions, albeit using so far unchanged definitions.

The interest in improving the documentation of women's work in informal and domestic settings has resulted in a growing interest in industrialised countries in 'housework' and its value (Goldschmidt-Clermont, 1982). In regions of the developing world such as West Africa it is women's unpaid agricultural production and home-based trade in particular which suffer from under-reporting, and these have now become the focus of increased attention.[2]

Over a decade ago, ILO employment missions in Africa were pointing out that much of the important work women did was unaccounted for. Indeed, an attempt was made in the 1973 Kenya mission to evaluate the usefulness of the labour force statistics on women's work. The mission report emphasised the uselessness of a preoccupation with conventional labour force definitions where the majority of the population are rural and poor. It pointed out that in the rural areas most women work in the fields, and usually for much longer hours than men. They accounted the division between economic and non-economic activities to be arbitrary and meaningless.

Some of the practical problems involved in the collection of data on women's work in developing countries have recently been outlined (Anker, 1983a and b). For example, as Pittin notes below, males may be more likely than females to understate the labour force participation of female household members and male interviewers may cause a downward bias in the reported level of female labour force participation (see Lattes and Wainerman, 1979). Again the divisions made in questionnaires between 'work' and 'housework' are often quite arbitrary.

At the 1982 Conference, the ILO recommended that labour force participation figures should include

> All persons of either sex who furnish the supply of labour for the production of economic goods and services as defined by the United Nations system of national accounts and balances.

'Economic activities' should include 'production and processing of primary products whether for the market, for barter or for own consumption'. In practice those areas where women are active are in fact often not considered to be labour force activities. Benería (1982) and others have questioned such arbitrary distinctions between 'housework' and production or processing in contexts in which all people, regardless of sex or age, use time and energy daily for the purposes of subsistence and accumulation.

Data and Development Plans and Policies

The question of inadequate documentation of women's activities is not merely an academic one, for the underestimation of women's activities in different fields leads to the under-allocation of resources and opportunities to women and programmes that affect them. A prime example is provided by the underestimation of women's agricultural activities, which has led to a lack of resources, training or extension services to answer their needs.[3] Home science rather than farm science has continued to be taught to women (Boserup, 1970; UNECA, 1975; Lele, 1975, p. 77). Only now, in some areas, is the full extent of their contribution becoming recognised, with consequent attempts to rectify the earlier imbalances in the allocation of resources.

Bukh (1979) has given a relevant example of women's lack of access to extension support among Ewe women farmers of Tsito. Until 1977 none of the women she interviewed had ever been visited on their farms by an extension officer. The extension service always concentrated on the so-called 'progressive male farmer'—the 10 per cent involved in large-scale production and primarily growing cocoa. She argues that the Ghanaian extension service suffered until the beginning of the 1970s from European concepts of women's roles in agricultural development, which was seen in terms of large-scale mechanisation of cash cropping operated by male farmers. 'Women's participation in agriculture was seen as reminiscent of the traditional forms of production and the role that was shaped for them within a future modernized agricultural system was primarily that of home workers.' As she noted, however, with the developing food crisis that became apparent in Ghana around 1970, women's activities in food production slowly came to be recognised. Appropriate action followed with the establishment of a new home extension branch under the Ministry of Agriculture directed towards improving women's productive activities in rural areas. This was set up in 1971 and expanded slowly, its main emphasis being upon food production and nutrition education.

Among the conclusions of the ILO Tripartite African Regional Seminar on Rural Development and Women held in Dakar, Senegal, in June 1981, it was clearly stated that although rural African women form a large part of the agricultural labour force and are almost solely responsible for food processing, conservation and storage, yet national plans and agricultural policies perceive women only as housewives and mothers and not as farmers. Noted among the results of this situation were the denial of access to land, credit, extension services, improved technology and other forms of institutional support. As the seminar report emphasised, one outcome of this situation is that women's time-consuming and laborious tasks are characterised by low productivity and wastage, thus hindering achievement of the goal of self-sufficiency in food production. Furthermore, women's multiple labour burdens are detrimental to their well-being and that of their dependent children.

Attention was accordingly called to the need to reconsider the work of women in rural production and distribution, both to improve women's working and living conditions and to improve their productivity and to the need for improved documentation and understanding of sexual divisions of labour and how they may be changing.

In this first section, different types of data on women's work in two West African countries are examined, including data from censuses and household surveys at both the national and the village level. The first chapter treats the case of

Hausa women in northern Nigeria, showing clearly how large numbers of women remain in home-based production and processing for the market, work which has been continually omitted in national census exercises over several decades. The second chapter is based on a survey of women's activities carried out in Mali, a country with a predominantly rural population where women in rural areas do a large proportion of the work, and a number of studies of time budgets have demonstrated women's excessive work load inside and outside the home (Mondot-Bernard, 1981). They produce, process and sell agricultural produce and are often overworked and undernourished. Miscarriages, premature births, and repeated child-bearing also contribute to their exhaustion.

Domestic Organisation

The automatic assumption that males are 'household heads' and 'breadwinners', maintaining dependent women and children, is one of the basic reasons why women's work and their maintenance of their dependent children is so often overlooked (see Rogers, 1979). Men are even classified in this way when they are absent migrants.[4] Such stereotypic classifications regarding control of resources and labour and responsibilities for maintenance have very far-reaching planning implications, since they may seriously affect the re-allocation of land or become the basis for the allocation of extension and other services. Indeed, on the assumption that males are household heads with control of land, crops, finances and the family labour of wives and children, agricultural and rural development programmes have been aimed almost entirely at them, channelling agricultural inputs exclusively to them.

The validity of such assumptions has been challenged by Dey (1980), who has graphically documented the case of the Mandinka of The Gambia, among whom the women cultivate the rain-fed rice and have ownership or use rights over rice land, while the men control the upland areas and customarily grow groundnuts and millet. Both also cultivate other crops. Three development projects introduced irrigated rice-growing, giving men control of the land and the crop. Women were effectively excluded from owning irrigated land and from receiving the credits necessary for cultivating irrigated rice on their own account. But their labour, particularly for transplanting and weeding, was none the less crucial for the success of the projects. According to the customary division of labour, women were under no obligation to work for their husbands, so women had to be found who would work for wages. But the women themselves stated clearly that they would prefer to grow their own rice. Dey's conclusion was that by failing to take into account the complexities of existing farming systems, and by focusing upon the men to the exclusion of women, the irrigated rice projects have wasted valuable female expertise. Again, while resources were poured into expensive capital-intensive irrigation schemes, striking results might have been obtained by a few simple improvements in the production of the women's rain-fed and swamp rice. By excluding women, the projects have also increased women's dependence upon men, who are now in charge of an additional food and cash crop.

What is more, The Gambia has subsequently become dependent upon large quantities of imported rice, and a reason given for this shortfall is that women—the traditional rice growers—have not been allocated an appropriate share of relevant resources, including technology and agricultural credit. In spite of the poor record of irrigated rice-growing by men, the government's agricultural policy continued to favour investment in this type of crop rather than rain-fed rice, still grown by women under technically primitive and hence backbreaking conditions (Badoe, 1983). Since 1975, women rice farmers are reported to have had spent on them less than 4 per cent of the amount spent on irrigated rice, in spite of the fact that the area covered by rain-fed rice is 26 times greater. In these relatively deprived conditions, women still managed to produce over 80 per cent of the rice grown in The Gambia (Badoe, 1983).

Such an example points to the need to adopt more complex and cross-culturally applicable models of the functioning of domestic groups and the sexual divisions of labour, power and resources in which the variable and changing allocations of resources, tasks and power between the sexes and the generations will be more adequately accounted for. At the same time account must be taken of the fact that considerable numbers of households have no adult male 'heads' present (see Youssef and Hetler, 1984).

Ethnographic accounts of residence patterns and the organisation of domestic groups in West Africa have long described the intricacy and variety of household forms, the considerable autonomy of wives, the segregated patterns of conjugal role relationships, the lack of joint conjugal funds or resources, and the 'openness' of nuclear family functioning. Varied patterns of growth and fission have been described in terms of developmental cycles, and descriptions of the interesting varieties of domestic architecture have been related to the diverse composition and complex functioning of household groups (Goody, J. 1972). Some compounds accommodate one or more brothers and several wives and their children; others are the homes of lineage segments. In some cases conjugal family members, husbands and wives, parents and children, do not customarily live together but may live in neighbouring compounds and visit each other on a daily or nightly basis. Sometimes, compounds are precisely delineated, and surrounded by high walls and enclosing private spaces. In other communities individual rooms are scattered in such a way that the stranger may not be aware which belong to each other in terms of the relationships of the occupants.

Again, evidence of the extent to which relationships between members of domestic groups, including women and men, adults and children, are commoditised, and involve fine monetary transactions and calculations, has called into question the use of the concept of the household as an undifferentiated economic unity in a number of contexts, including that of the Hausa in northern Nigeria, discussed below. As Jackson (1978), Schildkrout (1981) and others have reported for the Hausa, a woman who makes groundnut oil may use the money given to her by her husband for soup ingredients to buy from herself for the soup that she will herself consume that evening. Likewise Hausa women are known to sell grain that they obtain in various ways to their husbands. They also lend money to their husbands. Furthermore, they expect to be rewarded for agricultural work they do and so on. As a number of ethnographers in the area have noted, financial transactions are likely to play an extremely important part in the relationship between husband and wife (e.g. Abu, 1983).

The two chapters in this section confront such issues. First, Pittin demonstrates clearly how false ideas about domestic relations and the functioning of domestic groups have been associated with inadequate documentation of Hausa women's work and simplistic and erroneous documentation of patterns of production and consumption. Wéry then raises some of the practical problems involved in surveying complex household forms in Mali with traditional questionnaires, and in documenting the variety of activities performed by women and their sources of income and maintenance and the extent to which conjugal relationships form the basis for economically bounded or self-sufficient units. As he graphically demonstrates, conjugal divisions of labour and forms of dependence and maintenance may be incredibly varied, and conjugal relationships are most realistically viewed as links in complex webs of reciprocal obligations and chains of exchange between kin and affines, which connect not only different domestic groups and households but also migrant workers scattered both at home and abroad.

In recent years, many scholars have called attention to the need for more understanding of such household micro-processes. In particular there has been a focus on the fact that in pre-industrial economies there is for women a constant interpenetration between the producer and the homemaker roles, making it difficult, if not impossible, to separate domestic and non-domestic activities. As several observers have noted, the extent to which these two spheres interpenetrate depends upon the extent to which modes of production in agriculture and the marketing of goods have caused a spatial separation of activities, the extent to which they have changed the customary patterns of division of labour by sex, and the extent to which activities have become paid and removed from the home.

Notes

1 For expressions of concern over the omissions of women's work from national statistics in the past decade see, for example, Boserup (1970), p. 163; Standing (1978); Benería (1981). Standing (1978) summarised the problems of collecting female labour force data.
2 See Rogers (1979, pp. 152 ff) who emphasises that 'in order to produce food in edible form, an enormous amount of work is involved after the harvest—which is the point where the official measurement of 'work' usually halts. Threshing, winnowing, drying, boiling (especially for rice paddy) and other activities have to be undertaken between harvesting and storage of many staple foods . . . exhausting work is again involved in processing it before cooking . . . before cooking an adequate supply of water and fuel needs to be obtained, and these two requirements can take up to several hours a day.' See also Goldschmidt-Clermont, *Economic Evaluations of unpaid household work: Asia, Latin America and Oceania: A review of economic evaluations*, in Women, Work and Development series, Geneva, ILO.
3 The general lack of training programmes for rural women has recently been spelt out in an ILO document on training for rural women (ILO, 1983). Regarding lack of attention and resources for women farmers, see for examples Jackson (1978) on Hausa women; Caplan (1981) on the United Republic of Tanzania; Hirschmann (1985) on Malawi; and Burfisher and Horenstein (1985) on the Tiv of Nigeria.
4 Rogers (1979, pp. 66–67) has provided several examples from southern Africa of the ways in which this kind of stereotyping has hampered the collection and analysis of agricultural labour statistics and the development plans which should be based upon these.

1 Renée Pittin

Documentation of Women's Work in Nigeria
Problems and Solutions

The focus of this chapter is the secluded Muslim women of northern Nigeria.[1] It is contended that the profound contributions made by these women to the economic life of Hausa communities has been systematically ignored in surveys over the decades, and that at present this neglect is increasing rather than abating. Reference to census data in particular makes this situation abundantly clear, as will be demonstrated below. It is evident that surveys have been carried out with either total disregard or non-comprehension of the actual distribution of productive labour within the domestic unit. This is implicit in the formulation of the questionnaires, in the framing of questions, and in the choice of respondents. Indeed, some surveys appear to have been designed to reinforce the already all too prevalent myths regarding domestic labour, which assume an economic dependency on the part of Hausa women altogether out of keeping with the actual patterns of income, and expenditure and labour in a Hausa compound.[2]

There are a number of factors which have contributed to the present parlous state of socio-economic data collection. One vital factor is the male- and Western-biased approach to the meaning, nature, and parameters of work. Such definitions and guide-lines as have been employed have tended to ignore or submerge women's occupations, and to produce and perpetuate an image of women as economic parasites. Of equal importance are the misconceptions and ideologically loaded constructs surrounding the concept of the household. In Nigeria, discussion of the household is also a foray into the omnipresent and pervasive male-dominant ideology, with assumptions of male authority and female socio-economic dependency, in a gender-based hierarchical structure. The domestic group is often seen as monolithic, clearly bounded, and unchanging, except in so far as the domestic cycle produces changes in personnel. This view is in the Hausa case reinforced by the practice of seclusion, inasmuch as women are not seen moving about in the community. It will be demonstrated, however, that these perceptions are misleading, and that they produce a picture of Hausa domestic life which is contradicted by available micro-data. Findings from micro-studies show a much more fluid social structure, and a far wider system of networks cross-cutting domestic units and uniting women of different households, than is or could become evident from the standard survey questions and procedures. It is thus incumbent upon us to examine critically the very question of the utility of the domestic structure as an analytical unit.

The suggestions presented concerning survey techniques and format are immediately related to the situation of Hausa women, but they also have wider application. This study of the economic participation of Hausa women is therefore used here as an illustrative case study. It furnishes detailed and accurate information concerning the women's actual economic roles, the factor of seclusion adding a further dimension to the problems of women's visibility, and provides a counterpoint to the better-known lifestyles of southern Nigerian women. We shall demonstrate further that the kinds of errors perpetrated in the Hausa case also bedevil other regional censuses, and have been a continuing problem in obtaining and analysing national census data.

Much of the data regarding Hausa women's roles and activities discussed here are based on the author's own research, carried out from 1971 to 1973 in the Nigerian city of Katsina, located in the northern part of Kaduna State, which borders on the Republic of Niger. 1971 tax assessment lists show a population of 76,060 for Katsina City and environs. For centuries, the urban economy has been centred on agriculture, commerce, and administration; this was still the situation during the period of research. In the past few years, industry has come to Katsina, most spectacularly with the commissioning in December 1982 of the multi-million Naira steel-rolling mill, located just outside the former city walls.

For ease of administration, the city was divided into four quarters,[3] and further subdivided into wards. A study carried out in two of these wards, Yarinci and Marina, produced a wealth of data concerning women's socio-economic roles, details of which are discussed below. Participant observation, extended case studies, and the administration of a series of closed- and open-ended questions to over 400 Yarinci and Marina women, were among the procedures employed to obtain comprehensive and detailed information about the kinds of opportunities and choices open to urban Hausa women. The findings showed that the vast majority are economically active, and display an economic independence seemingly at odds with their spatial confinement.

Seclusion is not a new phenomenon among Hausa women, although the apparent rapidity and extent of its recent growth is. In the cities, seclusion has been the norm for decades. At present, although a small number of educated élite Hausa women work and travel outside the home, most married urban women remain secluded. At the same time, in the rural areas, large numbers of formerly unsecluded women are joining the ranks of their urban sisters, and are opting, or have opted, for seclusion.

Seclusion is most strictly observed in the first few years of marriage, but acts as a constraint throughout the child-bearing years, and indeed beyond them. So pervasive is the ideology of seclusion that it binds even women who are no longer married. Senior male kin may forbid non-married women[4] to move freely in the town, but usually such control is unnecessary, for the women themselves have internalised the rules and restrictions and find no real role for themselves in public places. Older non-married women may and do travel from house to house visiting friends or relatives, but they do not seek to build themselves a niche in the market, or find work outside the compound. As the only adult women of marriageable age who move freely through the streets, and sit outside their houses, are prostitutes, 'excessive' movement has its own pitfalls.

All urban women, married and non-married, live their lives largely within the compound, although the basis on which they reside (e.g. as wife, sister, compound head) will alter with changes in marital fortunes, and with the inexorable modifications associated with birth and death. Most women pursue at least one, and often more than one, trade or craft, the proceeds from which are inalienably their own. The type of trade a woman chooses depends on its likely profitability, the availability of raw materials (which may be seasonal), the woman's own economic resources, her age, her responsibilities, such as young children, her perceived and desired status, and the purposes for which she is earning money. Thus, for example, a woman with young children may engage in an activity such as embroidery, which can be put down at any time and as easily resumed, and which will not hinder her domestic and child-care duties, in terms of the time and concentration required. An older woman seeking to earn enough money to provide for her pilgrimage to Mecca may pursue a number of cash-earning economic activities simultaneously, or undertake a trade which is particularly arduous and/or time-consuming, and which may require considerable initial expenditure, but which should realise a high financial return. The preparation and sale on a large scale of meals such as rice and soup is one such activity.

Certain women are prevented by physical disability or convention from working. In the former category are women who are too old, feeble or ill to work. In the latter category are women who have recently married: women in their first year of marriage are expected to be utterly and totally dependent on their husbands. There is one significant difference between the two Katsina wards, in the growth of a phenomenon of conspicuous leisure, which appears to be confined to, and indicative of, women of the urban élite (Pittin, 1976). Where all women have the leisure afforded by seclusion, the ultimate confirmation of wealth and superior status is in the non-utilisation of available time for personal economic advancement. Younger women in Yarinci, married to well-to-do civil servants, form the majority of this category of women. Most women in Yarinci have cash income-earning occupations, however. Of the 191 women included in the 1973 socio-economic survey sample, 122 women, or 63.9 per cent, were engaged in individual income-earning work.

Marina, with its preponderance of artisans and traders, reflects more closely the wider urban population, and indeed the commonfolk (*talakawa*) who make up the bulk of Hausa society, rural and urban. Of the 211 women included in the survey in Marina, more than four-fifths (176 women, 83 per cent) were independently economically active.

The high proportion of women with income-earning occupations is consonant with long-standing and widespread attitudes concerning women's work.[5] In Katsina, a woman's own social status has some bearing on the categories of occupation she might choose to pursue, while the types of work engaged in, to some extent, reflect the class and occupational composition of the wards, and demonstrate the wide range of activities available to women. Many women have two or more occupations, which may be concurrent or consecutive.

In both wards, and generally in Hausa communities, the preparation and sale of snacks is a popular occupation, whatever a woman's age or social status. In Yarinci, it is the principal economic activity of almost half the women, and in Marina of more than a quarter. Hausa domestic consumption patterns assure a continuing market for the various prepared foodstuffs and titbits. It is usual for a family to buy prepared food for at least one meal, or at least to supplement a meal with a tasty snack.

So separate is a woman's trade from her roles as wife and mother that a husband is expected to pay for food prepared for sale by his wife, even if the purchase is to feed their family. Similarly, a woman may buy groundnuts from her husband's crop, for example, if the couple can agree on a mutually acceptable price. Some of the oil which she processes may then be sold back to her husband, for use in her cooking. A woman's degree of participation in snack preparation will depend on her inclinations, her other obligations, and the available market.

Embroidery, knitting and sewing are largely an avocation among élite Yarinci women, a means of passing the time rather than of making money. For more than a quarter of the Marina women, however, these activities provide a significant source of income. The most important of these crafts is the embroidery of the closely stitched men's caps. Distribution and sale of the finished products are through the agency of middlemen, who return to the women a portion of the price paid by the buyer. These crafts require a minimum of capital, and can be done at the women's convenience. As Marina includes a large number of dyers, tailors and other cloth workers, it is a logical base for women's textile craftwork also. Traditional crafts such as weaving and spinning are of limited importance, being more commonly practised among rural women, or as a secondary source of income for some of the Yarinci and Marina women.

The selling of one's labour for money, as in the activities of grinding and pounding, is considered to be low in status, and is generally the preserve of poorer women. Domestic services such as washing children's clothes and cooking ware, cleaning the compound and preparing the food, are utilised exclusively by women of the traditional and modern élite, who may employ full- or part-time servants. The servants are often from families who have served the forebears of the élite for generations, and they may live with the family they serve.

Petty trade is of limited significance as a woman's occupation, partly because it is the work of so many men, who can move freely in the town. Some women, however, keep a supply of non-perishable items which their neighbours frequently need to replace, or they may specialise in, say, plastic storage containers and dishes, or washing soda. Other women trade on a small scale in kolanuts, tobacco, sugar cane, and other perishable goods with a rapid turnover.

The women who engage in large-scale food processing or trade make profits and deal in quantities quite out of proportion to the small number of participants. Some processed food, such as groundnut cakes, are taken by the lorry-load to Lagos and other southern cities. Women in large-scale trading generally buy in bulk, and in season in the rural areas, and sell in the urban areas, often storing the goods for a price rise. Women participating in large-scale food processing or trade need a substantial sum of money to begin, and require some degree of free movement and independence to pursue their work. These women tend to be in their thirties at least, and they are often no longer married, or living in non-co-residential marriage.

Preparation and sale of complete meals is not done by any Yarinci women, and is the work of only a small percentage of Marina women. It takes a great deal of time, must be done on a regular basis and therefore demands diligence, and requires a reasonably large sum of money initially. No young woman undertakes such work (all women carrying on this trade were in their thirties or older).

Salaried employment was available only to Yarinci women, who had the necessary contacts and, in a few cases, the necessary education. Salaried women were among the few women who could not be in full seclusion. The others are found mainly in the final category, 'other occupations'. These include water sellers, praise singers, and messengers. Others in the final category, whose work was carried out in domestic units, were three unmarried women assisting their mothers with the mother's trade, two hairstylists, two midwives, a fortune teller, and a caretaker. One woman was seeking employment.

An income-earning activity which is *not* significant for women in the urban area is the rearing of poultry and small livestock. Fodder is expensive and not easily available, and there is little convenient grazing land. In rural areas, however, this is an important source of wealth for women, who own most of the sheep, goats and poultry.[6] Simmons points out that the animals 'are considered strictly as a form of individual cash savings, with the offspring regarded as interest on the investment, rather than as sources of food' (1976a, p. 19).

This description of women's occupations in the two wards thus demonstrates that women do participate actively in commodity production and trade in spite of their seclusion and, in part, because of it, since they are freed from the tedious trips to well, market, bush and farm which are the lot of unsecluded women. While some women await customers within the confines of the home, most women distribute their wares through the children, male and female, who form a vast army of hawkers in the towns and villages of Hausaland (Schildkrout, 1981).

We have concentrated above on the variety of occupations women pursue, and on the integral and essential part women's production plays in the daily life of the community. In demonstrating the overall pattern, however, the extent of individual industry becomes submerged. For example, only the most important income-earning activity of each woman was recognised in discussing the range of occupations, even though many women have several crafts or trades which they may engage in concurrently or consecutively.

The women engaged in the many occupations noted herein include married women living with their husbands, married women living away from their husbands, and women who are widows and divorcees. All women have complete control over their profits, which are funnelled mainly into the gift-exchange networks which loom so large in the lives of Hausa women, and which indicate and reinforce the bonds of kinship and friendship, the subtleties of status, and the dependence of women upon each other in Hausa society. Given a high divorce rate, differential longevity of women and men, and the fact that women in their forties rarely remarry, and even women in their thirties may not remarry, it is clear that a woman works for her own and her children's security, and does not tie her fortunes to those of her husband.

A husband's formal responsibilities towards his wife are limited: the minimal requirement is to provide food and shelter; failure to do so is grounds for divorce in Muslim law, though unsecluded rural women may spend several days each week working on the very farms from which their husbands will 'support' them. A husband is also expected to clothe his wife, or wives, and children on the festival of Id el-Fitr, but there is no formal obligation to clothe them for the rest of the year, nor is his failure to provide clothing for his wife grounds for divorce. The responsibility of clothing herself and the children is often left to the woman, who is also expected to take care of any additional niceties, such as jewellery for herself and her daughters.

Although some urban wives find themselves virtually supporting themselves and their children, it appears that the division of marital responsibilities generally puts greater burdens on rural than on urban women. And in addition to their greater responsibilities for themselves and their children, rural women have the additional duty of processing the cash crops and foodstuffs producd by their husbands. If the wives are secluded, then the crops are brought to the compound for the women to deal with there (Konan, 1975, pp. 18–19). This work may be remunerated, or it may be treated as part of a woman's 'contribution' to subsistence. All women, whether rural or urban, are responsible for all domestic duties relating to housekeeping, cooking, and the care of their children.

Sixty Years of Census Data

Hausa women's entrepreneurial activities, real enough to provide many of the basic commodities needed in the community, are often as 'invisible' in censuses and surveys as the women themselves. Such women are doubly discriminated against: as is the case elsewhere in the world, their domestic labour as wives and mothers is not treated as work; in addition, their income-earning occupations, carried out in the home and providing an independent and not infrequently lucrative source of income, are unseen and all too often unrecorded.

In examining the extent to which women's multiple economic roles have been recognised in Nigerian surveys, we shall focus primarily on the data available for Katsina, as the most complete existing comparative material is from Katsina City. It is particularly informative to follow the fortunes of the Nigerian census over the course of the past 60 years. Data concerning the occupations of Nigerian women have been sought as an integral part of the census programme, almost from its inception. At the same time, virtually every error and bias which could serve to reduce the apparent economic participation of women has been evident in one or more censuses. Interestingly enough, recognition of these problems, and their effects upon general perceptions of women's roles in the Nigerian economy, are most clearly stated in the earliest of the socio-economic censuses, and have been noted only occasionally thereafter. A review of the successive censuses will highlight some of these difficulties, and will also demonstrate the steps taken (and not taken) to alleviate them.

Nationwide censuses have been carried out in Nigeria since 1911, although this first census was a population count only and very superficial. The 1921 census was an ambitious project, designed to elicit information on male and female occupations, as well as on education, age, religion, and other areas seen to be of interest to the colonial government. Its success was necessarily limited, given the vast physical area to be covered, the large and scattered population to be interviewed, and a corps of personnel which was grossly inadequate in numbers and training for the task before it. With regard to women's occupations, some of the problems which would plague future censuses too had already arisen. The anthropologist C.K. Meek was in charge of analysing and publishing the census data. He admitted that 'The collection of occupation statistics occasioned ... the greatest difficulty. There are no doubt many omissions, especially as regards the occupations of women, which, in some districts, were not obtained at all.' (1925, p. 172). Elaborating upon this later, he said that 'The returns of the occupations followed by women were particularly unsatisfactory, owing no doubt to the multiple and occasional character of ... [their] occupations ...'(p. 213).

The census statistics which included Katsina covered a much larger and more populous area, and no detailed local data are available. Almost half of the Kano Province women are classified as agricultural workers, with another 30 per cent described as textile workers, presumably engaged mainly in spinning, judging from subsequent census information. Almost all the remaining women (21 per cent) are included in the 'domestic and miscellaneous' category, which comprises housewives, and women with unidentified and unspecified occupations.

These figures contrast strongly with those from the neighbouring Sokoto Province, which has an ethnic composition, culture, and physical environment very similar to that of Kano Province. There almost all women (96 per cent) were included in the 'domestic and miscellaneous' category! Sokoto is one of the areas noted by Meek as not gathering data about women's occupations, mindlessly relegating women instead into the category of wives and mothers. Categorisation decisions must have been made at a provincial supervisory level for the results to be so strikingly different in the neighbouring provinces.

In Nigeria's earliest census seeking economic information, then, such wild discrepancies were already evident. The multifaceted nature of women's economic contributions was recognised, but only in some areas. The census designers, supervisors, enumerators, and analysts, however, were unable wholly to come to terms with women's multiple roles either in that census, or in the censuses which followed. In many respects, though, the handling of the data for the Katsina area was more satisfactory in the 1921 census than in any subsequent census except its immediate successor, the census of 1931.

Katsina City was fortunate in being part of one of the six northern districts bordering on Niger, which were the focus of an intensive census in 1931, carried out at the same time as a general census in the rest of the country. Many of the better trained census staff were centred in the intensive census area, and the data sought were more extensive, and more carefully collected, than in any other part of the country. The results were considered to be very accurate indeed.

Instructions to enumerators were to designate 'the principal means of livelihood of all persons who actually do work and carry on business ... [as well as] any subsidiary occupation ...' (1931 Census, Vol. II, p. 40). Women in the Magajin Gari District are included in 25 categories of 'gainfully employed' individuals (working men fall into 57 categories). However, 70.9 per cent of all women are crowded into one occupational classification, that of spinning. Selling cooked foods included only 2.9 per cent (498) of the women in the district, surely an underestimate. But at least in this census, virtually all women are treated as economically productive members of society, engaged in craftwork or trade. This appraisal of women's roles was destined not to be repeated in any subsequent Nigerian census.

The accuracy of the Nigerian census of 1952, in relation to gross population figures only, has been a subject of contention among scholars. The presentation and analysis of women's economic activity, on the other hand, was indisputably a disaster. Problems and difficulties which had not arisen before now became insurmountable, while the approach to women's roles showed a naivety and lack of forethought which are inexplicable in a country which had already cut its demographic teeth on two previous censuses. The errors began with the categorisation of women's work. The entire gamut of women's occupations was crushed into a derisory *three* groups while men's work was fitted into six broad occupational groupings. Women's work was to be included in the categories of

(a) agriculture, fishing, and agriculture-related occupations; (b) trading and clerical occupations; and (c) others. Categories (a) and (b) would immediately exclude all the women engaged in spinning in the 1931 census, unless they themselves happened to sell their work outside the home, in which case they could perhaps be treated as traders. There *was* a male occupational category for craft workers; apparently it was thought to be unnecessary for women, in spite of the evidence of its importance in previous censuses. There was also an occupational category for men not in the 'labour force', although there was no similar category for women.

In the Magajin Gari District, 90 per cent of all females fell into the category of 'others'. The government statistician included the following disclaimer:

> The three occupational groups for females have not provided as useful an indication of primary occupations as the male groups. This was not merely because females were classified in fewer groups. Most females undertake some of the work on the farms, and many are partly occupied with home crafts or in trading. Undoubtedly Enumerators had great difficulty in deciding whether the duties of 'housewife' were or were not the *primary occupation*. (Government of Nigeria, 1953, p. 9; emphasis in text).

The question of what constitutes part-time work, and the classification and priority of the role of housewife, were difficulties which had already arisen in 1921. By 1952 there should have been solutions, not reiteration of the same old problems. A new difficulty in the 1952 census was the utter unresponsiveness of the occupational categories. Besides the general criticisms, there is a particular lacuna with regard to the large number of women who were housebound commodity producers, their wares sold mainly by children. Census designers emphasised the extra-domestic nature of trade, writing of trading establishments, stores, shops, market stalls and pedlars. The work of women in producing and selling foodstuffs and other goods, via children, and the vital importance and extensiveness of this work, were largely unrecognised in the census.

How serious this error was became apparent with the final census figures. In only one northern province with a culture similar to that of Katsina were women's economic activities recognised even minimally, with a third of the females included as traders. This apparent anomaly prompted a response from various writers, but the explanation given was either that there *was* 'no ready explanation' (Prothero, 1956, p. 175), or that women in that province (Kano) might have been 'forced to supplement family production by trading and craft production' (Mabogunje, 1968, p. 166). This is also incorrect. Women in Kano, as Hausa women in Katsina and elsewhere, control their income individually and inalienably, and are no more or less involved in economic pursuits than other Hausa women.[7] The anomaly was produced through inaccurate perception of the nature of northern women's economic participation, as demonstrated in the Katsina census figures, and the data for every other Hausa area outside Kano. There was little recognition of the tremendous economic contribution of Hausa women in general, for this had remained hidden within the awkward and inadequate classifications of female economic activities, and the less than·effective preparations, procedures, and supervision of the 1952 census.

A basic procedural error which surely exacerbated the difficulties associated with ascertaining women's occupations was the emphasis on eliciting information from the household head, rather than from other members of the household. Since the household head is generally assumed to be male, since a male is usually sought, and since the husband is always assumed to be head of the family unit, information was usually obtained from men, primarily if not totally by male enumerators. The problem was very likely most acute when it came to establishing women's occupations, especially in relation to married women's domestic and maternal roles.

The census instructions were straightforward and clear-cut. The designation of homemaker was to be entered for 'married women who have *no occupation* other than their own household duties' (Government of Nigeria, 1953, Schedule 2, p. 50; emphasis added). That these instructions resulted in difficulties must have been as much a function of (male) respondents' own biases as of enumerators' biases, confusion, or inability to establish occupational priorities.

One other reason for a husband or household head to deny a woman's economic activities would have been the fear of taxation. Concern about taxation has been given as one of the main reasons for the under-count in the 1952 census, and could well have been significant in the lack of recognition of women's occupations. Only men were counted in the payment of headtax, but there was doubtless strong suspicion that after the census women, or at least women with income-earning occupations, might also be taxed. Information about such activities would therefore be hidden. Based on the Katsina research, however, it is our contention that many other factors also come into play, each of which may influence men (verbally) to minimise participation by women in any activity apart from their roles as wives and mothers. These factors will be discussed later in this paper.

With all its defects, the 1952 census nevertheless had one great mitigating virtue. This was the easy availability and extensiveness of the documentation surrounding the census, including census preparation, forms, procedures, and analysis. The opposite end of the spectrum was reached with the census of 1963 which, following hard upon the nullified 1962 census, was both politically sensitive and a demographic disaster. The political problems which brought about the ruin of the 1962 census had not been solved by 1963, and when the data were presented there was no accompanying explanation or analysis. Rather, the following proviso was included: 'The Statistical Tables are put out without any comment; this practice is considered necessary at this time' (Government of Nigeria, 1963, Vol. I).

With regard to women's roles as portrayed in census data, there are still lessons to be learned. Perhaps the most important concerns the 'labour force', a term which was gingerly used in the 1952 census but which became a basic, albeit unexplained (and inexplicable), concept in 1963. Exactly who was, and was not, included in the labour force is nowhere clarified, except in so far as certain occupational categories are specifically included. However, as the labour force also includes other persons whose occupations are 'inadequately described or unspecified', the criteria for being in the labour force remain unclear. Suffice it to say, though, that men tend to be 'in', and women tend to be 'out'.

In Katsina Province, of the 715,662 females of 15 years of age or more, only 27,176, or a total of 3.8 per cent were considered to be in the labour force. This compared with an astounding figure for male labour force participation in the province of 94.2 per cent. That the physical invisibility of women, hidden in their homes, was a factor in the skewed labour figures is evident both in the importance of categories such as 'street vendors' and in the comparison of regional labour statistics. While the Northern Region included only 12.8 per cent of its adult female population in the labour force, this figure jumped to 32.4 per cent for the Eastern Region, and 62.1 per cent for the Western Region, home of the Yoruba with their long tradition of women trading outside the home. These comparative statistics demonstrate the failure of the census to recognise and effectively quantify secluded women's economic production. The statistics raise more questions than they answer, however, for it is not possible that such a small proportion of eastern women, for example, who are farmers, traders, and entrepreneurs par excellence, should be included in the labour force. This is contradicted by the evidence of every anthropological and sociological study ever done of the region. In part, presumably the dual careers of women, as wives and as workers in other areas, affected the figures regarding women's occupations throughout the Federation. Otherwise, the statistics concerning women in the labour force could not have been so ridiculously low, however the labour force had been defined.

It is also likely that the Nigerian data in this area suffered from the inbuilt disabilities of similar labour force studies elsewhere, in which it has been noted, for rural women in particular, that 'the demarcation line between "economic" and "non-economic" activities "is statistically arbitrary and for purposes of indicating living standards, meaningless" ' (Singer and Jolly, 1973).[8]

One other striking example of male bias in the 'labour force' statistics in the 1963 census must be noted. This concerns the category of 'inadequately described or unspecified' occupations noted above, among workers in the labour force. Throughout Nigeria, it was women's work which continually fell into this category. The end result was that almost one-fifth (18.9 per cent) of all women in the labour force worked at these 'unspecified' occupations, while the corresponding figure for men was an infinitesimal 0.4 per cent! Thus, within the labour force, as well as outside it, the content of women's work is ignored, inadequately classified, or inadequately understood. The labour force occupational categorisation scheme was created for men, and has value only in relation to men.

No results other than gross population figures were ever released from the last census of 1973. Reference to the 1973 *Population census enumerator's manual* suggests, however, that some of the problems which had dogged earlier censuses had not been solved, and that the work of secluded women in particular (who would have increased in number in relation to the female population as a whole, given the spread of seclusion to the rural areas) would again sink into oblivion, as would the work of vast numbers of other women. This is evident from the directions, explanations and examples contained in the *Enumerator's manual*, where it is made clear that a 'homemaker', i.e. 'a person of *either sex* [emphasis in text] aged six years and over who was wholly engaged in household duties and was not paid for this work' was not to be included as an unemployed person (Government of Nigeria, 1973, p. 29). It appears, however, that the homemaker was also not to be included as an *employed* person,[9] because 'homemaker' was the first category in a list of eight in the *Enumerator's manual* (p. 29), which included the disabled, the retired or pensioned, the elderly, prisoners and the voluntarily unemployed. Judging from the categorisation of homemakers in the *Manual*, and from the treatment of women in the 1963 census, it seems unlikely that housewives would have been included as participants in the labour force. Even now, women's domestic labour as wives and mothers is commonly excluded from labour force statistics, in spite of international recommendations to the contrary.[10]

It is not apparent from the census manual whether houseboys and housegirls, who are fed and clothed by their employers, often their kin, would be treated as 'not being paid' and therefore as homemakers. Perhaps they and the wives of the house would fall into the same category of homemakers which, judging from the exceptions which follow, is aimed particularly at housewives. It might be argued that clothing, food and shelter are payment for the servant, but are a marital obligation and not payment with respect to the wife. In this case, it is possible that the six year old girl helping with the housework might be in the labour force,[11] while the wife, doing most of the work, would not.

The exceptions were interesting. The following categories of people were *not* to be categorised as homemakers:

(a) A housewife who traded for a few hours each day during the reference week.

(b) A housewife who worked on her husband's farm without pay for *at least* [emphasis in text] three days during the reference week.

(c) A housewife who worked in her own shop (Beauty Parlour, Beer Parlour etc.) for at least a few hours each day during the reference week (Government of Nigeria, 1973, p. 29).

Also to be excluded as homemakers were women who had 'similar particulars' to the above. Category (b) and (c) rule out urban Hausa women immediately, while category (a) has, yet again, the added spatial component. Trading is assumed to involve contact between buyer and seller, and so loses secluded Hausa women. There could have been a further exception: '(d): A housewife who engaged in house-trade, commodity production, or services for a few hours each day', which would have included the majority of busy, income-earning Hausa women. There was no such category, however, and there is excellent reason to believe, based on decades of neglect, that Hausa women would have been no more recognised in 1973 as having 'similar particulars' to (a), (b) or (c) than they had been in the past.

Category (b) is particularly worthy of note, for as it is phrased it is bound to result in the loss of thousands more women from the labour force. Generally, every effort is made to carry out the Nigerian census during the non-farming season, because of the long hours worked by farmers during the agricultural season, and the difficulty of finding the respondent population at home. The reference period for the 1973 census was 'from zero hour of Sunday 25th November 1973 to midnight of Saturday 1st December, 1973' (Government of Nigeria, 1973, Appendix D, p. 1), which is most definitely the dry season in Nigeria. There might perhaps still have been crops to be harvested, which might have been ready for harvesting during the reference week, but there easily might not. According to census instructions, family members who work without pay on the family farm (or in the family business) were expected to have worked *three or more days* during the week preceding the census, if they were to be included in this category of workers. Even if the housewife had prepared the land on her husband's farm, and had then sowed, weeded, and harvested the crops thereon, none of this would have been recognised in the census unless she had put in the required three days during the reference week, an unlikely event during the dry season. On the other hand, a farmer on his/her own farm was required to have spent only *one* day on the farm during the reference week. If he/she had not, then the farmer was to be categorised as unemployed. It is not clear if the wife noted above, who had not put in her three days, would then have become a homemaker (outside the labour force) or an unemployed person (inside the labour force).

In the midst of the numerous retrograde provisions of recent Nigerian censuses, one positive modification must be noted. This is the decision to treat a wife living away from her husband as head of her own household, consisting of herself, her children (if any), and any other persons staying with her. This is a small step in the direction of more accurate census data regarding women. Proper understanding and analysis of women's roles, however, demands a very serious reappraisal, and radical reorientation, of the approach, procedures and categories to be used in census collection and analysis.

Hausa Domestic Groupings: Obstacles to Analysis

Let us protest immediately against the utilisation of the household as a basic unit of study in surveys and censuses. No other single term has been defined in so many different ways, producing so many different results (which are then all too often compared with each other, as if all were based on the same criteria). And no other single collective term in sociological use has contributed so greatly to the obfuscation of women's roles, activities, and interests. Using the data before us, we can demonstrate this point with reference to Hausa social structure and domestic patterns.

Much of the material published in the past few years concerning the Hausa has been the product of surveys carried out by rural sociologists and rural economists. Taking their cue from M.G. Smith, a number of these researchers have divided Hausa domestic groupings into three. There is the spatial unit, the compound, which is a walled or fenced residential unit. This may be partitioned when, for example, 'the head of the compound has an adult son or dependent adult male relative living with him. A social unit which is often synonymous with the [partitioned unit] is the . . . individual family which usually includes a man, his wives and his dependent children. Finally there is the household or work unit which is "a separate unit of domestic economy with common production and consumption of food, a single head, a common pot, a common granary, and a common farm" [M.G. Smith, 1955, p. 19]. This work unit may consist of one [individual family] or two or more [individual families] combined together forming a household' (Norman, 1974, p. 4).

Before turning to the criteria of production and consumption, and the doubt which must be cast on their utility as indicators of single social units, it is worth noting the bias and the lack of clarity which are associated with the concepts of the household and the family noted above. The bias is in the emphasis on male family heads, and on the lack of formal recognition of women except as wives, a situation which is demographically and socially inaccurate in Hausa society. Saved by the judicious use of qualifiers (usually, often, for example), the author presents an ideal, and stops short of presenting the real. The above researcher was particularly interested in the relationship between labour and land, and so was not concentrating on domestic relationships. But the same assumptions, and emphasis on married men and women, are evident in the research of workers whose subject matter should have led them to more careful analysis.[12]

The Katsina data suggest that 'unmarried' adults are women who have been, but are no longer, married. Considering the two Katsina wards together, the total population of men who had never married was 366, while the figure for women was 682. Among the men, a small proportion of this total (6.3 per cent) were not married at the time of the initial survey. Among the women, the proportion was far higher (20.5 per cent). Using Hausa categories, the women can be classified as follows: two-thirds of the adult women fit the standard 'wife living with husband' expectation; one-third (277 women) do not. Twenty-three women live in Hausa non-coresidential marriage (*auren skilkiti*). Generally, the wife lives in her own home, bought or inherited, and her husband, who is also married elsewhere, visits her occasionally. This would be on her allotted days, if they live near each other, the husband spends two successive nights with each wife. If husband and wife live further from each other, visits will be less frequent, although they may be of longer duration. In either case, the wife is often the *de facto* compound head, and runs her life with limited reference to her husband.

The 76 women categorised as non-married are, in Hausa terminology, *jawarawa* (s. *bajawara*)—women who are still marriageable, i.e. who are young enough to be candidates for remarriage. This is not to say that they will remarry: two years after the initial survey, a follow-up study which included 52 of the non-married women established that only two-fifths (21 women) had remarried. Women aged 50 or more, 'old women' (H. *tsaffi*, s. *tsofuwa*), will not remarry. Even women in their forties rarely remarry. Men, on the other hand, remarry until (and sometimes after) they are doddering and senile. The remaining women, 'others', include women in transition: women who have left their husbands but have not been divorced, women whose husbands have deserted them, and women who have returned home for childbirth. The all too common emphasis on the conjugal unit or the household has thus negated the significance of the alternatives to marriage, adopted by choice or perforce, by a significant proportion of the female population.

The Hausa farming unit of production is often treated as coterminous with the domestic group. But in rural areas women's farming activities are being reduced through the spread of seclusion, and women's other income-earning activities play a limited part in production for the family as a whole. Even where women do participate in agriculture, they still engage in their own individual economic pursuits. Certainly, the productive and reproductive roles of women in performing domestic tasks, and in child-bearing and rearing, are a significant part of the entire economic output, but this monolithic approach to individuals' roles through the domestic unit masks women's own economic production, which is personal rather than family-oriented, the profits being individually owned and utilised. The fact that a childless woman (or a woman whose children are too few, too young, or too old) can and does hire other children to do the hawking of her goods weakens still further the case for equating the domestic unit with the production unit.

The separation of husband's and wife's economic endeavours is most clearly evident in the trading and bargaining between spouses regarding the woman's purchase of produce from her husband's farm, or the husband's purchase of commodities produced by the wife, to be used for feeding the family. But in other areas also, and even where husband and wife live in the same residential unit, production is often undertaken for distinct and non-coinciding purposes. Moreover, property is individually owned. Thus, for example, women own most of the sheep, goats and poultry in rural areas, and do not use them for consumption within the compound (unless an animal is bought by a compound member, or is ill and likely to die).

By repeatedly treating the production unit and the domestic unit as synonymous, researchers have done Nigeria a major disservice, for their findings have had profound consequences on the direction and (lack of) effectiveness of agricultural development projects. Many of the consultancy firms hired at vast expense by former Nigerian governments to do feasibility and impact studies for the multi-million naira agricultural programmes, such as major irrigation schemes, have digested and regurgitated, unquestioningly, the same untruths about the Hausa farmer's certain access to free family labour, both female and male, and have made this the linchpin of their arguments for approving the project designs (C.C. Wallace, 1978a, 1978b). The heads of farming units did not have year-round availability of family labour in the past, and the situation has now been exacerbated by the new projects which are based on two or more harvests a year. The present critical shortage of farming labour has induced many young men to hire out their own labour for cash, rather than working on the family farms. Lacking the family labour force so casually and incorrectly assigned to them, and often lacking the cash or credit to hire wage labour, as well as to pay for the inputs required for irrigation agriculture, small farmers are being systematically forced off the land and turned into wage labourers themselves, leaving to the wealthiest (often absentee) farmers the prime irrigated land, on which to farm and prosper.

The Nigerian Federal Office of Statistics lays emphasis on common consumption to define a family. This method is also favoured by the Institute for Agricultural Research, Zaria, in addition to, or *instead* of, the criterion of joint production, even though the criterion of production is often used for a group wider than the family, and the criterion of consumption is frequently limited to a conjugal family, or other form of small family group. The model includes in one unit 'all those who eat from one pot'. As some individuals may well have servants, other clients, and Koranic students eating also 'from the same pot', this definition seems on the face of it a non-starter. This kind of inconsistency emphasises the obvious limitations of the analytical method. In other respects, also, the criterion of consumption is even more deleterious than that of production in its effect of amalgamating individuals, especially women, into a pattern of seeming dependency. Reference to the networks of food bestowers and recipients in Katsina illustrates the problem.

One of the striking features of the women's world in Katsina is the spatial and social autonomy of the women, many of whom live near, but not in the same compound with, their close kin. The fact of receiving food from a compound does not alter this autonomy. A woman with several sons, for example, may receive food daily from each of them, but this does not incorporate her into, or make her a dependent in, the respective households or family units. Bestowal of food on a continuing basis may be a token of kinship, friendship, or patronage. Acceptance does not merge the recipient into the domestic group of the donor.

Outside the residential unit, as well as within it, the formula of common consumption is not only unwieldy but positively misleading. A woman who cooks meals as her trade may well send some of this food to her close kin. They, concurrently, may send her food from their own compounds. Many compounds have multiple sources of food, and are equally distributors of their own cooking, and of foods received which are in excess of their needs. A single compound, even a single individual, may thus be both a recipient and a distributor of food. To reduce these bonds to unilateral dependency, or to fail to recognise the recipient's own social and/or economic autonomy or semi-autonomy is to overlook the complexity of relationships involved in food bestowal, both in terms of donors and ultimate recipients, and in terms of the multiple ties which bind the participants.

Another factor, broader-based and covering more aspects of an individual's behaviour, militates against a unitary and bounded approach to domestic groupings. This is the segregation of male and female roles, evident in marital relationships and running through and beyond individual domestic groups. The use of the concept of the household assumes or suggests a congruence of purpose, goals and activities within the unit. Such joint role behaviour is not evident in the

Hausa domestic unit, and to emphasise it is to impose an alien and inappropriate framework upon the actual system. In fact, husbands and wives do not work together, eat together, go out together, share domestic tasks, or share the same friends. Women's and men's time and social activities, and much of their income, are vested in same-sex networks, generally favouring their kin. This segregation of relationships is reinforced by and reflected in the domestic spatial arrangements. All women thus move freely within the women's section of all houses, while men are denied access to the inner part of most houses, and often feel uncomfortable even in the women's section of their own family or marital compound. This is the logical outcome of a system which turns sons out of the women's quarters from pre-puberty, and which seems to demand justification for any prolonged subsequent visit thereto.

Men's attempts to control women are also reflected in housing patterns: the husband's own room or rooms are generally positioned between the entranceway of the house and the women's rooms beyond: the husband is then 'intermediary' between his wives and the outside world. In fact, control is strictly limited, given the wide separation between the men's and the women's worlds. In so far as a woman is married, and secluded, there is a spatial constraint. But as we have seen, women do not necessarily remain married, and their activities are frequently directed towards the establishment and maintenance of countervailing networks which run parallel to, and can replace, the marital support system. Indeed, to view the domestic unit as a bounded entity, with its members' activities centred in and around it, is to seriously limit and misconstrue the actual interests and affiliations of its constituent population.

Kin solidarity and interdependence, which have been demonstrated in terms of food consumpton patterns, are equally important in other areas. In providing financial assistance, child-care services, and other moral and more tangible forms of support, members of the kin group help each other within and beyond the individual's marital home. Living links between kin are forged through the institution of fostering, whereby women may raise and take on all responsibility for one or more children of their close kin, caring for them until they reach marriageable age, and shouldering also the costly and time- and energy-consuming responsibilities associated with the celebration of marriage in Hausa society.

Women's ultimate security is based on their kin, their children, and themselves. With their independent economic activities, women participate in female networks which may largely exclude other household members. Women who are unhappy with marriage may 'vote with their feet' and leave the marital home; the major constraint is the loss of their children, the custody of whom Hausa custom grants to the father.

It is ironic that, because of seclusion, women are seen as the immobile and constant residents of a household. In fact, women are the real migrants in Hausa society, signalling every change in marital status or career choice by physical movements, from family home to marital home, to family home, to new marital home, and so on. A woman who opts for prostitution moves, initially, far from her kin and friends, later moving back to remain near them.

It is clear from the above that men's and women's careers, residential patterns and roles, even within marriage, diverge sharply. The household, far from being a corporate group with corporate aims, interests, production, and consumption, is rather an artificial construct, with changing personnel whose salient ties are equally or more with their own kin elsewhere than with other household members, with whom their association may in any case be temporary. In a comparative study of domestic groupings in Ghana, C. Oppong emphasised that

> . . . no assumptions should be made as to the congruence of the sets of people who perform various domestic functions of production, consumption, reproduction together, i.e. that those who cook together also eat together or jointly provide the food or farm together . . .

> . . . *jointness* [shared decision-making, task performance, etc.] in any activities between spouses should not be assumed but should be investigated.

> . . . *closure* or functional individuation of the conjugal family may never be assumed but is a subject for enquiry [in as much as] individuals may cooperate with several sets of others to carry out various domestic functions, or [may] carry them out alone (1976, p. 27).

Each of these methodological warnings represents an abyss into which the unwary researcher plummets, using Western assumptions about the nature of domestic relationships. The lack of fit between actual Hausa domestic relationships and the kinds of off-the-rack organisational groupings into which researchers have tried to cram them amply bears out the importance and need for strictures such as these. All aspects of domestic organisation must be analysed before meaningful (and comparative) statements can begin to be made about roles, relationships and authority structures in the domestic setting.

Given the many factors which militate against the use of the construct of the household, or the family, it is imperative that a different, non-sexist analytical framework be employed in studying women's roles in domestic groupings. Possibly the most fruitful approach for future research is that suggested in the Oppong study noted above (1976, pp. 27–28), and later expanded by her into a detailed and cross-cultural format (Oppong, 1980). This approach rejects the conjugal or domestic unit as the framework for analysing women's roles, and focuses instead on the multiple roles of women, relating these to the activities, pressures and influences of significant others, and to the constraints and benefits of various organisational and domestic groupings.

In the Katsina case, a viable approach was to use as an organisational base the one unit with clear spatial parameters, which did not assume prima facie any form of dependency, responsibility, joint production, or joint consumption. This unit was the compound, walled off from similar units, with a single entranceway to the street. The networks of social relationships within and outside the compound could then be analysed on the basis of actual ties, interests and authority patterns, rather than on the basis of the male-dominant assumptions so commonly tied to discussions of the household or the family. Women-centred and women-only compounds were equally weighted with all other spatial units. Using this spatial criterion, 355 compounds lived in by Hausa men and women were analysed. About one-fifth of the total number were headed by women. More than one-quarter of the non-married women and older women were compound heads, as were more than half the women in non-coresidential marriage. In some cases the unit was limited to the woman herself, living alone, while in other compounds the woman lived with one or more of her grandchildren, nephews or nieces, whom she was fostering. Some compounds contained multi-generational women-centred units, as, for example, a widow with her non-married daughter, the daughter's children, and the children the widow herself was fostering. The women worked together at a particular craft, and the children assisted in its distribution. By combining labour and resources, the women could engage in economic ventures on a larger scale than the individual could undertake alone.

The number of women-headed units is not large, by world standards, but women-headed units are a reality in Katsina, and may well be common elsewhere too, although they are at present hidden by the emphasis on conjugal units. As long as women are not seen as individuals, but rather as wives, mothers and daughters, domestic analysis will remain stereotypical, ignoring the real roles, rights and relationships of women.

Measuring Women's Work

We have concentrated here on women's income-producing roles, in order to rectify the statistical misrepresentation which has been demonstrated in survey and census data over the decades. In concentrating on income-earning activities, however, we have neglected the ceaseless domestic labour which is expected and required of women. Though Hausa men treat women primarily as wives and mothers, the labour associated with these roles is not thought of as 'real' work, but rather as an adjunct of women's unalterable biological functions. To the extent that any woman is engaged in unpaid and undervalued or unvalued domestic work, and in agricultural and other endeavours as an unpaid family member, it may be said that her labour is invisible.

Measuring women's work—even recognising or securing the admission that women's work exists—is fraught with difficulties, some of which have been outlined on preceding pages. Many of these problems are related to the implicit challenge to male domination inherent in the kinds of questions asked, and the answers given may be inaccurate partly in response to this challenge and partly because of the difficulties of defining and separating the many dimensions of women's work. The study of women's work demands much more intensive effort than it has for the most part received, and should be based on a combination of (participant) observation and survey techniques. A relatively small sample studied in depth will be of far greater value than a large sample studied only superficially, which means that the quantitative data so beloved of census statisticians must be supplemented by carefully collected qualitative information.

One type of participant observation, especially among people with a low level of literacy, which is utterly crucial to any study of women's work, is the collection of data on time use, or time allocation. A time allocation component should ideally be an integral part of any investigation of women's labour. No other single research instrument is so effective in demonstrating the extent of women's work, the comparative time spent working by men and women, and the reality of gender-based division of labour.[13] A time allocation study requires that, for the period chosen (e.g. 24 hours, 14 hours, 'daylight hours'), every activity performed by the individual subject is registered, and the length of time taken for the particular activity noted. It is necessary to keep a running and immediate account of all activities.[14] The beauty of a time allocation study, and its major failing, rest in the fact that a day has only 24 hours, or 1440 minutes, and that this basic unit of time, or a portion of it, is a non-varying foundation on which to examine women's, and men's, work. The positive side of the technique is that the time constant provides a simple and clear-cut framework within which to measure women's work. The negative side is that women's work is not linear: women often do two or more kinds of work concurrently, especially in relation to their domestic activities.

Nevertheless, even given the difficulty of registering adequately all aspects of women's work, some of which may be carried out simultaneously, the time allocation technique has demonstrated dramatically the heavy burden of work that women must shoulder, and the inequitable relationship between husband and wife with respect to the tasks expected of, and performed by, each.

A conceptual framework incorporating seven roles and statuses of women avoids the pitfalls and assumptions associated with household or family studies by centring directly upon women 'within the networks of significant relationships and within their institutional and cultural contexts, including varied types of domestic organisations' (Oppong, 1980, p. 6), and by examining the activities and expectations associated with the roles of given categories of women in particular contexts. Using this framework, data on women can be collected, including detailed case histories, in order to determine changes in behaviour and expectations over time, and to recognise changes in production patterns associated with changes in reproduction and other factors related to women's changing maternal and domestic roles.[15]

The conception, design, explanation, administration and analysis of labour force surveys demand particular care and forethought. In conceptualising women's work, survey planners need to take into account from the start its multiple dimensions. Questionnaires need to be designed to permit the inclusion of more than one type of activity. And sufficient space must be provided on the form to describe women's work properly, so that it does not subsequently fall into an 'inadequately described, unspecified, or miscellaneous' category. The inclusion of different kinds of labour should end, finally, the constant juggling and misrepresentation of women's roles. Moreover, instructions should clearly specify that the work of domestic maintenance, or 'homemaking', is work, so that it is consistently included among other forms of labour. The range of women's income-earning activities must also be recognised and recorded. Activities will then include, for example, the commodity production taking place within the home, from which women derive income directly, and the labour expended on family farms or in family businesses, wherein the income does not necessarily accrue to the woman directly, if at all.

Wider occupational categories for women's work, created for the purpose of analysis, need to be directly based on women's work, rather than being derived, as in the past, from male categories. By recognising and reporting the myriad forms of work in which women engage at the enumeration level, and utilising these in classification, the extensiveness and richness of women's occupational roles, and their importance to the economy, will begin to be understood, and this vast economic effort will perhaps begin to be respected for the tremendous contribution it is.

For the most effective and accurate data collection and presentation, however, surveys should be used in conjunction with, and as a supplement to, individual-oriented research methods. It is important to have quantitative data on a large scale to support or refute particular hypotheses, but it is even more important to have a clear understanding of the respondent population before unleashing upon them a large-scale survey.[16]

Through a judicious combination of qualitative and quantitative techniques, research concerning the many and varied facets of women's work can be carried out productively and accurately. Such research should afford the investigator(s) a depth of understanding concerning the extent of women's work, and a recognition of the constraints hindering women's entry or involvement in other socio-political and economic activities, which goes far beyond the knowledge attainable through any single research method, or simple survey type of investigation. The findings and insights which are the product of such a multi-stranded enquiry comprise the factual basis vital for comprehension of the present gender-based division of labour, and for the design of effective development plans which will gain for women what is their right: full participation in the organisation and management of the society which has all too long withheld recognition of women's work and worth.

Notes

1 A longer version of this chapter has appeared as No. 125 in the World Employment Programme working paper series, ILO Geneva, 1982. See also Pittin (1984).
2 There have been some excellent micro-studies of the Hausa, to which the objections raised here do not apply. In fact, given the data available, it is all the more unacceptable that Hausa women should be categorised as economic hangers-on. The painstaking work of E.B. Simmons on the rural Hausa, for example, which concentrates particularly on nutrition and the domestic economy, gives considerable detail concerning women's food-processing, and trading activities, and their independent income and expenditure. P. Hill's 1969 article on Hausa women's house-trade is relevant here, while her other publications also include much information on Hausa women's roles and activities. Mary Smith's Baba of Karo, the autobiography of a Hausa woman, gives a running commentary on women's lifestyles in narrative form. Additional, supporting information is available from studies on Niger, such as that of Nicolas (1975). See also the recent work of Schildkrout (1981) and Longhurst (1982).
3 In 1981, Katsina City was redivided into two Local Government Areas.
4 'Non-married' refers to women who have been, but are no longer married. 'Unmarried' refers to women who have never been married.
5 M.G. Smith found that all of the 421 women enumerated in his 1949–50 Zaria study had at least one 'subsidiary' occupation (i.e. any occupation for which the woman receives direct remuneration, and which is not a part of her required duties as wife and mother), while some women had up to four or five (1955, p. 244). The situation appears not to have changed in Zaria, for Simmons reports that '. . . it is socially unacceptable [for a woman] not to have an occupation . . .' (1975, p. 158). P. Hill makes it clear that in Batagarawa and the Kano close-settled zone, virtually all women worked. The husband's social status did not affect women's participation in income-earning activity, or choice of occupation, in Batagarawa, where '. . . the wives of poor farmers are as apt to participate in [housetrade] as those of richer farmers, including the [aristocracy] . . .' (1972, p. 268). In Kano, all women trade, but '. . . the wives of rich men . . . are those most likely to flourish . . .' (1977, p. 173)
6 See, for example, P. Hill (1972), pp. 317–318, for Batagarawa; Goddard et al. (1971), p. 15, for rural Sokoto; Simmons (1976a), p. 19, for rural Zaria. Mortimore and Wilson (1965), p. 90, note women's ownership of goats and poultry in the Kano close-settled zone.
7 E.g. see Bashir (1972), p. 11, for Kano. For other Hausa areas see Nicolas (1975), p. 97; P. Hill (1969), p. 398; and M.G. Smith (1955), p. 115.
8 B. Rogers notes, although such distinctions are 'meaningless . . . they lie at the heart of planners' categorization of the labour force which treats women as marginal workers, if indeed they exist at all' (1979, p. 63).

9   This must have been particularly awkward and confusing for enumerators, as the census form included only the two categories, employed and unemployed.

10 See, for example, United Nations (1975a), pp. 43–44.

11 There seems to be no data available regarding the classificatory framework to be utilised in the 1973 census. The labour force was apparently to have been based on the population from the age of 6 years.

12 M.M. Konan, for example, writing on Hausa occupations and family patterns, notes in passing (1975, p. 2) that the research village included 241 married men, 336 married women, and 133 unmarried adults. She interviewed only married men and women, however, and nowhere gives any information about the family ties (or lack of same) of the 133 unmarried adults (almost a fifth of the adult population!) who are not even distinguished as to gender, much less in terms of social or economic roles. Judging from the questionnaire forms, information concerning the family relationships and marital status of all these other adults was collected. All the more annoying, then, that it was so totally ignored, that this large proportion of the population was excluded even from a study ostensibly of family patterns, certainly the kind of study which should be the first to recognise the alternatives and variations on the constant theme of husband, wife and children.

13 The use of time allocation studies has long been advocated by the United Nations (see, e.g., Szalai, 1975), including the Economic Commission for Africa, which has incorporated a time allocation format in its suggested design for the examination of women's roles (UNECA, 1977, Annex, p. 3). The Burkina Faso/UNESCO/UNDP Project for Equal Access of Women and Girls to Education included a time allocation study, described by B.G. McSweeney (1979), which gives graphic proof of the many obligations which occupy a woman's time, and which place strong constraints upon her participation in other kinds of activities, particularly in relation to opportunities available to men.

14 McSweeney discovered that 44 per cent of women's work was unaccounted for when using the technique of recall rather than direct observation (1979, p. 380). This finding reinforces our belief that merely asking women about their work, as in a survey situation, is an inadequate approach if the aim is to gain a full understanding of the extensiveness and ceaselessness of women's work.

15 The 'seven roles' are well-nigh exhaustive, including as they do women's parental, occupational, conjugal, domestic, kin, community and individual roles. The parameters of each role are outlined, and the roles are then related to: associated activities; acquisition, allocation, management, and control of specific resources, including time, knowledge, and money or material goods; power and decision-making, and relationships with significant others. Its comprehensiveness makes the seven roles framework an ideal baseline guide for research concerning women in general, and a jumping off point for research on specific roles, or aspects of women's roles, expectations and aspirations. See also the associated field guide (Oppong and Church, 1981) and subsequently Oppong and Abu (1985). For potential complexities and variations in conjugal relationships (polygyny, polygamy, monogamy, polyandry) see Oppong (1985b).

16 Anker (1980) presents a number of sample surveys for possible use, with necessary modifications, by researchers interested in women's roles. See also Anker 1983a and 1983b.

2

René Wéry

Women in Bamako
Activities and Relations

In this chapter are discussed certain demographic and socio-economic characteristics of a sample of women surveyed in Bamako, the capital of Mali, which is one of the poorest countries in the world, with an average per capita income of probably less than US$100 per annum. It is still a relatively small city (its population was estimated at about 400,000 in the 1976 population census), but it has experienced a growth rate of around 10 per cent per annum since Independence. The sample of women reflects this large in-migration as well as the diversity of the Malian population, which comprises a majority of Bambara as well as Peule, Sarakole, Malinke and Wolof, and has been differentiated according to the women's reported economic activity.[1] The sample includes 48 compounds located in Ouolofobougou, a central district of Bamako, and in Sabalibougou on the outskirts. One hundred and twenty-eight women were surveyed in these compounds.[2] The women are married and are categorised according to their reported activities including salaried employment, self-employment, exclusively domestic activities and occasional income-generating activities in addition to one of the other three.[3] These four subsets of women are compared in respect of activities, resources, conjugal relationships and demographic factors including family size.[4] Our goal is to explore, at the level of the individual woman and her domestic group, similarities, differences and apparent interactive effects between types of activity on which major energy is expended, access to resources in money and food and their processing and allocation, exchange relations and division of responsibilities and resources with husbands in relation to declared domestic power and modes of decision-making, and family size.

Several populations of what was formerly known as Western Sudan have been subjected to extensive study, mainly ethnographic, from the 1930s until the beginning of the 1960s. In the 1960s, interest shifted to the socialist transformation that Mali was experiencing, but socio-economic data collection remained very limited. It is only recently that efforts to gather demographic and socio-economic data have started, although on a small scale. In addition, the first population census took place in 1976, but its analysis has been somewhat delayed. The present survey was only intended to be a modest means of increasing knowledge of problems relevant to a planning exercise aimed at satisfying basic needs. Its exploratory nature must be emphasised.[5]

The 128 women in the survey have been classified into four subgroups. The first is made up of 19 women who declared in either the first or the second round a salaried job, usually in the civil service, as their main activity. The second includes nine women who considered their main activity to be economic, and who were self-employed or independent. The third group is made up of 64 women who declared their main activities to be household tasks, but in one of the two rounds said they had certain other activities. The majority of these women were petty traders (elsewhere in the text, we refer to this category as women with secondary activities). The fourth category comprises all women declaring only home-based activities. The first and second subgroups are mutually exclusive; in contrast the performance of a secondary activity did not preclude salaried (two cases) or self-employment at the same time (one case).[6]

The average age of the four populations was approximately 35, and most of the women were currently married, those in the salaried and self-employed groups being more likely to be in monogamous marriages. Few salaried women had ever divorced, in contrast to those in other groups. The women were mainly the wives or daughters-in-law of the heads of their compounds.

Bamako attracts large numbers of rural inhabitants, and many of the women were migrants. More of the salaried women (and their husbands) had always lived in Bamako; they were also more likely to speak French and have a higher level of education than the rest, of whom one-fifth had not been to school. The self-employed were distinguished by the fact that half belonged to the Union Nationale des Femmes Maliennes. A few others belonged to women's associations.

About one in ten husbands were involved in some kind of agricultural activity, but a very high.proportion were reported as economically inactive, retired, unemployed or sick, and approximately one in three reported themselves as simply inactive. Of the active husbands, about half were self-employed and half salaried. The activity rate is the highest for the husbands of the women not working outside the home and the lowest for the husbands of those with secondary activities and the self-employed. Most husbands whose wives were salaried were employed, mainly in administration and the civil service; these were also the men who most frequently said they had a secondary activity.

One can tentatively explain the participation of self-employed women and those with secondary activities by the high rate of unemployment among their husbands or, more precisely, the lack of economic activity. The women's level of education was generally low and they had to perform tiring domestic tasks, and the petty trade in which many were engaged left them enough time to fulfil their domestic obligations. Approximately half those with a secondary activity reported that they gave part of their income to their husbands, and many of these women used their income to purchase food. A high proportion of men whose wives had no outside activity were also not economically active, while many of the economically active husbands of the women involved only in domestic tasks were self-employed.

Migration of husbands was quite common in all groups, especially the self-employed, who were also more likely to have a child or step-children living elsewhere. This was less common among the other groups of women, and least common among the salaried employees.

Domestic Organisation: The Compound

The house or compound inhabited only by a husband and his wife or wives and their children is unusual in Bamako. The predominant residential pattern is more complex, often including a man and his wives, his married sons and brothers, and their wives and children, plus unmarried children. Variations are wide, some compounds being extended horizontally or vertically or presenting a mixture of the two. Among the compounds studied, there were more than 50 people present in the largest on the day of the survey, and it was not uncommon to find a compound with five or six or more domestic groups within it.

The various domestic groups living in a compound usually pool their resources, at least as far as cooking is concerned, which for people with low incomes, as in Bamako, is by far the main expense. It is virtually impossible, using survey techniques alone, to study, at the level of the compound, the various income sources and levels of different inhabitants of the compound, as well as their expenses and expenditures, and the contributions by the head and other members of one domestic group to the expenditures, including communal food preparations, of that particular group and of other groups and at the same time to keep the survey data broken down according to the type of activity the women are engaged in. Due to the number of women in a compound, salaried employees, home-based women with secondary activities, and women with no outside activities are sometimes found in the same compound. Moreover, we would hesitate to claim that all possible flows of resources between members of one domestic group and between domestic groups within compounds have been correctly surveyed. In Appendix 2.1, we have represented certain features of the organisation of one compound selected in the survey. This shows, among other things, the multiple sources of income and its redistribution between members and kin.

In spite of the complexity of modes and degrees of sharing resources, however, and the varied nature of the organisation and distribution of tasks between domestic groups, we did try to see how the activities undertaken by a woman in the compound, in particular cooking, might be linked to the type of activities undertaken by the other women living there. We have therefore tried to establish a relationship between the number of women in a compound and the distribution of activities undertaken by all of them.[7] In Ouolofobougou generally the larger the compound, the higher the probability of finding women engaged in different sorts of activity, some in salaried jobs, others mainly home-based with secondary occupations, and others without any outside activity. In Sabalibougou, by contrast, whatever the number of women in a compound, they tended to have secondary activities even in compounds where there were only one or two women.

Food preparation

With regard to cooking, the responsibility for preparing meals for everyone in the compound (known locally in French as *être de corvée*) rotates among domestic groups and within a polygynous group, among wives. In large compounds, two women may cook at the same time for subsets of compound members. A woman living in a compound where there are several domestic groups may, for example, be responsible for cooking for the compound for a whole day twice a week and be free for the rest of the week. In addition, a woman not responsible for the preparation of the common meal that day may well prepare an additional meal for her husband and children, depending upon available resources and tastes. The compound meal is often prepared only with the resources of the domestic group in charge although redistribution among groups can take place, as shown in Appendix 2.1. In large compounds, resources can differ widely among domestic groups according to the

Table 2.1   Mean number of hours spent per day in meal preparation by wife's main activity

Meal preparation	Activities of respondents			
	Salaried employee	Self-employed	Occasional income generating activities	Exclusively domestic activities
N	(19)	(9)	(64)	(46)
Common meal [1]	4.0(2.9)	3.4(2.7)	5.8(5.2)	4.4(3.6)
standard deviation	1.9(2.4)	2.2(2.5)	2.3(2.8)	1.8(0.3)
Other meals 1.1	4.0	1.8	2.4	
standard deviation	.9	—	1.5	1.5
Children's meals	1.2	1.5	.7	1.0
standard deviation	.6	.7	.6	nd
Compound cooking per day [2]	3.0	2.0	3.1	2.5
standard deviation	2.2	2.7	2.9	1.6
All meals/day [2]	3.3	2.9	3.4	2.9
standard deviation	2.2	3.1	2.9	1.9

1 Numbers in brackets, include women not cooking.
2 Hours spent in cooking multiplied by the number of *corvée* days per week. [8]

activities of the various members, so that the richer ones may not be satisfied with the basic meal prepared by the poorer ones. Moreover, women make it a point of honour to outdo each other, mainly through their own contributions. This distribution of duties between the women frees them when they are not involved but otherwise occupies them considerably. A women may spend eight hours or even more preparing a meal for all the compound members.

It is only when there are several domestic groups in a compound and/or several wives in a group, that the cooking rotation takes place. Thus the salaried workers and other women frequently found in monogamous marriages and single domestic group compounds are often responsible for cooking seven days a week, whereas women not working outside the home or home-based women with secondary activities usually live in larger compounds and so rarely cook for more than one or two days a week. Some women do not cook at all, in particular self-employed women and women not working outside the home.

The number of hours women spend on preparing meals thus depends on the frequency with which they are responsible for the compound meals, which differed in each subgroup (see table 2.1).

Only one self-employed woman in four devoted four hours or more to the preparation of a meal. Salaried women and those working outside the home tended on the whole to spend the same amount of time on meal preparation; about one-third spent less than four hours, one-third four hours, and the rest more than four hours. When home-based women with secondary activities were responsible for compound cooking, they tended to spend more time on preparing meals. More than half the women spent more than four hours in the preparation of a meal (frequently as much as seven or eight hours). In addition to the preparation of meals for the compound, some women in all subgroups also cooked additional meals on the days they were not responsible for the compound meals, mainly for their husband and children; salaried women, in particular, prepared special meals for their children.[9]

In sum, a woman's activities outside the compound do not appear to influence significantly the amount of time she spends on food preparation, either for all members of the compound or simply for her own domestic group. The way cooking time is allocated and spread throughout the week differs considerably, however, as does the composition of the set of kin and in-laws for whom she cooks.

Income and its disposal

Wide differences were also apparent between salaried women and to some extent self-employed women on the one hand and the two other categories on the other regarding disposal of income.[10] Nine salaried women kept their wages and disposed of them freely, generally to purchase clothes and sometimes food. Six shared their income with their husbands, two gave it entirely to their husbands, and two reported using it to purchase food. Self-employed women shared their income with their husbands (more than one woman in two) more often than salaried women. One woman in three kept her whole income and devoted it mostly to buying clothes. Sharing was also frequent among home-based women with secondary activities and those with no outside activity (slightly less than one in two). Few women with secondary activities claimed to keep their income for themselves, but a relatively high proportion used it directly to purchase clothes.

The average wage of husbands of salaried wives was approximately three times higher than that of husbands whose wives were home-based but had a secondary activity and approximately twice that of husbands of women involved in housework only.[11] (The figures in table 2.2 include husbands without economic activity and therefore give an idea of the average income of the whole group.) The important income differentials between the three main subsets were not, however, reflected in the contribution made by husbands or heads of the compound (see Appendix 2.1) when their wives were responsible for the compound cooking. The average contribution to the main meal cooking was 15 French francs (figures in table 2.2 are computed on the whole sample) though the contribution made by husbands of self-employed women was around half the average of the others, which can be attributed to the high rate of inactivity among them. One should add that the contribution to the *corvée* is relative; one would need to know the number of persons participating in the meal, and so on, to appreciate more fully the standard of living involved.

Approximately one woman in four declared she had not received money from her husband during the preceding month, including more than one in three of the self-employed but only 10 per cent of home-based women with secondary activities. In absolute terms, however, the average sum received by the women in the different subgroups was surprisingly similar, even when one includes women not receiving anything. Much greater differences are seen in the relative monthly contribution made by the husbands.[12] Husbands whose wives were salaried gave their wives approximately 20 per cent of their average income. In contrast, those whose wives were economically inactive or had only a secondary activity gave between 45 and 50 per cent of their income to their wives. Thus while salaried women were somewhat better off than the other groups in absolute terms, in terms of the sharing of their husbands' resources the salaried women appeared less well-off. However, their husbands were also the most likely to go to the market to buy food, which might compensate somewhat for their lower monetary contribution.

The incomes of wage earners and self-employed women provide them with greater independence for personal expenses, but also make it possible for them to contribute to household expenses. Self-employed women, and home-based women with secondary activities covered many domestic expenses other than food, and the majority of salaried women contributed to cooking expenses. Some economically inactive women did manage to contribute to household food expenses, possibly through transfers from relatives within the compound or living elsewhere, but the survey does not give information on this.

Table 2.2   Husbands' mean income per month and contribution to household expenses by wife's activity

	Activities			
	Salaried employee	Self-employed	Occasional income generating activities	Exclusively domestic activities
N	(16)	(8)	(49)	(34)
Average salary of husband (in French francs)	878	374	339	551
standard deviation	300	—	194	157
Idem plus benefits	1015	374	371	645
standard deviation	432	—	206	200
Husband not contributing to expenses (%) [1]	26	34	12	28
Husband's contribution to corvée (in French francs) [2]	10.4	7.3	10.7	11.3
standard deviation	11.1	9.8	12.5	10.8
Average contribution of husband per month [2, 3]	231(313)	158(284)	201(230)	172(240)
standard deviation	193(154)	211(210)	183(178)	173(160)
Husband only contributes to food (%) [1]	74	56	81	85
Respondent contributes to food purchase (%)	74	77	63	52
Respondent contributes to other expenses (%)	79	89	78	39
Husbands do shopping for the family (%)	69	50	33	44

1 Women's responses.
2 Contribution of husband and/or head of the compound—whole sample; husband's declaration.
3 Figures in brackets exclude cases where husbands do not contribute.

Table 2.3   Indebtedness and financial responsibilities, difficulties and preoccupations, by women's activity (in percentages)

	Salaried employee	Self-employed	Occasional income generating activities	Exclusively domestic activities
N	(19)	(9)	(64)	(46)
Has debts	26	55	31	15
Family owes money	16	22	8	7
Others owe money	32	22	25	7
Sends money regularly	74	55	50	39
Receives money regularly	42	67	56	52
Urban life is hard because:	74	45	45	45
it encourages spending	13	—	50	75
is expensive	50	—	22	—
Prime needs:				
clothes	33	44	61	50
compound	39	33	12	15
Main worry:				
health	32	44	38	57
child	42	44	33	12
money	11	—	11	7

Self-employed women and those with secondary activities seemed to be the most in debt (table 2.3). Perhaps they borrow money to buy goods for sale or take things for sale on credit. Self-employed women also seemed to lend money frequently, either to relatives or non-relatives. In contrast, salaried women and women with secondary activities rarely lent money to their relatives but frequently to other persons. Regular transfers of money or presents to and from family and friends living outside the compound were common; salaried women made transfers more often than other subgroups, but less frequently received money from relatives (see Appendix 2.1). Salaried women's husbands were those most frequently in debt, and the most likely to be involved in regular transfers of money or goods to or from relatives not living in the compound. More frequently than the others, salaried women considered that life in Bamako on the whole was more difficult than in the rural regions, mainly because it was expensive (table 2.3).

Decision-making

Questions for domestic decision-making include the purchase of consumer and durable goods and activities outside the household, including taking a job, educating the children, their marriages, fostering, and so on. Salaried women reported the greatest decision-making power in matters relating to their children and day to day matters (see table 2.4). They thus distinguished themselves from women in the other groups in that they felt that they had a certain control over their lives. The women who felt they had the least decision-making power were those without economic activities; among these most such decisions would either be

Table 2.4   Power and decision-making (mean scores), and perception of control of destiny, by wife's activity

Decision-making power*	Salaried employee	Self-employed	Occasional income generating activities	Exclusively domestic activities
N	(19)	(9)	(64)	(46)
All decisions	285	171	173	79
standard deviation	161	192	138	237
Decisions relating to children	125	42	44	25
standard deviation	86	129	89	134
Day-to-day decisions	160	128	128	54
standard deviation	87	108	87	131
Perception of control of destiny (%)				
yes	26	11	2	4
no	63	78	89	91

* For definitions, see footnote 13.

taken jointly by them and their husbands or other relatives, or they did not participate at all.

Family size and planning

Table 2.5 gives the main data on births and deaths of children, attitudes to motherhood, and knowledge and use of contraception. The average number of living children was four to five. A sadly striking feature was that a majority of women in all activity groups had suffered the loss of a child, particularly among the inactive women and those with secondary activities. With respect to family size, the most remarkable factor was the higher number of living children of self-employed women and their larger family size desires (table 2.5). Salaried women, in contrast, gave birth to their first child at a slightly higher average age than the rest, lost fewer children, had a lower fertility, and more frequently declared that they were satisfied with the number of children they had. They also saw the cost of educating a large number of children as the main disadvantage in having a large family, and they were the only category which used contraception to any extent. Three groups rarely saw the time spent on child-care as a problem, whereas it was often cited by the self-employed women, who seldom considered the cost of rearing children as a disadvantage. Like the women with occasional income-generating activities, the latter also saw the help children give to their parents when they are old as a major advantage of having more children.

Child-care

Fostering

As elsewhere in West Africa, the fostering of children by non-parental kin was quite common among these women, and may be viewed as consistent both with reproductive behaviour and attitudes and with the need for assistance occasioned

Table 2.5   Births, deaths, perception of children and family planning, by mother's activity

	Salaried employee	Self-employed	Occasional income generating activities	Exclusively domestic activities
N	(17)	(8)	(59)	(40)
Average no. of living children	4.1	5.3	4.4	4.1
standard deviation	2.4	3.9	3.0	3.2
Average no. of births	5.3	6.4	5.7	5.1
standard deviation	3.0	4.3	3.5	4.0
Average age at birth of first child	19.1	18.0	17.8	17.7
% with infant deaths	58	50	64	60
mean no. of loss	1.0	1.3	1.5	1.3
% want more children	60	83	67	72
Advantages and disadvantages in having numerous children				
Expensive	71	33	77	64
Take time	—	33	6	11
Bring joy	21	16	8	25
Help in old age	29	50	68	44
Knowledge and use of contraception				
Has heard about it	100	83	60	42
Has made one visit	50	16	10	14
Uses contraceptives	29	—	4	8

by the type of economic activity. The highest incidence of out-fostering (20 per cent) and the lowest incidence of in-fostering were found among economically inactive women (see table 2.6). Out-fostering was least common and in-fostering common among the self-employed, who tended to have the largest families and to want still more children. For them, child labour was an asset. Again, approximately one salaried woman in four had fostered children. As described elsewhere, high-status urban West African women are under pressure to raise the children of more indigent relatives, and also desire domestic help to alleviate the conflicts between their domestic and occupational responsibilities (cf. Oppong and Abu, 1984).

Weaning and feeding
Salaried and self-employed women, on average, weaned their children approximately two months sooner than economically inactive women and those with secondary activities (see table 2.6). Weaning ages varied considerably, however, and this weakens the relationship between economic activity and weaning. In each subgroup, some women weaned their children abruptly, perhaps at 18 months, without having gradually introduced them to foods other than milk, whereas others completed breastfeeding at an early age (6 months, and, in a very few cases, even earlier).

Table 2.6   Fostering, child-feeding and health practices, by mother's activity (in percentages)

	Salaried employee	Self-employed	Occasional income generating activities	Exclusively domestic activities
N	(17)	(8)	(59)	(49)
Has children brought up elsewhere	16	11	17	20
Has fostered children	26	22	11	13
Breastfeeding finished (average age in months)	11.2	10.3	10.8	11.3
standard deviation	6.3	5.7	6.6	7.4
Child weaned (average age in months)	18.2	18	21.2	20.9
standard deviation	9.8	n.d.	6.8	9.8
Child starts adult food (average age in months)	18.8	13.8	17.0	18.4
standard deviation	9.9	7.0	9.6	9.9
Has prepared children's meals	87	67	82	61
Age at which she stopped (average age in months)	21.3	17.5	19.8	24.9
standard deviation	9.5	8.2	8.5	12.5
Has children vaccinated	82	50	73	58
Goes to dispensary for children	87	66	77	81
Goes to dispensary for herself	58	22	31	41
Consults a traditional healer	11	—	13	4
Knows it is important to boil water	95	78	64	72

More frequently than others, the salaried women and the mainly home-based women with secondary activities prepared special meals for their children. The earliest age for stopping this practice was recorded among the self-employed women, and the latest among women without economic activities. The economically inactive women seemed to be the most consistent in giving their children pap at about one year, introducing it to adult food at 18 months, weaning it completely two months later, but continuing to prepare special meals until it is 2 years old. The incidence of bottle-feeding is low.

Health

In rural zones the main preoccupation of women appears to be health. Concern about health seems to be somewhat less in Bamako, and those least concerned with health matters were salaried women, for whom the main preoccupation appeared to be the education of their children. They were, however, aware of health hazards, such as the need to boil drinking water. Vaccination of children was far from being general, but was more common among the salaried women and those with secondary activities, among whom about three women in four were likely to have their children vaccinated in contrast to only two out of four for the other two subgroups. Attendance at health facilities was relatively high among all subgroups, with salaried and economically inactive women using them more frequently than the women in the other two subgroups, and more often for the benefit of the child than for the mother.

Conclusion

The present survey has attempted to cast light on the activities and lives of a sample of women in Bamako, but it has at the same time raised several questions, showing the complexity of the productive and reproductive life of African women without, however, being able to offer any exhaustive analysis. The majority of the population lives within highly complex networks of relations, as tentatively shown for one compound in the appendix. The survey has only been able to indicate certain fragmented features of the behavioural networks, covering the nuclear families of the women surveyed, their domestic groups, the compounds in which they lived, and other compounds where relatives, kinsfolk, neighbours, etc. lived. Understanding of these networks of relations is a basic prerequisite for explaining the behaviour of individuals, as well as the transformations occurring in the systems of production and reproduction and community and domestic organisation. It is also essential for the design of appropriate policy measures to improve standards of living and to effect demographic and economic change. Among the interesting points raised by the survey is that the fertility behaviour of self-employed women seems to be different in many ways from that of the home-based women with secondary activities, although they live in similar types of compound. Moreover, there were striking differences, not reported here, in the distribution by compound of activities undertaken by the women, between the districts of the more traditional Ouolofobougou and the more recently developed Sabalibougou. More in-depth and larger-scale data collection exercises would obviously be necessary, both to study the pattern of activities developing in Sabalibougou, on the assumption that this district may be representative of several contemporary trends, and to relate them to the macro characteristics contrasting Sabalibougou with Ouolofobougou.

One of the objectives of the survey was to explore other concepts of 'household' than that used in the 1976 population census—a definition which was adopted for lack of viable alternatives, but judged not to be fully appropriate to describe the existing residential patterns and socio-economic relations. The notion of 'household' used relied primarily on the marital status of the males living in a compound. Marriage normally leads to certain decisions being taken independently from the head of the compound. Thus, once each male relative of the head of a compound is married, his wives and children are considered to be his direct dependants and are taken to constitute a 'household'. By the same token, on the basis of independence of decision-making, lodgers also constitute separate households. As described, however, this unit is not the usual cooking and eating unit (the common meal is shared by different units of this type, possibly including lodgers).

Although the present survey was limited it did indicate that data useful for social development policies need to be associated with a range of units—the individual, the conjugal family, the parent-child dyad, the domestic group, the residential compound, and the scattered range of effective kin.

With regard to women in modern sector salaried employment—better educated, urban women—factors associated with their smaller family size are apparent. They are aware of the costs involved in raising and educating children to the standards they think appropriate. They have more influence in domestic decision-making and are more able to realise their own wishes. They also start child-bearing later because of their protracted education, and there are indications that they have fewer infant deaths and provide more medical attention and special foods. Their greater say in decision-making may be related to their greater financial independence and greater contributions to household expenses as well as to their education and other social attributes. These women, however, represent only a tiny fraction of the urban population and their number is not likely to increase rapidly whatever the pace of socio-economic development. They do not necessarily point the way, therefore, to any widespread changes in fertility behaviour.

Notes

1   These considerations are based on a two-round household survey, carried out in April and September 1982, within the framework of a project of the Direction National de la Statistique et de l'Informatique du Ministère du Plan in collaboration with the ILO, under a project funded by the UNFPA. The survey was designed following a systemic approach, in which we tried to collect information on demographic, sociological and economic issues, in rural and urban communities. There were questionnaires for the heads of the compounds, for the heads of domestic groups and, lastly, for their wives. Two additional questionnaires served to gather information at the community level and certain anthropometric measures relating to all persons living in a compound. Due to the approach and to budget constraints, and the consequent small sample size, the survey should be considered as a pilot survey more than as a source of representative information on Malian populations.

2   In rural areas, the compound ('concession' in French) refers to an economic unit which, in traditional societies, receives from the chief of the village the right to use a piece of land belonging to it. This notion has been extended, under French colonial rule, to the dwelling unit conceded to a family in urban areas. The compound comprises a variable number of domestic groups, normally but not necessarily related. One finds several cases of lodgers in Bamako, and in rural areas, descendants of 'domestic slaves'. In rural areas all members of the compound devote several days a week to cultivating its land, in addition to the independent cultivation of land by some domestic groups. In urban areas, productive activities are much more diversified. The compound is normally the sleeping unit, but this was not always the case in one of the villages surveyed. As to the consumption unit, more details are given below.

3   Although we discuss here the results of the urban survey, some remarks on the manner in which the activities other than housework have been surveyed in rural areas are in order, because they throw light on possible measurement biases in surveying economic activities in the urban zones. In rural zones, we did not attempt to assess whether the

women interviewed could be classified as being in the labour force or not, as from an early age any woman who is still physically fit cultivates the compound's land. On the other hand, we did try to see whether the respondent, in addition to her obligations in relation to the compound's land performed on her own account certain productive activities, such as the cultivation of a plot, raising animals or handicrafts, possibly providing her with a disposable income. In the design of the questionnaire, we supposed that the cultivation of a plot of land would include a garden where rural women grow onions, tomatoes, okra, etc. which constitute the main, and often the only, additional ingredients to make the sauce for the cereal dish. If selling garden produce has been declared as an activity, as well as the cultivation of a plot in which the women grow millet, maize or groundnuts, the most striking point is that gardening has nearly always been omitted from the list of activities carried out by the women in addition to their household tasks.

We do not know to what extent the same problem applies to the urban survey. A large proportion of women said they were petty traders but, because of a too aggregated classification of activities, the survey does not tell us what they sold or whether these products came from the woman's garden or were bought at the market and retailed. Indeed, many women reporting petty trade activities lived on the outskirts of Bamako, which would tend to show that this type of trade constitutes an important element in the distribution of goods.

The second omission or lack of detail which otherwise could have helped to correct the first, results from a weakness in the questionnaire. Detailed questions on self-employed income-generating activities were put only to women who declared that their main activity was not traditional domestic tasks. These questions on activities outside the home were not asked of the women who declared that domestic tasks were their main activity. These were only given an abridged set of questions, the aim of which was to determine whether the respondent had some occasional, possibly income-earning activities such as selling goods in the market, doing the neighbours' washing, dyeing 'boubous', sewing, etc. The analysis of the first round of the survey has shown the resulting loss of information but because of the short period between the two rounds it was not possible to redesign the second round questionnaire to cover these secondary activities in more detail. This remark also applies to the cultivation of a vegetable plot.

4   The sample size obviously limits any extrapolation within the sample itself by completing missing values on the basis of the average, and extrapolation to other populations, both in Bamako and outside.

5   The other objective of the survey was to test the questionnaire design of the series of household surveys which are to be carried out under the PADEM (Programme africain d'enquêtes auprès des ménages). The survey therefore contained, for instance, modules to collect anthropometric measures, data on nutrition, agricultural techniques, etc.

6   The total number of cases with the classification retained amounts to 138, which results partly from the three cases mentioned but mainly from the change in status between the two rounds, especially from the inactive class to one of the other three or vice versa. It should be noted that we had expected seasonal changes to be pronounced as the first round took place during the dry season, whereas the second round took place when certain crops are being harvested, such as maize, which is usually sold by women on their own account. The questions on the seasonality of secondary activities have shown that women in petty trade or similar activities perform these more or less regularly throughout the year. Women performing secondary activities were concentrated in Sabalibougou on the outskirts of Bamako. The three other sub-samples were more represented in Ouolofobougou, in the centre of the city.

7   A Chi square test gives a significant probability at 2 per cent of dependency (although the number of cells with less than 5 observations is large). When the sample is split between the two districts of Ouolofobougou and Sabalibougou, we still obtain a statistically significant dependency at 2 per cent in Ouolofobougou but in Sabalibougou it is not statistically significant.

8   This puts on an equal footing a woman who is *de corvée* for two days every week and spending 9 hours each day, and a woman living in a nuclear household *de corvée* each day. The Chi square test on the number of hours per day crossed with the activity is significant at 7 per cent, considering either only the time she is *de corvée* or also including meals prepared outside *la corvée*.

9   There may be some confusion in a few cases between meals prepared for children and those prepared, in addition to the common meal, for the husband, and sometimes for the children too. Meals prepared for children do not in theory include meals prepared before weaning.

10 One question in the survey concerned the way in which women dispose of their income, both wages and the gifts they receive. The way in which the question was put was slightly ambiguous, and so the question permitted several replies. Some women declared first how they disposed of their income and then how they used the money that was left, whereas others immediately declared for what purposes the money they had was used without making clear whether these expenditures were freely incurred or whether they had first given the money to their husbands.

11 Because of the difficulty in estimating the net income of the self-employed, only wage earners are used in this comparison.

12 Certain discrepancies were noted between the replies from the husband and those of the wife regarding the husband's contribution to the domestic expenditure. One source of discrepancies is that the husband may give his income or a part of it to the head of the compound, to be subsequently redistributed between domestic groups. This type of flow has not been properly recorded. Moreover, it often seems that the woman will remember receiving a small amount of money (maybe FF25–40) while the husband does not remember giving it. The different structure of questions in both questionnaires may be partly responsible for these discrepancies, but on the whole they are minor.

13 As the list of decisions was long we tried to summarise the information in a global symmetrical index, giving a score that varied from -10 to $+10$ according to the person making the decision and weighted by the frequency of the decision made. For instance, if the woman alone made the decisions the score would be 10; if decisions were entirely taken by the mother-in-law or more distant relatives, the score would be -10. Joint decisions, according to whether the woman put herself first, and who was the joint decision-maker, would be scored between these two extremes. There is an aggregate index covering all decisions and two sub-indices, one covering decisions relating to children and one covering all others. The first index ranges from -600 to -600, that relating to children from -280 to $+280$, and that relating to other decisions from $+320$ to -320.

Appendix 2.1

Description of certain patterns of organisation within and outside a compound

To illustrate some of the points raised above, particularly the difficulty of identifying a single unit of analysis, we have selected in the survey one compound and tentatively represented some of the flows between its members. The flows dealt with are the flows of money and/or goods between the members of a domestic group—mainly the contributions of spouses to the group expenses, flows between the domestic groups that make up the compound where the redistribution of income is prevalent, and flows between compound members and persons not living in the compound. These latter are of interest because of their redistributive functions, but at a higher level of aggregation they also involve a redistribution between rural and urban areas, and indeed between countries, because of the transfers of emigrant workers.

The compound which has been selected was the first compound in the file for those surveyed in Ouolofobougou which is a central quarter in Bamako, ethnically fairly homogeneous (mostly Bambara). It was a relatively large compound comprising five 'nuclear' households, with 56 persons reported as living there in the first survey round. In terms of the number of households, it is not exceptional for Ouolofobougou, nor for certain other regions of Mali. As to the number of persons, the compound was one of the largest surveyed, but in a recent survey carried out in rural western Mali, it was found that many compounds were as large and a significant percentage had more than 100 members.

In the compound chosen, six male members, head's sons, brothers and nephews, were absent at the time of the first round, having emigrated, which is reflected in the transfers to the residing members. During the second round, two households (persons 6 to 9) were not re-interviewed. One household had migrated and the other was not present the day of the interview. Several persons, including a married son and his family, had returned but they were not interviewed.

This compound might be slightly different from average in that the overall educational level of its members was higher than the average in the compounds surveyed and because of the relatively high labour force participation of members, including women in the salaried sector. However, precisely because of these two factors—indices of modernisation—the compound considered is interesting.

Symbols used

△ ○ are respectively the men and the women interviewed. The chief of the compound is numbered (1) and his wife (2); she declared herself self-employed during the first round. The household of his brother is composed of members (3, 4 and 5). One wife had no activity other than household tasks, and the other had occasional income-generating activities. The two households of his married sons are (6, 7) and (8, 9). The fifth household is that of a nephew (10, 11), whose relationship with the head's brother was not identified in the survey. The wives of the two sons of the head and the nephew were salaried workers either at the time of the first round or the second (the nephew's wife).

☐ are parents (not living in the compound).

◇ are friends, neighbours (not living in the compound), institutions.

← are monetary flows: the direction of the arrow points to the beneficiary.

A shaded ☰ or ⧩ represents a debt with a parent or friend, either actual or recently reimbursed, as for the head of the compound who reimbursed a debt to a friend between the two rounds. Alternatively, according to the direction of the arrow, the flow represents someone in debt to the respondent.

A big 'pot' represents a 'common meal'. A small 'pot' ○ represents the preparation of a meal either out of *la corvée* or in addition to the common meal, usually for the respondent's husband and her children.

□ represents expenses other than food, including clothing and fuel, the most common expenses mentioned.

Description and comments on flows

(a) Redistribution of income between 'nuclear' households of the compound

The son (6) and the brother (3) gave their whole income to the chief (1). The son (8) only gave him a part of his income. All men interviewed declared that they gave their wives some money. In addition the chief (1) gave money to the wives of his brother (3) and to the wife of the son (6). The wife of the son (8), who gave the chief only part of his income, did not receive anything. It appears that the wife of the son (6) also received something from her mother-in-law, which was presumably fuel or money to buy fuel (the nature of the transfer was not identified in the survey but it is common for the wife of the head to cover the fuel expenses of the younger women).

(b) Redistribution of income between compounds

The most remarkable outcome was the frequency of income transfers in the compound, transfers of goods are less common though cereals, blankets, jewels and other gifts have been mentioned in the present case, the more so as only the previous month's transfers were recorded in the first round, and in the second round only those that took place between the two rounds (about a five-month interval).

Some of the receipts result from the out-migration of household members outside Bamako and outside Mali. The head had received, for instance, a month before the first round, money from a nephew in France, from one in Niger, and from one in Timbuktu. This type of transfer is normally sent to the head of the compound, though the wife (10) of the nephew (11) had received money from a brother in Niger.

Several members also exchanged money and gifts with relatives living outside and inside Bamako. The head's wife, for instance, gave money to a son living outside the compound but in Bamako as well as to a brother-in-law living in a province. She said that she received money from a son, a daughter and a daughter-in-law, all living in Bamako but not in the compound. One of the brothers' wives (11) sent money and goods to a foster child living in the countryside and to a grandchild, while she received money from a brother, a nephew and another relative. The wife (7) of one of the head's sons takes care of her mother living somewhere else in Bamako, and the wife (9) of the other son supported her family (mother, uncle and 'other' relatives) living elsewhere, while she in turn received money and goods from unidentified relatives.

The frequency of these transfers can obviously be explained in the present case by the migration of family members and/or the work status, among others factors, of the women. The dependency on emigration for family survival is quite common, however, especially in view of the present drought in the Sahel, and the high population mobility in western Africa is well known. More generally, as transfers in other compounds would show and as has been documented in the region, the interdependence of households and compounds is very widespread. Even from this one case, one can see that loans to and from kin or friends and neighbours are common both for men and for women.

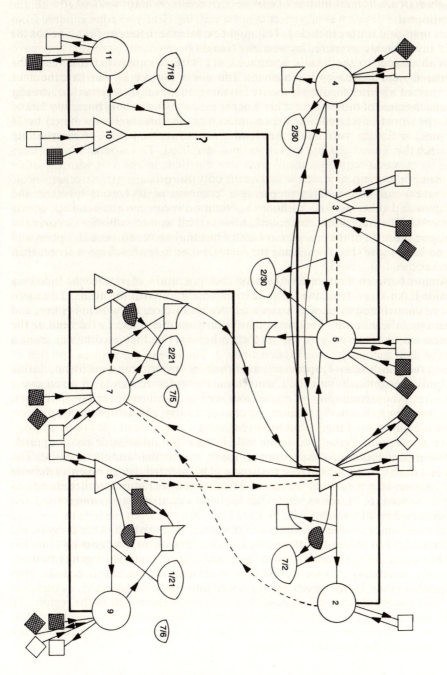

Diagram 2.1: Resource Flows in a Compound

(c) *Redistribution and cooking within the nuclear households*

Concerning cooking, all women, except the head's wife, cook a 'common' meal. It should be noted, however, that the brother's wives claimed to cook for 30 persons whereas the head's sons' wives said they cooked for 21 only. The reason for this difference was unfortunately not investigated. Although women were asked the numbers of adults and children of each sex the 'common' meal was shared with, the questionnaire design was imperfect in not specifying clearly whether children from other households were included. This might explain the discrepancies as well as the 'additional meals' prepared by women (7) and (9).

With respect to the head's household, the wife reported that the meals she prepared were shared by her husband and a son but not by her. It cannot be ascertained whether she simply omitted to mention herself or whether she actually shared the meal of other households. For the nephew's household (members 10 and 11), the woman declared that the common meal she prepared was shared by 18 persons, including two adult men and three adult women. The relationship between this household and others was not identified. This woman also declared that there was a 'common meal' each day but that, in contrast with the other women of the compound, she would be the only one preparing it. (In other words, we have a case of a woman preparing a 'common meal' for her husband and children and other persons without the 'rotation' principle characteristic of the *corvée*). In the traditional compound, however, all women, whether *de corvée* or not, give the head of the compound a dish when they cook. This could explain why the nephew's wife (11), not sharing the *corvée*, nevertheless feeds more people than just her own household.

Arrows between 'household members' and 'pot' and 'other' have the following meaning. An arrow from the husband to his wife shows that the husband declared that he contributed to his wife's expenses. An arrow from the wife to her husband means that the wife gave her husband her salary or other sources of income. In the present case, the two wives of the head's brother said that they gave their husband a part of their income (cf. the broken arrows). The wife of the nephew and that of one of the head's sons (7) apparently kept their income without explicitly declaring so, and devoted it to buying food, clothes and things for their children. In contrast, the wife of the second son (9) declared that she kept her income for herself, though also devoting it eventually to food and clothes. Lastly, the wife of the head gave a response out of the range of answers envisaged.

An arrow going to the 'pot' or the 'other' (note that differentiation is not made between contribution to the 'common meal', and to the 'additional meal') and coming from that one linking the husband and his wife tells which expenses the wife had to cover with the money she received (from her husband and from the head). In the household (6, 7), for example, the husband's contribution covered food and other expenses; in household (8, 9), only food. Arrows from the wife to 'pot' and 'other' tell that the wife contributes to the household expenses with her personal income. All women, except the nephew's wife, did so. Arrows coming from the husband and going through shaded 'pot' and 'other' represent the fact that the husband declared that he went personally to the market (regularly or occasionally) to buy 'food' or 'other' goods for the household.

Part II

Fertility, Parenthood and Development: Yoruba Experiences

Whereas for the demographer fertility signifies achievement in the production of offspring by a specified total population, for the anthropologist it signifies the achievement of parenthood as a culturally defined status of individuals, which initiates and to be complete must embrace the process of socialising offspring—turning offspring into children, so to say (Fortes, 1978, p. 18).

In the West African situation . . . there is first of all the principle that no one is a complete person until he or she marries and achieves parenthood . . . Secondly there is the deeply ingrained idea that normal men and women should continue to beget and bear children throughout their fecund years (ibid., p. 45).

A crucial dimension of the national development process of any country is the numbers of offspring reproduced by the individuals in the reproductive age span and the extent to which the resources needed for rearing this next generation are available and allocated to this purpose. Decisions about such allocations take place at every societal level, governmental, community and familial, and the ways in which the associated tasks and responsibilities are spread, and the amount of concern and interest invested in child-care and development, are among the important differentiating facets of the world's cultures. Moreover, the extent to which parental resources are increasingly used for child-rearing and the diminution of reliance upon child labour are recognised as being important components of demographic transition.

West African societies remain extremely pro-natalist, but with significant changes in values and practices among small segments of the population. There is also considerable evidence of widespread abortion, indicating that not all conceptions are welcome and that there is scope for expansion of such meagre family planning facilities as exist—a topic to be explored in Part III. Both in the recent past and in the present major transformations are taking place in the ways in which offspring are socialised. The most noticeable is the increasing part played by formal schooling in the past several decades, and at least for some people the extent to which biological parents rather than kin groups are becoming responsible for, and personally involved in, the care and socialisation of their own children, in contrast to the time honoured and widespread practices of fostering and shared child-care. Again, as wage employment and mechanised farming take the place of household-based modes of agricultural production and trading, child labour within the kin context has decreased, opening the way for children as a schooled leisure class on the one hand or as child labourers in the farms and businesses of strangers on the other.

At the national level, concern for the development of the next generation has been demonstrated by the large proportion of the national budgets of West African countries allocated to education and the mammoth attempts to introduce universal primary education in areas which had been hitherto neglected. At the same time, however, there is a general lack of legal protection of minors from exploitative child labour. No countries of the region have yet ratified Convention 136 on the minimum age for employment.

Parenthood

In West Africa, in order to become a socially recognised adult, even in some cases to have proper mortuary rites performed, a woman or man must first become a parent, and tremendous pressures are exerted on those deviants who postpone the event beyond the age regarded as normal. Marriage is meant for child-bearing, and in many societies it is the occasion for elaborate and protracted exchanges of gifts and goods between the kin groups of the individuals concerned (Oppong, 1985b). Infertility results in acute anxiety, and a search for ritual and medical assistance. Parenthood provides the pivotal social role for individuals.

Total fertility rates of seven or more are not uncommon in the region, being recorded in Ghana, Guinea, Mali, Togo and Burkina Faso. The physical strains involved in such repeated births and prolonged lactation for women have recently been emphasised, and Harrington (1978) has devised an index of physical and nutritional stress which measures the proportion of a woman's reproductive life spent either pregnant or breastfeeding. Her Nigerian data demonstrate that in some communities more than half the women who have ever been pregnant have spent more than 60 per cent of their adult lives pregnant or breastfeeding. Indeed, women can expect to spend 20 years or more of their lives bearing a child every third or fourth year, as more than half who live to 50 bear a child in their forties and births to teenagers remain common (Ware, 1983, pp. 20–21). In some countries nearly a quarter of girls aged 15–19 give birth in any one year, and a small minority are mothers by the age of fourteen (ibid.). As table 3 in the Introduction shows, teenage mothers contribute 15–16 per cent of the total fertility rate in West African countries. Some differences in family size are observable by type of employment, education level, and place of residence (urban or rural).

Parenthood and Fertility among the Yoruba

In this section there are five essays which focus upon aspects of parenthood and fertility among rural and urban sectors of the Yoruba population of Nigeria, in the light of prevailing and changing socio-economic circumstances, in particular the expansion of education, labour market demands and opportunities, urbanisation, and rural development. The aspects considered include family size preferences and achievements, investments in children and expectations of returns from them in terms of labour, maintenance or old age security, and the stresses for mothers as child-rearing becomes more costly and as home and work become, at least for some, increasingly spatially separate spheres with rigid and conflicting schedules of activities and responsibilities.

The potential connections between reproduction and economic factors have been examined in a few earlier studies of the Yoruba. Ware (1975) indicated the link between favourable attitudes to fertility regulation and lower family size on the one hand and perceived costs of raising children and lack of resources on the other. Caldwell (1977a, 1977b) discussed the perception of educational costs and their impact, postulating that while children still provide net economic benefits fertility would remain high, an economically rational strategy. Adepoju (1977a) noted the continuing inputs of labour by children into domestic economies and thus the continuing rationality of high fertility. Adeokun has linked traditional birth spacing practices to the physical development of the last child in relation to the mother's work patterns and goals.

Here the first essay by Farooq and associates examines survey evidence of some of the correlates of differences in preferences and achievements for parenthood already noted, including education and urban living. In the subsequent chapters, Orubuloye and Adeokun attempt to see how and why values regarding numbers of offspring may be changing as a result of parents' altering perceptions of the costs and values of children. They take into consideration children's labour value, costs of educating them, and the kind of income and security they may provide for their parents in later life. Adeokun attempts this task by comparing Yoruba and Creole data, the latter being partly of Yoruba descent and subjected to forced migration, settlement, and decades of education and urban living in Sierra Leone. Each of these essays, like earlier ones, highlights the need for more multifaceted data sets from individuals, communities and domestic groups, in addition to survey responses, if we are to gain a clearer understanding of the mechanisms through which fertility-related values and practices begin to change. They point to the need for more understanding of socio-economic transactions between parents and children, husbands and wives, and kin, of the allocations within and between households of resources and power, and of decision-making processes and the associated norms, values and beliefs.

Several approaches can be adopted to analyse intergenerational and lateral flows of income and wealth (Ben Porath, 1982a and b). Flows designed to have an impact on the future earning capacity of the next generation can be analysed within the framework of human capital theory. Flows between the generations can be viewed as part of implicit contracts in which the family substitutes for imperfect or non-existent markets and flows can be viewed as an outcome of the altruistic nature of family relationships. Since such flows occur as an aspect of parental/filial relationships, they are perforce shaped by the cultural norms, laws, values and beliefs attached to parental and filial roles which vary widely in different ethnic groups, as well as being subject to prevailing resource constraints and under pressure for change from various quarters.

To understand such flows and exchanges in West African contexts there is need for more household-level micro-research which would help us understand demographic and economic processes of change (Adepoju, 1977a). Moreover, the household economy is intricately interrelated with family structure but the latter is generally not considered in the type of aggregate data analysis frequently found in demographic and economic accounts. There is thus need for more detailed, in-depth studies of small communities and families, which could examine at the micro-level the impact of such critical demographic phenomena as rural–urban migration, different modes of rural production, and household income levels and labour utilisation, not to mention fertility (ibid.).

In the last two essays in this section there are attempts to document such aspects of domestic economies, changing familial roles, parental resource constraints, and pressures for change. They try to document in more detail the role expectations, activities, conflicts and strains of sets of working mothers, and how they are altering: one set is in a rural trading co-operative, the other in urban homes and workplaces. In both cases several types of data are used in addition to survey responses, including observations, focused interviews and group discussions.

Chapter 6 by Patricia Ladipo thus reports on an action research project which was carried out within the scope of an experimental rural development project, the Isoya Rural Development Project, which was started in 1969 by the University of Ife as the pilot project in integrated rural development. The Isoya Rural Development Project had the objective of improving the living conditions of the rural people in the area around the university, and was also meant to serve as a laboratory for testing and teaching approaches to rural development. The project encompassed programmes in agriculture, intermediate technology, home economics and adult literacy. The emphasis was on agriculture, and by 1972 a high yielding variety of yellow maize had been successfully introduced as a cash crop. Women in the project villages had traditionally traded in food crops, while men did much of the marketing of cash crops; consequently the men took over the marketing of the new maize, from which women were excluded. At the same time, white maize became scarce and women's trading cycles suffered. Accordingly, with the help of the development project, multi-purpose co-operatives were set up for women.

Co-operatives have been in existence in Nigeria for 60 years. In a study of women's co-operatives in western Nigeria (Grant and Anthonio, 1973), two types were found—registered ones which provided thrift and credit, co-operative labour and marketing services, and unregistered ones, which encouraged direct production of agricultural produce, marketing, and the co-operative spirit, and gave loans to their members.

In comparison Okonjo (1979) reporting on rural Igbo communities has described contribution clubs devised to assist members in small-scale capital formation which fulfil some of the functions of a bank or an insurance society. Since the women did not use banks and few used the post office, the clubs were invaluable. The women she surveyed invested their money in education, trade and business or in a cloth-weaving co-operative which entitled members to instruction and supervision and guaranteed markets.

Women's involvement in modern co-operatives remains low, however, and as yet they have hardly been used as a vehicle for population education. A UNFPA/FAO sponsored field study and action project on the involvement of rural women in co-operatives in Nigeria, and the feasibility of introducing population education through co-operatives, has recommended not only that co-operatives societies should broaden their programes and objectives, so as to attract more members, but that management skills should be developed and education provided for rural women in co-operative principles and practices as well as functional literacy (Osuntogun and Akinbode, 1980). It was further recommended that formal population education be introduced into the curricula of co-operative training institutions. The data base for the study came from 543 respondents surveyed in 39 co-operative societies.

In the study described here, Patricia Ladipo documents what happened among a group of rural women when three types of planned innovations occurred: provision of credit support for co-operative formation, introduction of improved maize storage techniques, and provision of family planning information. This account provides an example of documentation combined with action at the individual and group levels and, while demonstrating change and the capacity and desire for change, also reveals the continuing barriers to economic and demographic innovation in rural agricultural settings, including the lack of primary health care and the consequent ever-present fears of infant mortality.

In the last essay in this section, Catherine Di Domenico and associates examine the case of urban employed mothers and their dilemmas in trying to reconcile conflicting domestic and occupational activities and responsibilities in contexts in which help from kin and offspring is dwindling and fathers usually play a minimal part in the daily care of children and domestic chores.

As a prelude to these discussions, a brief background on some essential features of Yoruba society follows.[1]

The Yoruba

The Yoruba are one of Africa's largest ethnic groups, totalling an estimated 20 million and more in Nigeria alone. Given this population size, generalisations are difficult. Consequently, what is presented here is a highly abstract sketch of the society, highlighting the antiquity of the people, the recent but rapid spread of mass formal education, and the persistence of aspects of the traditional family system, in spite of apparent socio-political pressures for change and the rapid growth of urban centres, many of them of ancient origin.

The majority, like people in the rest of West Africa, remain predominantly rural peasant cultivators whose major food crops are yams, cassava, cocoyams and plantains. Cocoa has remained the major source of cash earning among the Yoruba since the beginning of the century. The methods of cultivation are generally crude, and the holdings usually fragmented. The men do most of the hoeing of the fields while the women sow, reap and husk and prepare and market farm products.

Archaeological evidence supports the great antiquity of Yoruba civilisation as well as the role played by the family in the transmission of skills from one generation to the next through the process of apprenticeship. Agricultural pursuits traditionally constituted the dominant activities of the adult population, often in combination with the practice of some trade. In the administration of land and of society, the population was organised into progressively more complex units starting from the domestic group and descent group of mutual obligations, headed by the oldest male, through the village, containing a group of inter-related kin groups under a *bale*, to the group of villages, claiming common descent under a crowned king who traced his ancestry to Oduduwa, founder of the Yoruba. A period of protracted warfare among the different subgroups of the Yoruba did not destroy their coherence, which was built around a common language, culture and customs.

In a century of colonial and European contacts and administration, changes in Yorubaland were gradual. Christian religious contacts were first established, before schools, modern health institutions and infrastructure were introduced. The physical presence of Europeans was patchy, and the geographical spread of the territory large. The colonial administration placed its reliance on local institutions and resources. This arrangement limited the extent and intensity of the transformation of some aspects of society, which had begun through the establishment of schools and churches.

The process of agglomeration of populations based on primary occupations predates these colonial contacts and the advent of modern rural–urban migration. This process was accelerated by the administrative framework adopted by the colonial administration, and by the clustering of paid jobs in administrative centres.

Urban centres

Two of the major urban centres which feature as the settings for the employed mothers in Chapter 7 are Ibadan and Abeokuta. Ibadan is the largest commercial, educational and administrative centre in Yorubaland outside Lagos. It is the site for a wide range of industries from cigarette-making to heavy vehicle assembly, and it has become the publishing centre for the nation. Abeokuta contains somewhat smaller-scale industries, particularly food processing and textiles. Although its growth rate has been slower than that of Ibadan, both cities are increasing rapidly in size and area, both because they share the high national growth rate and because they are the dominant migration destinations for their region. Both cities are 'traditional' in the sense that they have histories which antedate the period of European colonialisation.

The populations of both cities are still composed mostly of indigenes of the respective cities, although migrants from other parts of Yorubaland, Nigeria, and elsewhere do co-exist with the local inhabitants. At least 90 per cent of the population of the cities is estimated to be of Yoruba origin. Of these, at least one-third were not born in the cities but have migrated from elsewhere. Some have come from other large towns in Yorubaland, but the majority come from outlying villages and hamlets in search of modern amenities and employment opportunities.

Female labour force participation in these towns is high, and may be estimated at about 90 per cent of that for men. According to the 1963 census figures and recent survey data, two-thirds of the women in the labour force appear to be engaged in commercial activities. Most of these are saleswomen, the majority of whom work as traders or petty hawkers in the local markets. This commercial class is predominantly female.

The social structure of Yoruba urban life is a complex interweaving of two hierarchies: a traditional ladder determined by age, family status and office; and a more modern ladder the rungs of which are marked by wealth, income and education. At the top of the first hierarchy is the Oba (roughly equivalent to a king) and his chiefs. These are generally men of advanced years and appropriate sagacity, although they may have little formal education. The latter hierarchy is headed by the new elites: professionals with high levels of education or business people with large incomes. Both groups, but particularly the wealthy, may engage in highly conspicuous consumption that contrasts starkly with the poverty of the urban masses. The small but growing middle classes are dominated by civil servants and higher level wage-earners in the public and private sectors.

Like the urban society itself, the services of the city are changing rapidly. Expanding education facilities and requirements dominate the social consciousness, especially of the young.

Education

The mass transformation of the Yoruba population began with the introduction of formal, free and nearly universal primary education in the mid-1950s, until all levels of education became free in the new Yoruba states of Ogun, Oyo and Ondo, which were carved out of the former western state of Nigeria and to which the data for this study refer. Given the potency of education for the change of traditional society, it is not surprising that the impact of mass education can be observed in different aspects of the society. Most notably, there has been a steady increase in the proportion of educated persons in younger cohorts of the population. For example, while less than 20 per cent of the female respondents involved in the KAP survey born before 1921 were educated, as many as 60 per cent of those born since the introduction of free primary education had received some education. There has also been a corresponding increase in the employment of both sexes outside agriculture. The free circulation of population, for purposes of trade in farm produce and in manufactured goods, has also encouraged migration into the cities. Increasingly, a range of responsibilities has been transferred to non-family based organisations. The school plays an increasing part in the formation of values. Civic duties have increased. Payment of taxes, greater participation in political and public sectors of the economy, and the increasing social welfare content of government programmes have reduced the functions of the family.

September 1976 saw the launching of a national programme of universal primary education, which encourages all children aged six and above to attend free schools. This change, along with the expansion of secondary education, has significantly restricted the availability of older children for the supervision of their young sisters and brothers or for domestic or agricultural employment. Health facilities are also expanding but are still inadequate for a rapidly growing urban population.

One outcome of the various changes in the area as a whole is the ageing of the farming population and the farming family through the out-migration of the younger and better educated groups.

Procreation and its context

Both fertility and mortality levels remain high in this region, with a crude birth rate estimated at around 50 per 1,000 population. Notions about desired family size, fertility limitation practices and birth spacing in different sectors of the population have been documented in a number of demographic studies and surveys (e.g. Caldwell, 1982, Chapters 2 and 3). In addition anthropologists have described traditional and changing socio-economic activities and institutions including marriage, kinship and domestic organisation (e.g. Lloyd, 1955).

The bonds of kinship, the status due to seniority, and the separation of the sexes are some of the principal elements in traditional Yoruba society that act as stabilising factors, persisting even in contemporary urban settings as well as rural areas. Kinship entails loyalty, co-operation, mutual help and tolerance, and seniority guarantees deference and obedience to authority (Fadipe, 1970, p. 118). The proximity and availability of people, control of required resources, and choice have all become more important factors shaping familial relations. In the case of residence patterns, for example, there have been changes in the technology and inputs into various aspects of home construction which have led to a reduction in the proportion of inexpensive family compounds simply constructed of mud, wood and thatch and an increase in expensive individually financed and owned, immediate family housing, which is much less amenable to expansion and thus the accommodation of large and increasing numbers of kin.

Traditions of kinship which have persisted include worship of ancestors, reckoning of ties of descent over great distances and through time, and the love of periodic festive reunions of kin; all these encourage the persistence of customary modes of behaviour and expectations in more modern settings. It is in this context of change and tradition that the Yoruba family must be viewed.

Marriage is regarded as expressly for the purpose of procreation and often breaks down if the couple fail to have children for several years (Orubuloye, 1977). Polygyny is one of the the traditional practices which continue to flourish and the majority of women are likely to spend part of their life in such marriages. In addition, segregation of conjugal roles persists in the economic, social and emotional spheres. One anthropological observer concluded that males and females live almost in separate worlds (Marshall, 1970). This separation is sometimes spatial with husbands and wives living in separate domestic groups. The father–child link is traditionally one of authority and often physical distance. It is the mother–child bond in which the greatest emotional cohesion and physical proximity are customarily witnessed. Sibling bonds are often close too, with older brothers and sisters caring for the younger ones, especially children of the same mother.

The pressure on the Yoruba woman to support her own children and thus to make money is great, in view of her knowledge that her husband may at any time take another wife and beget other children who will also make demands upon his limited resources. Moreover, in the case of separation or divorce, she may become the children's main or only support. Both married and unmarried women are thus expected to play an active part in economic affairs alongside their family roles. For centuries they have been economically involved as craftswomen, traders and farmers, and they are still actively encouraged by their families to follow courses either in Western education and skills or in more traditional crafts. Indeed, a girl is often not considered fit to marry until she has acquired some training. This results in a relatively late age of marriage among the Yoruba compared to neighbouring peoples. Yoruba women also have a higher recorded rate of labour force participation in both the formal and the informal sectors than other Nigerian women, and are more likely to undertake apprenticeship training. If a woman fails to work and contribute to family expenses she is often regarded with contempt by her peers, her husband, and her family.

Despite their eagerness to enter the modern labour force, women face legal barriers in their attempts to play a full part in the modern economy. Laws set up to protect women, relating to maternity leave provision and protection against night shift work, are seen as serving to reinforce employers, especially in the private sector, in their negative attitudes towards employing women workers. These negative attitudes are also reinforced by the fact that women are overwhelmingly responsible for child-care arrangements and day-to-day household management. Managers tend to assume that women will more frequently be late and have higher rates of absenteeism than men, although there is no proof that they are correct in this assumption. These and related issues, and the consequent evidence of labour market segregation on the basis of sex, have recently been documented by Di Domenico (1983) and Adeokun et al. (1984).

Family size

Although there is a traditional preference for male children, all children are normally welcomed into the Yoruba family and regarded as a blessing. Most Yoruba wish to have many children, are worried if they have few children, and dread having none and being left without descendants. If this arises from infertility a variety of solutions, from divorce and remarriage to polygyny, is generally attempted, as the wife rather than the husband is usually blamed for this state of affairs. Death of children may also be a cause, however, and high infant mortality rates may partly explain why Yoruba fertility is still high and why there is as yet no sure evidence of a decline in any part of society. Little attempt is made to control fertility except by periods of sexual abstinence after birth and after reaching a certain age. Many Yoruba continue to believe in unrestricted fertility. The belief that economic limitations should restrict fertility is found mainly among the educated middle classes of the cities.

Traditional socio-economic and political institutions as well as high infant mortality levels provide powerful motivation and support for high fertility, while everywhere the lot of the childless woman or man is to be deplored. Among the Yoruba, childless couples are looked upon with sympathy and suspicion. Both individual and community efforts are mobilised to offer sacrifice to the gods of fertility to solve the problems of childless women.

Breastfeeding

Breastfeeding practices are closely related to socio-economic characteristics of Yoruba women such as age, occupation and education. Traditionally, most babies were weaned between the ages of two and four years. More recent studies have found breastfeeding to last 18 months to two years. Women with higher levels of education nurse for shorter periods than those with low education because their jobs are likely to make breastfeeding for long periods impracticable. Di Domenico and Asuni (1979) found that among women in a more 'traditionally-styled' working environment in Ibadan, where young children can accompany their mothers, there is a definite tendency to breastfeed longer than among those in more 'modern-styled' environments where the child must be left at home and where working hours are less flexible. A combination of breast and bottle appears to be the pattern increasingly adopted by Yoruba women (ibid.). The increased use of bottle-feeding has now been recognised as a problem at both the national and the international levels. The medical profession in Nigeria has started a campaign in favour of breastfeeding, and the World Health Organisation has adopted a code of practice severely restricting the sale and advertising of breast milk substitutes.

Evidence suggests that prolonged breastfeeding plays a vital role in the suppression of ovulation. Another aspect to birth spacing is cultural. The length of time the Yoruba mother breastfeeds her baby relates to the taboo on intercourse while nursing, based on the belief that the semen will spoil the breast milk. Prolonged sexual abstinence after the birth of the child is a major constraint on the fertility of Yoruba women and abstinence almost always lasts longer than lactation (Okediji et al, 1976). Although the traditional emphasis on prolonged periods of post-partum abstinence (lasting for about three years) has diminished due to increasing levels of education and migration to urban areas, the practice is still an important aspect of Yoruba culture (Orubuloye, 1981; Adeokun, 1983). In the cities, and especially among the more educated, abstinence is gradually being replaced by the use of modern contraceptive devices. However, these have not as yet significantly affected overall fertility or the desire to have a large family (Orubuloye, 1981).

Child-care

Child-care and rearing of infants and young children in West Africa is typically shared by parents, siblings and kin (cf. E. Goody, 1978). When mothers go to farm or market, the older and younger members of the household look after the very young ones. Moreover, most traditional farming and trading activities of women permit them to carry their small babies with them wrapped in cloths upon their backs. West African mothers are thus not rendered economically inactive because they are married and rearing children. The Yoruba pattern is no exception (Di Domenico, 1980). As Chapter 7 demonstrates, however, in urban areas, where most people work outside the home, the picture is different. Because of migration, the smaller, less flexible size of dwellings, and schooling, brothers and sisters and other relatives are often not available to care for infants and small children. In spite of such changes women continue to play an active part in economic activities outside the home, and according to the 1974 National Manpower Sample Survey in Nigeria, about one-half of the total urban female population were engaged in some form of economic activity other than farming (Federal Republic of Nigeria, 1979). In the Yoruba urban setting, where most women are engaged in traditional occupations, the presence of children at home does not seem to diminish the level of women's economic activity outside the home (Lucas, 1976; Fadayomi et al., 1979). Motherhood can frequently be combined with income-producing work because there are still substitutes to take on maternal responsibilities—house-helps, nannies, grandmothers, and in recent years day-care and nursery centres.

Education leading to work in the more modern sector of the economy with inflexible hours and away from home is likely to increase the pressures on the married couple, however, thus adding to the strains of having large numbers of children. For there is evidence of frequent changes of inexperienced child care-takers and accidents due to their carelessness and a general desire for the traditional now dwindling support from the grandmother and other relatives. There is also a growing awareness of the need for good modern alternatives in the way of day-care facilities, which at present are in some cases so inadequate as to put the children at risk. As we will see in the fourth chapter of this section, there is thus increasing strain and conflict for urban employed mothers as the traditional supports crumble and new institutions fail to develop rapidly enough to cope with the rising demand.

Current Awareness

In the past ten years there have been a number of conferences, meetings and publications on the topic of the Nigerian population, particularly women and children. These have been partly inspired by an increased awareness of problems during the International Women's Decade and the International Year of the Child (1979), and the World Population Conference (1984).

Of special importance was the meeting held early in 1985 in Ibadan—A Plan of Action Workshop on a Population and Development Programme for Nigeria. At this meeting reports of the economic demographic situation of the country and projections of possible futures were presented and discussed by senior government officials from all concerned ministries. Analyses were considerably hampered by the lack of basic statistics on population size and fertility and mortality levels, thus

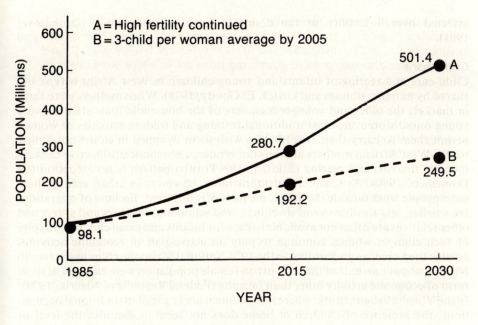

Figure 3.1: Nigeria: Population growth under different fertility assumptions, 1985–2030

Source: The Futures Group (1985): Nigeria: The effects of population factors on social and economic development. Washington, RAPIO

possible projections had to be based upon informed estimates. The report of the Washington-based Futures Group raised considerable interest and debate. With regard to possible patterns of population growth till the year 2030 under different fertility assumptions and taking the 1985 population as 98.5 million, the report demonstrated that with a fertility rate of 6.34 children per woman and a population growth rate of 3 per cent the population would grow to over 500 million. If fertility were reduced to replacement level over the next thirty years, that is two to three children per woman, the population would still rise to nearly 250 million by 2030. This growing population was set within the current context of agricultural growth patterns and the rates of depletion of natural resources, as well as population needs for employment, health services and education. The potential consequences of such rapid population growth gave planners and decision makers much food for thought (see figure 1).

Following the workshop, an Inter-ministerial Consultative Group was set up, comprising representatives from various federal ministries and nongovernmental organisations. A sub-committee drafted the Population Policy document for Nigeria which has recently been submitted to Government for ratification. The draft population policy sets out concrete objectives and operational targets aimed to moderate the rate of population growth, enhance the status of women, raise the minimum age of marriage and reduce infant mortality rate, among others. Each executive ministry—Labour, Agriculture, Health, Education, Social Development, etc.—is charged with the responsibility of implementing and monitoring the performances of their respective activities within the overall population programme, especially the delivery of family planning services. Workshops and sensitisation activities at the state and local government levels have followed.

Interest has also increased in examining the ways in which women's activities affect the process of development and the reciprocal impact of urbanisation and formal sector employment on women, children and family forms. In Ibadan alone in the past decade various conferences have been held which have been directly relevant to the topic of working mothers and their pre-school children.[2] In Nigeria as a whole the debate has been vocal. Various international and national bodies have encouraged research and writing on the topic (Fadayomi et al., 1979; Fapohunda and Fapohunda, 1976). A number of resolutions have by now been presented to decision-makers in government circles and elsewhere based on these conference proceedings and research reports. The following studies also have some clear policy implications. Chapter 6, for example, is of practical importance to the design of integrated population and development programmes for agricultural communities, combining as it does accounts of three types of planned innovation: credit support for co-operative formation, improved storage techniques for an important cash crop, and family life education. It provides a nice example of research combined with action at the individual and group levels, underlining the fact that government assistance to women may need to be based on a different set of criteria from that given to men. Incidentally it demonstrates the inter-relatedness of women's reproductive and productive roles, and highlights continuing barriers to demographic change, such as the lack of accessible health facilities and high infant mortality rates. Chapter 7 calls attention to the increasingly difficult predicament of working mothers whose occupational activities cannot be combined with child-care and the consequent need for nurseries and crèches attached to places of employment.

Notes

1   The following text incorporates passages by Adeokun, Di Domenico et al., Ladipo and Orubuloye, authors of four of the subsequent chapters.
2   See, for instance, the 1981 Recommendations of the National Workshop on Working Mothers and Early Childhood Education in Nigeria held by UNESCO and the Nigerian Institute for Social and Economic Research, which looked at the problems associated with women's work and the care of pre-school children. The recommendations included tax relief for employers who set up day-care centres, government encouragement of day-care co-operatives in rural areas, programmes for the training of nursery assistants, and maternity leave of four months. In addition it was proposed that nursing mothers should be able to leave work at 1.30 p.m. to go home and feed their babies for six months after returning to work at the end of maternity leave. The need for family education for men and women was noted, and the need for parents to send their daughters to school. The grave lack of nurseries, kindergartens and play groups for toddlers was noted, and the lack of data on the situation of children in Nigeria. As was stressed, for planning, more data is required.

3 Ghazi M. Farooq, Ita I. Ekanem and Sina Ojelade

Family Size Preferences and Fertility in South-Western Nigeria

The available Nigerian evidence shows that both fertility and mortality levels are high; with a crude birth rate of around 50 per 1,000 population, Nigeria ranks among the highest fertility countries in the world. There are, however, notions about desired family size, and fertility limitation and birth spacing are practised, as well as terminal abstinence to prevent further pregnancies. The task in this chapter is to explore the potential influence of several social and economic factors on fertility. This is achieved partly through a parallel analysis of rural and urban fertility patterns, given that it is in the urban centres that the most marked social change is likely to take place.

Like many other West African countries, Nigeria lacks a national vital registration system. The national censuses are not reliable sources for direct fertility estimates,[1] and only a few demographic sample surveys have been carried out.[2] Most of these surveys were very limited in their geographical scope. It was with this apparent urgent need for a national body of demographic data that the national Fertility, Family and Family Planning (FFFP) Survey of Nigeria was launched in 1971. The present study is based on the western phase data of the survey which covered the four states of south-western Nigeria.[3] More recent data not treated here have been provided by the Nigerian segment of the World Fertility Survey.

Fertility information in the survey was obtained only for currently married women between the ages of 15 and 50.[4] Such women constitute less than one-quarter of the total sample population, due to the young age structure of the population—about one-half of the total sample is below 15. Average age at first marriage is 18 years; 88 per cent of all women aged 15–49 are currently married. By the age of 25 almost all women are married, and remain so throughout the reproductive years as a result of the widely practised custom of inheritance of wives by the brothers of deceased husbands. Separation or divorce is relatively limited. As table 3.1 shows, polygyny is widely practised. In this sample, about three-fifths of women in rural areas and more than two-fifths in urban areas were in polygynous marriages. The majority of eligible women in both urban and rural areas were illiterate, but the proportion with at least primary education (42 per cent) was quite large in urban areas.

Table 3.1   Selected socio-economic characteristics of currently married women in the sample[a] by residence, south-western Nigeria, 1971

Characteristics	Urban %	Rural %	Total %
A. Type of marriage			
Monogamous	57.6	40.3	47.7
Polygynous	42.4	59.7	52.3
B. Education level			
None	53.2	77.4	66.9
Primary	24.2	14.6	18.8
Secondary	15.7	5.5	10.0
College or higher	2.5	0.2	1.2
Unknown	4.4	2.3	3.1
C. Labour force status			
In labour force	77.4	77.5	77.5
Not in labour force	21.0	20.9	20.9
Unknown	1.6	1.6	1.6
D. Occupation [b]			
Farmers, fishermen, etc.	7.9	28.8	19.7
Professional, administrative and clerical workers	14.2	4.4	8.7
Petty traders	46.8	48.0	47.5
Other sales workers	15.6	2.1	8.0
Craftsmen, production process, transport and services workers[c]	15.2	16.6	16.0
E. Wife's annual income (in ₦)[d]			
Less than 50	43.1	59.6	52.4
50–109	16.2	16.2	16.2
110–209	11.4	7.7	9.3
210–309	12.9	4.5	8.2
310 or more	5.4	0.8	2.8
Unknown	11.0	11.2	11.1
F. Household annual income (in ₦)			
Less than 190	15.9	28.0	22.8
190–309	12.1	13.8	13.0
310–609	17.1	17.7	17.4
610–1009	17.5	11.4	14.1
1010 or more	14.5	17.5	16.2
Total %	100.0	100.0	100.0
Number	1 908	2 472	4 380

Notes
(a) Excludes women with unknown fertility history and women below the age of 15.
(b) Total excludes women with unknown occupation (U = 1473; R = 1914).
(c) Only 17 eligible women in urban and 14 in rural areas reported themselves to be transport and service workers.
(d) At the current exchange rate, ₦1.00 = US$1.60.

Table 3.2 Relationship between additional number of children wanted and surviving number of children by education, south-western Nigeria, 1971

Surviving children	Additional children wanted (%)							
	Zero		1–3		4–6		7+	
	Illiterate	Literate	Illiterate	Literate	Illiterate	Literate	Illiterate	Literate
Zero	—	1.7	2.0	1.8	7.4	12.2	13.2	10.7
1–3	17.6	2.0	49.7	75.1	68.7	79.2	69.1	82.7
4–6	64.8	57.5	41.6	22.5	21.8	8.0	17.3	6.7
7 or more	17.6	20.0	6.7	0.6	2.1	0.6	0.4	—
Number	125	120	197	325	285	336	220	75

Contingency Coefficient Literates = .589
Illiterates = .443

The economic activity rate increased continuously from 58 per cent for those aged 15–19 years to 82 per cent for those aged 30–34 years and stabilised at around 85 per cent for those aged 35 years and above. This high rate of participation in labour force activity is the result of the almost complete dominance of women in retailing. As table 3.1 shows, petty trading formed the single largest activity for economically active wives. This type of economic activity poses no conflict with the wife's child-bearing and rearing activities or any other home goods production. A substantial number of urban women had secondary or college education, and 14 per cent of the urban women workers reported themselves as being in the white-collar occupations of administrative, professional and clerical workers.

Family Size Preferences

A number of questions were included in the women's interview to explore attitudes to and perceptions of family size. Typically, an African survey finds large numbers of non-numerical responses to such questions. Almost all the respondents who gave a non-numerical response said that it was 'up to God' when asked about the number of additional children wanted. The numerical responses to questions on surviving and additional number of children wanted, however, indicate a mean preferred number of children of seven, 6.3 for urban women and 7.7 for rural women. A frequently advanced hypothesis is that children are a better production investment in rural areas than in urban areas since they provide agricultural labour at an early age. Moreover, the cost of raising children is lower in the rural areas. This may partially explain the rural–urban differentials. About three-quarters of the rural wives and more than four-fifths of the urban wives thought that children's chances of living to adulthood were improving—an important factor relevant to enhanced adoption of family planning.

Education level appears to be significantly related to lower family size preferences in both urban and rural areas (see table 3.2). Wives with college and higher education wanted 2–3 children less, on average, than uneducated wives. The differential was even wider among younger women. However, education levels among the present young married female cohort compared to the older cohort are not yet high enough to produce significant changes. Increasing education both

Table 3.3   Percentage distribution of stated ideal (healthy) birth interval among wives by education and residence, south-western Nigeria, 1971

Healthy birth interval	Education				All wives	
	None	Primary	Secondary	Higher	%	N
URBAN						
1–2 years	35.8	57.8	70.3	72.9	49.3	737
3–4 years	54.7	38.3	27.1	25.0	44.2	660
5 years or more	0.8	0.9	—	—	0.7	10
Do not know or unknown	8.6	2.9	2.6	2.1	5.8	86
Total	100.0	100.0	100.0	100.0	100.0	1 493
RURAL						
1–2 years	33.2	51.2	60.3		38.0	688
3–4 years	53.8	38.0	27.0		49.3	891
5 years or more	1.3	0.3	—		1.1	18
Do not know or unknown	11.8	10.6	12.7		11.7	211
Total	100.0	100.0	100.0		100.0	1 808

increases women's participation in paid economic activity, which is in turn more and more difficult to combine with child-care, and increases the cost of having children, as more education is desired for them too and their entry into the labour force is thus delayed. (The first of these issues is taken up in the chapter by Di Domenico below.) Furthermore, education may raise aspirations for material goods, and decrease the relative desire for children.

As noted above an important intermediate variable through which cultural and socio-economic factors influence fertility is the sexual taboo on coitus after a live birth (i.e. voluntary abstinence), which may form the single most important factor influencing birth spacing. Table 3.3 shows that a large number of wives still adhere to the traditional taboos and regard three to four years (mostly three years) as the healthy interval between two births. It seems that the custom has comparatively less influence in urban areas, but education emerges as a much stronger factor in relaxing the sex taboo than does urbanisation. Preference for a one to two year birth interval is almost twice as high among wives with secondary or higher education as among wives with no education.

More than half of the urban wives (56 per cent) and one-third of the rural wives (36 per cent) in the national survey approved of planning the number and timing of births. Education level is significantly related to approval rate: more than seven-tenths of women with secondary or higher education approved of family planning compared to one-third of the uneducated women.

A large majority of women were familiar with traditional methods of family planning such as abstinence, rhythm and breastfeeding. Knowledge of modern methods appears to be limited, however. Only slightly more than one-tenth of wives were aware of the condom or the pill. More than half of the respondents had used abstinence as the method of fertility control—a direct corollary of the prevalence of lactation taboos, while less than 5 per cent had ever used condoms or the pill. As expected, the extent of knowledge and practice of birth control methods increased consistently with the level of education and was higher among the urban wives.

Table 3.4   Current fertility rates [a] per currently married woman by age and residence, south-western Nigeria, 1971

Age	Urban		Rural		All areas
	Rate	No. of women	Rate	No. of women	Rate
15–19	0.351	111	0.317	145	0.332
20–24	0.368	418	0.358	475	0.363
25–29	0.296	561	0.295	606	0.296
30–34	0.238	362	0.248	475	0.245
35–39	0.158	241	0.173	318	0.165
40–44	0.057	158	0.101	277	0.083
45–49	0.053	76	0.034	147	0.040
Observed TFR	7.61		7.63		7.62
GFR standardised for age	0.240		0.250		
I_g[b]	0.588		0.589		0.588

Notes
a. Based on births during the 12-month period prior to the survey.
b. I_g is an index representing the ratio of births that the married women actually had to the number they would have had if they had experienced the highest recorded fertility schedule, i.e. that of Hutterite women. See A. J. Coale (1969).

Fertility Levels and Differentials

Table 3.4 provides marital age-specific fertility rates estimated from the number of live births occurring to currently married women during the 12-month period preceding the date of interview. Both urban and rural schedules depict high levels of fertility. As is typical of high-fertility situations, rates are uniformly high up to the age of 34, with 20–24 being the most fertile age group. After the age of 39 the rates drop appreciably.

Urban and rural specific rates follow more or less the same pattern, with one noticeable difference. Fertility among urban women below the age of 25 is higher but the gradient of decline after the age of 24 is steeper. This leads to higher rural fertility for women over 29. The net result is that the current fertility level, as depicted by the overall rate of marital fertility, is about the same in urban and rural areas. The urban pattern is in line with the patterns generally observed elsewhere. The rural pattern could largely be the result of stricter adherence to lactation taboos and extended post partum abstinence intervals, which follow from the higher incidence of polygyny and lower education level in rural areas, as discussed before. A rural wife would therefore tend to take a longer period to produce the desired number of children.

The overall total fertility rate of the urban married women (7.61) was virtually identical to that of the rural women (7.63) (see table 3.4). The standardised general fertility rate (GFR) values show that on average one out of four currently married women in the region have a live birth in any one year.

The retrospective fertility information on number of children ever born (CEB) indicates that rural fertility is slightly higher than urban (table 3.5). For all currently married women the mean CEB was 13 per cent higher in rural areas. The

Table 3.5 *Mean number of children ever born and living children per currently married women by age and residence, south-western Nigeria, 1971*

Age	Urban			Rural			All areas		
	Children ever born	Living children	Proportion of children surviving	Children ever born	Living children	Proportion of children surviving	Children ever born	Living children	Proportion of children surviving
15–19	1.0	0.8	0.8	.82	0.7	0.6	.85	0.8	0.6
20–24	1.5	1.3	.88	1.7	1.4	.83	1.6	1.4	.86
25–29	2.7	2.3	.86	2.9	2.4	.83	2.8	2.3	.84
30–34	3.6	2.9	.80	4.0	3.1	.76	3.8	3.0	.78
35–39	4.6	3.6	.78	4.7	3.6	.75	4.7	3.6	.76
40–44	5.1	3.7	.71	5.4	3.8	.71	5.3	3.7	.71
45–49	5.5	3.8	.69	6.2	4.1	.66	5.9	4.0	.67
Overall mean	3.0	2.4	.81	3.4	2.6	.77	3.2	2.5	.78
Age standardised	3.2	2.6	.81	3.5	2.7	.77	3.2	2.6	.78

differential is reduced to 9 per cent when overall mean CEBs are standardised for age. It appears that up to the age of 44 there is no appreciable urban–rural differential in cumulative fertility. Figures on the proportion of children surviving indicate a high incidence of infant and child mortality in both urban and rural areas. By the end of their reproductive age span (i.e. 45–49 years), urban wives lose 31 per cent of their offspring and rural wives, 34 per cent. Such a high level of infant and child mortality is most certainly one of the major factors responsible for pro-natalism.

Even if we discount the high incidence of infant and child mortality as a phenomenon of the past and, with the improving mortality conditions of recent years, assume that the majority of rural and urban wives genuinely believe their children will survive to adulthood, the actual reproductive level still falls short of the mean ideal or preferred number of children by about two live births in the rural areas. Unless the desired family size declines, which is not likely to happen in the short run, rural fertility levels are likely to increase with socio-economic advancement. For example, as discussed before, with socio-economic development the practice of lactation taboos may recede, thus shortening the present prolonged post partum abstinence period. Better nutrition, improving health services, including maternal, and better child-care will reduce the incidence of sterility, pregnancy wastage, etc., and will improve the natural fertility level. In urban areas, on the other hand, the desired family size is largely being achieved; though preferring a shorter child-bearing interval, it seems that couples may be engaging in voluntary fertility limitation. In contrast to the situation in rural areas, it thus seems likely that the effect of socio-economic advancement may be to lower the fertility level by reducing the desired family size.

Table 3.6   Mean number of children ever born per currently married women by age, education status and residence, south-western Nigeria, 1971

Age	Education					
	Urban			Rural		
	None	Primary	Secondary or higher	None	Primary	Secondary or higher
15–19	1.1	0.9	1.0	0.7	0.6	1.1
20–24	1.5	1.7	1.4	1.7	1.8	
25–29	2.8	2.8	2.5	2.9	3.1	2.5
30–34	3.6	4.2	3.4	4.0	4.3	3.6
35–39	4.3	5.9	4.8	4.8	5.0	
40–44	5.0	5.3	5.6[a]	5.3	6.4	4.8[b]
45–49	5.6					
Overall mean	3.3	2.9	2.6	3.6	2.9	—
Mean standardised for age	3.1	3.4	3.0	3.3	3.6	—

Notes
a. Consists of only 13 women.
b. Fewer than 10 women.

Fertility Differentials

Table 3.6 presents the mean number of children ever born (CEB) by women's education. The relationship in both urban and rural areas is of a curvilinear form. Women with primary education show the highest fertility level and women with secondary or higher education, the lowest. The pattern of differentials persists over most age groups. The overall standardised mean number of children ever born for urban wives with no education is 10 per cent lower, and that for wives with secondary or higher education 13 per cent lower, than that for wives with primary education. The mean CEB for ages 40 years and over largely matches the mean ideal number of children for wives with primary or higher education. It is the uneducated wives who do not attain their desired family size, falling short by 1.6 children in the urban areas and 1.8 in rural areas. This fits in with the early demographic transition hypothesis that in the initial stages of socio-economic development an increase in education will mean an increase in fertility, partly because of a loosening of the taboo on intercourse during lactation. The spread of education is also likely to have a negative effect on the incidence of polygyny, curtailment of which may have some positive effects on fertility level since fertility is consistently higher for monogamous women.

A negative relationship is usually expected between female labour force participation and fertility. The relationship is complex, however, and is significantly influenced by the level of economic development. Normally, the more industrialised and economically developed a society is, the more clear cut and more incompatible are the two roles of market activity and reproductive (and home) activity. In a traditional society, however, which lacks a substantial modern sector and in which there are no social customs inhibiting female labour force participation, children can accompany mothers to farm and market, so there may not be any serious conflict between the two roles. In such cases, *ceteris paribus*, the extent of female labour force participation may not have a significant bearing on fertility behaviour. This appears to be more or less the case for south-western Nigeria, as shown in table 3.7. Only women engaged in the relatively modern occupations of 'professional, etc.' and 'other sales workers' have a lower mean CEB, and it is these women who are responsible for the overall lower standardised mean in the urban areas, CEB for working wives being slightly lower than that for non-working wives. Most of these women are probably engaged in the modern sector, where conflict between occupational and maternal roles can lead to serious stress and strain, particularly when suitable child-care is difficult to find, as Di Domenico describes. Most of these women have also attained higher educational levels and want a smaller number of children. Significantly, women for whom children provide an important source of labour, namely farmers, have a higher standardised mean CEB (16 per cent higher) than that for non-working wives.

Standardised mean CEB in the urban areas increases consistently with wife's income until the middle income group (210–609 naira).[5] Close inter-relationships usually exist between education level, occupation and income level, so the curvilinear form of relationship between fertility and income level is in line with earlier findings. In the highest income category of (610 + naira), which largely consists of educated women engaged in white-collar occupations, the fertility rate is the lowest. Rural fertility rates follow more or less the same pattern, though not as consistently.

Table 3.7 *Mean number of children ever born per currently married women by age, labour force status, occupation and residence, south-western Nigeria, 1971*

Age	Economically inactive	In the labour force	Farmers fishermen, etc.	Professional, administrative, etc.	Petty traders	Other sales workers	Craftsmen, etc.
URBAN							
15–19	0.9	1.1	1.0	*	1.2	0.8	1.0
20–24	1.4	1.6	1.9	1.4	1.7	1.4	1.6
25–29	3.1	2.6	2.6	2.2	2.9	2.6	2.7
30–34	4.1	3.5	4.0	3.4	3.5	3.6	3.3
35–39	4.5	4.6	3.7	4.6	4.8	4.1	4.8
40–44	5.5	5.1		5.4	5.1	4.3	
45–49	5.2	5.6	5.8		4.0	**	5.9
Overall mean	2.8	3.1	3.4	2.6	3.4	2.7	2.9
Mean standardised for age	3.3	3.1	3.2	2.8	3.2	2.8	3.1
RURAL							
15–19	0.4	0.8	0.8	*	0.9	*	0.6
20–24	1.3	1.8	2.0	1.2	1.7	1.5	2.0
25–29	2.7	2.9	3.2	2.4	2.9	2.4	2.8
30–34	4.4	4.0	4.6	3.4	3.7		4.0
35–39	4.8	4.8	5.0	*	4.5	4.2	5.4
40–44	4.7	5.5	5.9	*	5.2		6.0
45–49	6.1	6.2	7.2	*	5.9	*	5.6
Overall mean	2.7	3.4	4.1	3.6			3.2
Mean standardised for age	3.2	3.4	3.7	3.3			3.4

Notes

* Contains only 20 women in the two combined age groups.

** Less than 5 women in the category.

Conclusion

The majority of the wives in the national Fertility, Family and Family Planning survey conducted in south-western Nigeria had a definite idea about the number of children they wanted. A complex of socio-economic and cultural factors with varying, often opposing, influences appeared to be operating on fertility behaviour concurrently with the socio-economic development in the region. Urban wives with primary or higher education, in monogamous marriages and engaged in relatively modern economic activities, seemed to be matching actual fertility with their desired family size. Given that their desired family size is small in comparison with traditional values, these women are likely to engage in active fertility limitation practices. Uneducated and polygynously married women in both urban and rural areas were not achieving their desired family size. Such women constituted the majority in rural areas. As noted, it is possible that in line with the early demographic transition hypothesis, with socio-economic advances and loosening of traditional constraints, their fertility may increase.

Notes

1   Three censuses with complete coverage of the nation have been undertaken. Only the first, that of 1952–53, provides a plausible age-sex structure for deriving indirect estimates of vital rates, although the total population was undercounted by about 10–15 per cent. In the 1963 census age reporting was found to be very erroneous (e.g. Ekanem, 1972).

2   E.g. Olusanya (1969); Caldwell (1977c); Umoh (1972). The most recent data comes from the Nigeria Fertility Survey 1981–82 (see World Fertility Survey, London, September 1984, Summary of Findings). A probability sample consisting of 250 enumeration areas was used and data collected from nearly 10,000 eligible women.

3   The data were collected by the former Institute of Population and Manpower Studies, University of Ife, with the help of a grant from the Population Council. Details of the survey methodology were given in Acsadi et al. (1972).

4   A household form was completed for each member of the household and a male/female questionnaire was completed for every currently married male/female respondent within the household. Questions included births and deaths (per household) during the 12-month period preceding the survey, fertility and pregnancy history, marriage history of husband and wife, including type of marriage; education; occupation; labour force status; income; desired number of children; knowledge, and practice of family planning and attitude towards it. Altogether 3,016 households were selected in the western sample, using the 1963 census population figures as a sample frame. Of these, 1,429 (i.e. 47.4 per cent) were urban. This corresponds closely to the census proportion of 50.9 per cent. The average household size was 6.7 for the urban households and 7.5 for the rural.

Survey statistics in Africa frequently contain large non-sampling errors. The present national survey is not free of such errors, and the results of the study should be treated with caution (Ekanem and Farooq, 1977).

5   Unfortunately, the least reliable information collected from the national survey is that on annual incomes. The findings from table 3.8, which give mean CEB by wife's annual income, should at best be treated as exploratory.

Table 3.8   **Mean number of children ever born per currently married women by age, respondent's annual income, and residence, south-western Nigeria, 1971**

Age	Income in naira								
	Urban					Rural			
	50	50–109	110–209	210–309	310 +	50	50–109	110–209	210 + *
15–19	1.0	1.0	0.7	1.0	0.7	0.6	0.8	0.9	**
20–24	1.5	1.8	1.6	1.4	1.7	1.7	1.8	2.0	1.3
25–29	2.8	2.7	2.8	2.7	2.0	2.9	2.8	3.3	2.2
30–34	3.7	3.8	3.5	3.4	3.3	4.3	3.7	3.8	3.4
35–39	4.5	4.9	4.9	5.1	4.9	4.7	4.6	5.6	4.9
40–44	5.3	4.6	6.4	4.6	5.0	5.2	5.8	5.6	4.5
45–49	6.1		6.3			6.2	6.2		
Overall mean	3.0	3.1	3.2	2.9	3.1	3.3	3.8	3.8	2.9
Mean standardised for age	3.2	3.2	3.3	3.0	2.8	3.3	3.3	3.6	2.9

Notes
*   Includes 21 women with income of N-610 or more.
** Less than 5 women.

4   *Oyetunji Orubuloye*

Values and Costs of Daughters and Sons to Yoruba Mothers and Fathers

Opinions have varied regarding the labour and monetary contributions of children to their parents in different socio-economic and cultural contexts and the impact of such help on perceptions of the economic value of children and consequently on desired and actual fertility levels. While educated urban parents have been shown in some studies to emphasise the psychological and emotional aspects of having children, rural parents by contrast are observed to emphasise the economic and practical benefits to be derived from children, including the child labour and the long-term benefits of security in old age (Fawcett, 1977). Bulatao (1980) has presented empirical evidence demonstrating the association between perceptions of the value of children and the prevalence of child labour in a range of countries at different levels of economic development. The benefits which parents expect from their children may vary with the children's age and sex and according to whether they have been to school or not. These expectations may also vary with the parents' age and social and economic position in the community. The aim of this chapter is to examine the extent to which Yoruba parents have different expectations of their female and male children and the potential implications of these expectations for fertility.

The economic contribution of children to the household economy in most traditional societies can be classified into two broad categories: directly productive activities (including farming, fishing, tending animals and other non-farm activities) and indirectly productive activities (such as cooking, washing, cleaning, baby minding, carrying water, collecting firewood, running errands and marketing for household consumption). It would appear that most parents in traditional societies expect economic help from their children. These expectations may affect preferences for children of a given sex and ultimately reproductive behaviour. Evidence from a study of the value and cost of children among the Yoruba of Nigeria (Okediji et al., 1976) confirms the active participation of children in the household economy.[1] Although children's participation in productive work is relatively insignificant under the age of ten years, the majority of parents in this

Table 4.1   Some of the good things sons and daughters can do for parents, western Nigeria, 1973

	What sons can do for fathers		What sons can do for mothers		What daughters can do for fathers		What daughters can do for mothers	
	Fathers	Mothers	Fathers	Mothers	Fathers	Mothers	Fathers	Mothers
	(N=1288)	(N=1274)	(N=1121)	N=1080)	(N=1193)	(N=1187)	(N=1277)	(N=1257)
When young child								
1. Help on the farm	41.6	44.9	5.5	5.4	11.6	10.8	2.6	1.3
2. Help in the house	36.2	33.9	69.7	72.5	51.6	50.4	66.5	68.6
3. Financial support when old	1.2	0.4	2.8	0.7	1.3	0.5	0.9	0.6
4. Help with physical labour in every way	9.7	8.3	10.7	10.0	8.5	8.3	9.8	10.3
5. Take him/her in/build a house	0.2	0.1	1.4	2.2	0.1	0.3	0.2	0.4
6. Wash his/her clothes	4.1	4.1	3.5	3.9	22.2	24.5	4.1	4.0
7. Help in business	6.8	5.0	6.3	4.8	4.6	5.2	15.9	13.5
	(N=1383)	(N=1394)	(N=1363)	(N=1368)	(N=1305)	(N=1348)	(N=1350)	(N=1385)
When older								
1. Help on the farm	7.2	8.7	0.9	1.0	3.7	3.1	0.3	0.3
2. Help in the house	3.0	3.9	5.6	5.9	9.4	11.6	13.6	14.9
3. Financial support when old	70.3	68.9	73.9	73.5	66.2	64.0	62.4	57.8
4. Help with physical labour in every way	6.7	5.2	5.4	4.5	3.8	3.3	5.0	5.2
5. Take him/her in/build a house	9.1	12.6	10.4	12.5	10.9	11.1	12.1	14.9
6. Wash his/her clothes	1.1	0.8	1.0	1.0	4.7	5.2	1.3	1.2
7. Help in business	2.7	2.1	1.7	1.5	1.4	1.7	5.3	5.8

Note Sample sizes vary due to missing information on particular questions.
Source The changing African family project: Nigerian segment, CAFN 2 (1974).

study believed that boys were more productive than girls of the same age.

The kind of assistance which Yoruba parents derive from their children varies not only with the age and sex of the children but also with the age and sex of the parents (table 4.1). When they are young, the majority of sons help their fathers on the farm and in the house, while daughters help their mothers with domestic activities. The physical support derived from daughters by fathers mainly takes the form of household help, including washing of clothes. As the children and the parents grow older, the physical supports are translated into monetary ones. An increasing proportion of sons and daughters provide accommodation either in the form of taking in or building houses for their parents. The various kinds of assistance noted conform naturally with the traditional occupation of the parents as well as the customary definition of sex roles for women and men. More men than women think that boys are generally the most productive.

The preference for sons is not only for economic reasons, however, but also related to the desire for continuity of the family name. Moreover, not only are boys thought to be more productive in an economic sense, but both women and men think that parents should spend more on boys than girls. Comparative evidence from Uyanga's (1980) study among 600 rural wives and husbands living in six villages in the Odukpani and Adamkpa areas of Cross-River State of Nigeria also indicates that parents spend more on their male children, particularly on feeding and schooling.

Schooling

The introduction of schools has brought about many changes in patterns of socialisation, male–female relations and exchanges between parents and children, while new social divisions have emerged between the illiterate and the educated. At first rural parents, among the Yoruba as elsewhere in West Africa, were dubious about the potential benefits of European style education for their children, and boys were given more educational opportunities than girls—a practice which continues to the present day, when positive discrimination in terms of free places is being used in some states to encourage parents to send their daughters as well as their sons to school. It is widely believed among the Yoruba and others that any benefits from female education will accrue to her future husband rather than her own kin. Hence, less attention has been paid to female education in many farming families.

Yet the possession of a formal education has become the new avenue to economic opportunities and social status. It has also created a new set of expectations for both parents and children. Parents spend more on schoolchildren than they do on children who do not go to school, and they expect very little physical labour in return from children who go to school. Educated children, however, are expected to translate all physical obligations into monetary returns as soon as they are in a position to do so—which may be as early as 15 years old, later for those who have an extended education.

There are differences in expectations of monetary returns from boys and girls. Boys are expected to contribute towards keeping their parents' farm or business going, building a new house for their parents, paying younger siblings' school fees, and paying their parents' taxes and church dues. They may even hire paid servants to look after their aged parents. Above all, they perpetuate the family name by marrying and raising children. The girls, however, are usually not under overt pressure to fulfil any of these socio-economic obligations to their parents once they are married. Their obligations are first to their husbands and their children.

Not all parents in fact believe their children will give them real assistance when they grow up. In the Changing African Family Project in Nigeria, respondents who were aged 40 or over were asked to indicate how many of their children gave them real assistance when they grew up. Eighteen per cent of men and 31 per cent of women said they received real assistance from all their children. A further 24 per cent of the men and 21 per cent of women received some assistance from nearly all of them. Given the widespread and continuing nature of economic support of parents by their adult children, expectations of such help must certainly affect family size preferences. Educated parents appear to be less likely to expect such financial assistance, however.

Sex Preferences

A preference for sons has been one of the factors affecting family size preferences in a number of West African societies (Orubuloye, 1977). Even more important than the economic benefits which parents derive from their sons are the socio-cultural benefits. In most Nigerian communities, the presence of at least one male child in the family is regarded as absolutely necessary. In the Changing African Family Survey, for example, about three-fifths of the men and about one-half of the women said they would like to have four boys and two girls in a family of six children. Practically all indicated that they would like to have at least one boy in the family. The main reasons why it is considered important to have sons include economic support, continuity of the family name, and their permanent residence near the ancestral home, unlike girls who leave at marriage. Eight out of every ten respondents cited the above reasons. In comparison, the main reasons for wanting to have daughters include the fact that girls are more useful in household chores, look after their parents in their old age, marry and link their parents and kin with other families, and of course bear children. More than four-fifths of both male and female respondents mentioned these reasons. Given these preferences and processes of reasoning, it is not surprising to learn that many marriages break down on account of the lack of a male child, while the arrival of the first son strengthens the position of the wife in the family.

Disadvantages of Large Families

The disadvantages of having a large number of children are recognised even in traditional agricultural settings. The popular saying 'Lots of children lots of misery' is one of the ways in which parents express their feelings about the size of their families. Quarrels and petty jealousy among siblings are frequently mentioned as major disadvantages of large families. Women with many children invariably work harder than those with fewer, as feeding, clothing and general care of the children are by and large the mother's responsibility. Although these and other disadvantages of having many children are recognised, the benefits which parents derive from these children appear to outweigh the disadvantages.

With the introduction of Western education, however, children are perceived as having new needs which inevitably raise the level of expenditure upon children. The demand for children's education is high in Nigeria and the cost has increased substantially in recent years. Education is generally regarded as the way to a better future and a major avenue for social mobility.

Potential Implications for Demographic Change

The traditional economic system encourages high fertility; child-care is delegated, and parents gain from the labour of their children. The expectations of mothers and fathers regarding children's labour and financial support are obviously major factors determining reproductive behaviour in Yoruba society. There is a clear preference for male children, partly because of traditional sex role differences and the longer-term economic and social expectations from male children. It is generally believed that boys are more expensive to bring up, but they more often live with their parents throughout their lives and are thus expected to bring considerable economic benefits to their parents.

The introduction of Western education has made possible new types of employment and income generation. Children no longer work side by side with their parents. The physical obligations of children to their parents are gradually giving way to monetary obligations. Boys are expected to contribute more than are girls. The continuity and perpetuation of the family name remains the exclusive function of the boys, who are also expected to provide some kind of old age security for the parents. At the same time, the emotional aspects of parenthood are still very important and boys are generally required for family cohesiveness. The significant differences in expectations regarding sons and daughters are likely to continue to affect the reproductive behaviour of parents, in that parents tend to continue to produce children until there are enough sons to serve these long-term economic, social and religious functions. In this way, continuing perceptions about the inequalities and differences between girls and boys serve to perpetuate high fertility values and practices.

Traditional perspectives and values regarding children are likely to change, however. The introduction of Western education, its extension to girls, and the equal employment opportunities offered to them, may influence the attitudes of educated urban parents. Meanwhile rural parents may continue to emphasise the need for children of one sex or the other because of the long-term socio-economic benefits which they expect to derive from them.

Note

1   The data employed here are derived from the Nigerian segment of the Changing African Family Project (CAFN2) carried out in the years 1973–75 in the then Western (now Oyo, Ogun and Ondo) and the present Lagos States of Nigeria. CAFN2 consists of a probability sample of 1,497 males and 1,499 females over the age of 17 years taken in 1973. The project was carried out by the Sociology Department, University of Ibadan, Nigeria, with the co-operation of the Demography Department, Australian National University. The late Professor F.O. Okediji and Professor J.C. Caldwell were the directors of the project, while the present writer was a field supervisor.

5   Lawrence A. Adeokun

Creole and Yoruba Households and Family Size

This chapter presents a comparative study of data from Creole households of the western area of Sierra Leone and Yoruba households of south-western Nigeria. The main aim is to show the extent to which certain aspects of traditional African family forms and relations persist in spite of the pervasive religious, economic and political changes which have taken place, and to link these aspects where possible to fertility prospects, in particular addressing recent hypotheses concerning the direction of flows of benefits between children and parents. The two groups have a common cultural origin but have been subjected to very different historical influences, including in the Creole case the traumatic effects of enslavement and compulsory migration and settlement followed by later resettlement in Sierra Leone.[1] Here the concern is to relate experiences of education and employment to aspects of contrasting family forms and to consider their potential implications for family size.

In particular, the possibility that parents can devise means or utilise circumstances at their disposal to continue to maximise the beneficial flow of resources from offspring to parents so that investment in children need not be a 'cost' but a 'benefit', has not been widely considered.[2] Granted that the data requirements for fully investigating power-sharing, decision-making and resource allocation among family members are varied, there are relevant propositions which can be usefully explored with the type and quality of data available on the Creole and the Yoruba.[3] The method of analysis used in this discussion consists of a comparison of the summary statistics of the data for several aspects of familial roles in the two populations. Comments on the features of the society that may have produced the observed patterns and modifications are presented together with the statistical evidence. Since the comparative study is based on the assumption of different historical experiences some background information on the Creole is first presented as a context in which the findings may be discussed.

The Creole of the Western Area of Sierra Leone

The Creole and 'Creoledom' are a creation of the history of slavery and emancipation. Two main population elements formed the basis of the society. The first were the descendants of freed slaves who had spent some time in either Europe or the Americas before settling in the colony established in the western area of Sierra Leone. This group came to the colony with various skills and great familiarity with Western values including monogamy, self improvement through education, and the acquisition of personal as opposed to community wealth and property (Spitzer, 1974). These Nova Scotians, Maroons and black poor of London were to play a major role in the formation of Creole society, even though the total number of them sent to the colony was less than 2,000 persons.

The second group arrived in the colony over a period of 70 years, from 1807 when the slave trade was declared piracy by the British government and slaves found on arrested slave vessels were forfeited to the Crown to 1870, when the effective patrolling of the West African coast made further transportation of slaves from the coast unprofitable and risky. These 'liberated Africans' did not get out of West African waters before they were freed from slavery and settled in a number of settlements strung around the hills of the western area of Sierra Leone. Although there are problems in reconciling the records of the numbers landed in Sierra Leone, there is no doubt that this group made up the bulk of the Creole population (Kuczynski, 1948).

The Creoles were intensively subjected to schooling and Christianity. In this process of conversion, the first group served the purpose of the colonial administration in the role of teachers, preachers and administrative assistants. In a single generation the conversion and identification with the values of the Church and school were so complete that the Creoles considered themselves, with pride, as Black Europeans. Adoption of the Christian faith involved rejection of traditional African practices, especially polygyny, and the emulation of European social graces. There were, however, early demographic circumstances which placed some strain on the outright adoption of monogamous Christian marriage by the Creole, including the small number of women among the recaptured slaves, which made the formation of families within the Creole group initially difficult. In addition, it has been suggested that common law unions were a response to a lack of the wherewithal to finance the socially approved expense of engagement and marriage, including the expensive 'trousseau' (Spitzer, 1974, pp. 29–30).

One outcome of the adoption of Christianity and schooling and the associated economic advantages enjoyed by the Creole was the marked distance which they maintained from the local Sierra Leone population. Links were kept to a minimum, although the occasional indigene could be absorbed into Creole society through a consensual union, adoption of Creole values, or outright marriage.

Some of the liberated Africans succeeded in retaining their own language and Muslim religion much longer than others. Such was the group of Yoruba Muslims. Ancestral worship also continues to this day among the Creole in the Yoruba family gathering, and naming ceremonies are given Yoruba terms. On public and festive occasions, a uniform dress is adopted as a symbol of family links. In this case we thus see elements of tradition and of change, the latter resulting from colonisation, education, migration, adoption of new religious beliefs and practices and new opportunities for economic survival and advancement.

Socio-economic and Demographic Characteristics of the Two Populations

Both populations, Creole and Yoruba, may be broadly classified as 'young' populations, each having more than half of the population under the age of 20. But while under-fives constitute less than 10 per cent of the Creole they form no less than 20.3 per cent of the Yoruba sample. Taking the older ages, the higher life expectancy for the Creole population is clearly revealed by the fact that those over the age of 65 make up 6 per cent of the total, compared to less than 2 per cent for the Yoruba sample. The comparison becomes even more remarkable when the population above 50 years is considered. Such persons constitute less than 6 per cent of the Yoruba sample, while they make up 17 per cent of the Creole sample. In effect, the ageing of the Creole population is the outcome of the substantially lower fertility and the higher life expectancy.

Level of education is a key correlate of change. As far back as 1842, the total commitment of the Creole to formal education was apparent in a school enrolment rate that was higher than those of some European countries at that time (Spitzer, 1974). Of the Creole sample, over 40 per cent had received primary and secondary education, and about 1.5 per cent had university education. These high literacy rates and high educational attainment are consistent with the observation that after their initial success in trading, the Creoles were pushed into white-collar jobs. The twentieth century therefore saw an emphasis on upward mobility through education of children rather than success in business (ibid., p. 64). In significant contrast, the very recency of the introduction of mass formal education into Yorubaland is evident from the overall literacy rate of 46 per cent; 29 per cent of the sample had received primary education, another 10 per cent had secondary education, and 1.4 per cent had university education. Although, as among the Creole, education is now accepted as the means of upward mobility, the current cohorts of parents have had little education themselves. Encouraged by the low direct cost of formal education, however, they have embarked massively on the education of their children, including girls.

A shift in occupation was forced on the Creole, largely by the increasing competition from European firms which made trading and allied activities less rewarding. In the event, the high literacy and education levels attained prepared the Creole for the domination of the white collar jobs, not only in Sierra Leone but in other parts of former British West Africa. The employed persons in the sample population numbered 830 (484 males and 346 females), and a third were in managerial, administrative, clerical and related occupations. Just under a quarter were in the professional occupations and another 18.3 per cent were in trading activities. Production work attracted 21.1 per cent. With the exception of the 6.6 per cent in transport operations, very negligible numbers were involved in other occupations, including agriculture.

While the employed population constituted just over a quarter of the Creole sample, 43.8 per cent of the Yoruba sample were employed. Three-quarters of the employed population were equally distributed between farming, small-scale trading and non-agricultural manual work. About 15 per cent of those employed were in teaching and other professional positions.

From these socio-economic and demographic profiles of the two populations it can be surmised that there are differences crucial for the determination of the nature and direction of changes in family relations and household forms, to a consideration of which we now turn.

Marriage

In the 323 Creole sample households in which both parents were present, and the form of marriage could be established with certainty, only one contained a polygynous union (with a non-Creole). In contrast, a third of the 1,925 Yoruba households in which the form of marriage was systematically established contained polygynous unions. Membership of the Muslim religion, to which a third of the Yoruba belonged, seemed to be an associated factor.

Among the Yoruba the mean age at marriage was about 18.5 years. The more educated and urban women married later than those without education or in rural areas. Lower age at marriage was also reported by those belonging to the Muslim faith, with some possible built-in effect of lower education levels among Muslims. A few Yoruba females in the age group 10–14 were already married. In contrast the youngest married Creole female was 19 years old. Moreover, while about one in every eight Creole females in the 20–24 age group was married, the corresponding proportion among the Yoruba was eight out of ten. And between the ages of 25 and 49, marriage was nearly universal among the Yoruba, with 95 per cent of the females in current unions. In contrast, a quarter of the same age range were not married among Creole women. Some were unmarried because of protracted education, but for the majority staying single was an accepted alternative. The choice was made easier since the single state did not preclude motherhood. To summarise, the Creole showed a greater preference for monogamous unions. In addition, the early mean age at marriage of about 18 years among the Yoruba contrasts with the late age at marriage deduced from the Creole data.

Composition of Domestic Groups

Table 5.2 shows that in the domestic groups of the two populations four major categories are recognised. First are the elementary groups of parents and their children. (Here are included Yoruba households made up of polygynously married parents and their children.) Second are the extended residential groups, the main distinction between this category and the first being the addition of other relatives, including relatives of both husband and wife. (In a few cases, one in seven among the Yoruba and one in five among the Creole, the categorisation was based on the presence of a domestic servant only.) In the third category there is only one parent in the household. (In the Yoruba sample, however, households were excluded in which there was no currently married woman.) The fourth and final category is that of non-kin households which accounts for less than 2 per cent of the domestic groups.

The ratio of extended to elementary households is higher among the Creole than among the Yoruba, six for every ten elementary families among the Creole, in contrast to 4.4 for every ten elementary families among the Yoruba. This finding is consistent with the observation that schooling, commercialism and Christianity have not had the effect of eroding the meeting of obligations to relatives in Creole society (Spitzer, 1974, p. 34).

A possible explanation of the apparent tenacity of kinship obligations among the Creole could be the limited opportunities existing for subsistence activities in Creole society. Consequently, people's ability to meet their obligations towards

Table 5.1 *Proportion of females married by age groups among Creole and Yoruba sample*
population

Age group	Creole (N = 1,256)	Yoruba (N = 4,475)
10–14	—	1.3
15–19	0.5	31.3
20–24	12.5	83.9
25–29	47.5	95.0
30–34	86.0	96.1
35–39	75.2	96.4
40–44	81.0	94.9
45–49	74.0	93.9
50–54	68.0	40.1
55–59	60.5	27.6
60–64	54.1	18.2
65 +	31.3	13.8

Source Author's analysis.

Table 5.2 *Composition of Creole and Yoruba domestic groups*

Composition of groups	Creole		Yoruba	
	N	%	N	%
1. *Elementary*				
(a) Head and wife	31	5.2	51	2.6
(b) Head, wife and children	169	28.5	1 314	66.5
2. *Extended*				
(a) Head, wife and others	23	3.9	43	2.2
(b) Head, wife, children and others	100	16.9	562	28.5
3.				
(a) One parent, children/others	221	37.3	n.a.*	
(b) Head, relative/others	36	6.1	n.a.*	
4. *Non-kin*	12	2.0	2	0.1
Total	593	100.0	1,975	100.0

* These categories are not applicable to the Yoruba, where eligible
households were selected on the basis of a currently married woman
being a household member.
Source Author's analysis.

their kin has depended on participation in the urban labour market. Those who
have access to some regular source of income, therefore, carry additional
responsibility for close relatives who do not have such access. Indeed, the co-
resident relatives were mostly unemployed, though in the economically active age
groups. Moreover, the incomes of those co-resident relatives in employment were
much lower than for other categories of employed persons. More older women

were present in these households than older men. It would appear, therefore, that the men required assistance when young and unemployed while the women needed more assistance in old age. Of the co-resident kin, 257 were relatives of the husbands in the households and 46 were in-laws of whom 38 were women who claimed to be married.

The Creole thus appear to make a pragmatic accommodation to obligations to relatives in the peculiar circumstances of the monetarised economy in which they find themselves. In contrast, the trend of modernisation in Yoruba society is to disengage from kin who can fall back on subsistence agriculture for primary survival.

Child-Quality and Socio-economic Status of Parents

A high proportion of surviving children stay at home. Among the Yoruba, for whom the information was available, 75 per cent of surviving children were living with their parents. Although information was not available about the Creole children living elsewhere, it is estimated that the proportion could not have been any lower than for the Yoruba because of the limited opportunities for Creole migration to other parts of Sierra Leone. In addition, emigration for purposes of advanced education comes much later in Creole society, when children have finished undergraduate education in the local university college. The proportion of the Creole sample classified as 'children' was 53 per cent compared with 35 per cent among the other Sierra Leone ethnic groups, and about 40 per cent for the Yoruba. There is no dramatic difference in the age composition, around 40 per cent being aged 0–9 and less than 20 per cent aged 20–29.

The marriage of children can be expected to precipitate their departure from home. This would appear consistent with the results. Only 2 per cent of Creole and 8 per cent of Yoruba children were married—much lower rates than one would expect from the age composition. In effect, the children who stay on at home stay out of wedlock for much longer than others. The delay in marriage may be considered as a mechanism and corollary of child-quality improvement, as it allows time for school attendance and vocational training prior to marriage. About 45 per cent of children in both groups were primary school attenders.

Less than 20 per cent of Creole children were not in school, and these were largely made up of those still under 6. In contrast, the illiterate elements in the Yoruba sample—35 per cent—were made up both of those too young to be in school and of a few who were too old to have benefited from the advent of free primary school education in the mid-1950s. More Creole children (35 per cent) were in secondary schools than the Yoruba children (17 per cent). One assumes the Yoruba situation will improve with the extension of free education to the secondary and university level.

Among the Yoruba, a distinction can be made between the educational attainment of children of illiterate parents and those of parents with some education. While those parents with some education had all their children aged six and above in school, parents with no education had a lower registration of that age group.

Among the other Sierra Leone ethnic groups, the Creole are by far the most educated. An illiteracy rate of less than 15 per cent among the Creole compares extremely favourably with a rate of 63.8 per cent for other groups, whose rates of school attendance also fall much below those for the similar Yoruba age groups.

Child Quality Investments and Direction of Wealth Flow

The next consideration is what, if anything, these data can tell us relevant to hypotheses regarding the costs and values of children and the direction in which benefits are passing. The costs of children are mainly visible, while the channels for returns appear to dwindle with the geographical separation of parents and children. Filial obligations can be met over a great distance, however, as the studies of migrants' remittances to parents and others have shown (Adepoju, 1974). Nor is there enough information on the critical moment of need on the part of parents, for which investment in children provides some 'insurance'. The life stages reached by parents and children can influence the effectiveness or otherwise of the returns on investment in child-quality. It may be possible to glean some information regarding the mechanisms whereby returns can be realised from investment by studying the living arrangements of children who stay with their parents. Two important considerations are their earning potential and the economic contribution they can make within the household economy. The employment status of children is thus examined, and the earnings derived from such employment, and the relative contribution that such earnings may make to the domestic budget in the light of the employment status and relative income of the parents. In the Sierra Leone survey precise information was available on income. Informed comments are made on the probable situation and applicability of points made to the Yoruba.

Sixty per cent of Creole sons and daughters living in households over 20 years of age are employed. Below that age education is nearly universal. In the sample there were 174 children still living at home and in employment. Because of their better education, the average income level was much higher than that of the other ethnic groups.

The status of the various heads of households in which employed children were found may be classified as follows:

(a) 36 children, or 20.7 per cent of the employed, were living with old female parents who reported that they were not in the labour force but were working in the house;
(b) 28, or 16 per cent, lived with retired parents, mostly males;
(c) 14, or 8 per cent, lived with disabled or aged parents;
(d) 8, or 4.6 per cent, lived with parents who were actively looking for work

The remaining 88 children, or just about half, lived with parents who were currently in employment, with various levels of income, some earning more and some less than their children.

The fact that half of the children in employment should have been so conveniently located to assist parents in need raises the possibility that devices may exist for assuring the presence of children during vulnerable stages of life, and that parents may knowingly exploit those devices. The older the parents, the older the children they may have living with them. Consequently, if circumstances discourage children from moving away from home, these circumstances will serve the interests of the parents. Such circumstances include the shortage of rented accommodation in Freetown, contrasted with the high rate of home ownership by the Creole parents. The choice between a high rent and free accommodation may appear the lure, but there is more involved than depending on the parents.

Children living in and earning are expected to make a financial contribution to the upkeep of the home, which in some cases may constitute a very significant proportion of the domestic budget. Furthermore, of course, successful children are a unique source of parental pride and enjoyment, especially when they remain close by.

Among the Yoruba also, a protracted period of education, coupled with the government policy of reducing the cost of education by restricting children to local day-schools, is delaying the depletion of families much longer than in the days when secondary schools were few and far between. Then, the move to secondary school and, for village children, to upper primary classes, constituted the classic first move in the process of rural–urban migration. It is now no longer unusual for children to live in until it is time for post-secondary education or training.

The reduced monetary needs of parents in old age, resulting from reduced social and economic aspirations, may call for more sensitive depictors of the form of returns on child-quality investment, which is not fully reflected in the objective study of quantum of cash flow. More imaginative analysis of various kinds of transactions between parents and children may be required. Children living at home have more opportunities for a variety of transactions than those living elsewhere. For the old, the disabled and the retired, it is not simply the generosity of monetary remittances but the much less tangible direct contact that 'insures' their old age against indignities. In effect, since some aspects of the exchanges of benefits are, of necessity, longitudinal along the life stages of two or more individuals, the limited data available from cross-sectional surveys cannot be expected to provide a conclusive testing of related propositions. Here attention has simply been drawn to the existence of compensatory mechanisms, within the living arrangements of children, that may allow for returns on child-quality investments. Caution is therefore advocated in the analysis of the economic and socio-psychological content of the costs and benefits of children.

Present Fertility Levels

Although information from the Sierra Leone survey, on which the Creole family and household analysis was based, was not enough for the derivation of acceptable measures of fertility levels, alternative sources, very close to the study data are available (e.g. Dow and Benjamin, 1975). Here the measure of fertility most readily compared for different subgroups of the population was the mean parity for women in the age group 40–49. For Creole women, the mean parity at this age group was 4.8. Other major Sierra Leone ethnic groups had a much higher figure, 6.4 for the Mende and 8.4 for the Temne. But within Freetown, these other ethnic groups had rates of 5.2 and 5.8, respectively, showing the possible impact of urban living on fertility and, by implication, on the depression of Creole fertility levels.

Information obtained from the Nigerian data set was adequate for deriving the Yoruba mean parity at the same age, which was 5.7. The total fertility rate was 5.4 and the gross reproduction rate 2.6.

Surprisingly, the Creole fertility rate did not reflect the low marital rates observed among them. The explanation is to be found in the fact that the mean parity at age 40–49 for never married women in Freetown, a category often encountered in the Creole data, was not much different, at 4.6, from that of 4.8 for all Creole women. The figure for married women was, however, 5.7, which reveals the fertility-inhibiting effect of women staying unmarried.[4]

Among the Yoruba, early age at marriage, universality of marriage, and large family size ideals all promote high fertility levels. Very few births occur outside some form of marital union. The one major influence on Yoruba fertility within marriage is the relatively long duration of breastfeeding and the associated long birth intervals (Adeokun, 1983).

Delay in marriage, increased knowledge and adoption of family planning, and a decline in infant and childhood mortality, which will in turn produce a decline in family size ideals, are some of the links thought to connect education with declines in fertility. The short-term evidence of the impact of education on fertility is, however, mixed. Higher levels of education for parents are correlated with higher levels of education for children. Parents' education levels do not appear to have a very marked effect on fertility levels, however. For the Yoruba, mean parity at 45–49 years showed a decline from 6.2 for women with no education, through 5.9 for those with primary education, to 5.3 for those with secondary education and above. Other studies among the Yoruba have revealed that the total fertility rate is highest for those with primary education only, with those of women with no education somewhat lower and the decline more marked for those with secondary education or higher.

In Freetown, mean parity for the 40–49 age group was 5.9 for those with no education, and 5.2 for those with one or more years of education. Education alone is obviously not a sufficient guarantee of decisive fertility decline, and in neither area is there evidence that widespread adoption or propagation of family planning is under way.

Cost and Value of Children

The direct cost of children can be raised or reduced by government actions, which may render more or less costly the education and training parents desire for their children. Again, as has been observed, the benefits from having children can be maximised by parents through the manipulation of the living arrangements of the former, most notably through the children delaying marriage and staying longer with their parents, and the consequent enhanced potential access of parents to their children's support and resources. As noted, the value that children may constitute to their parents cannot be fully accounted for in cash and tangible resource flow analyses.

With these uncertainties in the balance of the cost and value calculations, it is too soon to speculate that increasing education and thus child-quality investment will necessarily further dampen fertility prospects or cause an escalation of costs and decrease in benefits sufficient to neutralise completely the emotional assessment of the value of children. In order to test wealth flow hypotheses, a longitudinal or life span approach will be required in the study of the interdependence of parents and their children. The flow between parents and children while the children are young, the flow when both generations are employed, and the flow at a third stage, when the parents are no longer active or able to meet all their needs on their own, will need to be studied. The extent to which the needs of elderly parents are met by the various categories of kin living with them or living elsewhere will also need to be investigated. It should then be possible to assess the adequacy of family support and to interpret the significance attached to the 'old age security' expectations that parents have of their children.

What has emerged overall from this discussion of the two populations has been a picture of continuity in the midst of change. One society has adopted the monogamous norm, both have embraced the advantages of education, training and modern sector employment where possible, yet traditional values persist, such as obligations to kin, including the provision of accommodation, and an enduring pro-natalism and accompanying practices, which lead to comparatively large completed family sizes at least among the older people. There are indications that although they provide little in the way of physical labour, educated children provide important sources of support, security and comfort to their parents, especially when the latter are in need. There is, however, little evidence that in the preceding two decades education *per se* has caused such a significant rise in costs to parents, combined with such a dwindling of returns that the new middle-aged have been constrained to change radically their fertility behaviour and expectations. It remains to be seen whether those currently in their reproductive span will achieve the comparatively large family sizes of the generation who have now completed their child-bearing.

In order to test successfully hypotheses regarding the potential fertility reducing impact of changes in intergenerational flows of resources and benefits, it will certainly be necessary to increase the volume and sophistication of information on patterns of domestic investment and the returns which may be expected from these investments over the life cycles of parents and children.

Notes

1   For details of different aspects of the evolution of Creole society, see Porter (1963); Spitzer (1974); Kilson (1966). On Yoruba society, see Johnson (1969); Fadipe (1970), etc.
2   A stimulating exception is the work of Reyna. See Reyna (1972 and 1975), and Reyna and Bouquet (1975).
3   The data on the Creole used here came from the questionnaires employed for the second round of the household survey of the western area of Sierra Leone (Adeokun, 1974). It covered 593 households with a total population of 3,030 in which the head of household belonged to the Creole. One-person households were excluded because such households do not contribute to the main focus of this study. The predominantly Yoruba data was collected in 1971 as part of a national survey of family, fertility and family planning in Nigeria described in Chapter 4 above.
4   See Bongaarts (1978) for the precise implications of the phrase 'fertility-inhibiting effect'.

6

Patricia Ladipo[1]

Women in a Maize Storage Co-operative in Nigeria

Family Planning, Credit and Technological Change

The objectives of the study reported in this chapter included identifying several types of help Yoruba women co-operative members need and observing what happens when such minimal assistance is made available to them through their co-operative. Knowledge of practical use in designing programmes for women was thus gathered. The study was also useful for demonstrating to those who set the regulations regarding co-operative support measures and formation that women's groups, like the one at Aganran near Ife, are worth helping.

An earlier report noted that the introduction of maize as a cash crop and the subsequent marketing of maize by men instead of women, who had traditionally marketed food crops, had led to disruption of the women's trade cycles and eventually to the establishment of women's pre-cooperative groups (Ladipo, 1981). These groups were found to offer women the opportunity to acquire modernising skills and attitudes, as well as to accumulate capital for individual and group based trading and processing activities. In spite of the fact that one of the groups, located at Aganran village, showed considerable progress in terms of financial growth and group activities, it had not yet been granted government recognition and the assistance that would follow such recognition.

Before the study described here began, experience with the women at Aganran and in other villages participating in the University of Ife's Isoya Rural Development Project had suggested certain inter-related areas of women's individual and group activities in which assistance might be needed to help them to achieve their goals as producers and earners as well as mothers and wives. These included provision of information, access to modest credit facilities and introduction of improved technology. It was our aim to monitor and document the impact of these innovations, at both the individual and the group level, and on the basis of our findings to make appropriate recommendations.

There were thus three action-oriented, experimental aspects of the project, combining interventions with documentation. The first, with the help of a gynaecologist, was to provide information about ways of regulating fertility. The second was to make credit available to the women as a group through their co-operative. The third entailed helping the woman to build an improved type of crib for storing and drying their maize prior to sale. In each case the effects of making this kind of help available were to be observed. Provision of these kinds of advice and assistance and subsequent monitoring of change formed one part of the ongoing activities of the author and project staff, who normally carry out such work as part of their rural extension programme in this local area.

Intervention and Documentation

Remarks made by women in the earlier project had suggested that their interest in controlling their child-bearing might be stimulated by opportunities to enhance their income-earning potential and by the general effects of national development at the farm level. The latter included factors that affect the quality of life for farm families and the range of alternative opportunities available. Increasing inflation, for example, which contributes to food shortages on the farm; development pro- grammes which undermine women's ability to contribute to the family income (such as the above-mentioned introduction of maize as a cash crop grown by men); the increase in urban labour demand which drains away the supply of farm labour; the compulsory education of children which requires cash and makes child labour unavailable, following the recent introduction of universal primary education; and better communication with other areas, which brings awareness of more comfor- table life-styles.

Several women seeking family planning services had expressed the feeling that their lives were not what they had expected. The men they married had appeared to have known economic potential, but the situation had changed so much that the families' livelihoods had become unexpectedly precarious. In these circumstances, it appeared that the number of children was less important than the quality of each child. Women said that they must now do much more than bear and feed babies. They must see that their children were equipped to compete in the modern sector. As one component of this study, we therefore set out to explore possible changes in women's perceptions of their maternal roles, to see whether there is a growing tendency to want to limit family size by other than traditional spacing methods, and what factors are associated with such changes.[2]

Regarding the provision of credit we wanted to see what the women would do with credit if it was extended to them, and to know the details of how they trade and what makes one woman more successful than another. An interest-free loan of 2,000 naira was made available to the co-operative for distribution to members. The women were aware that in receiving the loan they would be embarking on a twofold experiment: (1) to demonstrate to government that women could handle credit; and (2) to let the sponsors (the ILO) learn about how women trade. The members accepted the challenge for the benefit of their own group and other, similar groups. They agreed that anyone taking the loan would make herself avail- able for frequent interviewing and that she would answer the confidential ques- tions freely.

The co-operative members decided that since the money came from an outside source and not from members' contributions, the loan should be distributed equally rather than on the basis of amount of accumulated capital, as is usually done. They also decided that N500 of the money should be kept in the bank to satisfy a government requirement about the minimum bank account. The rest of the money was divided among the 25 women who were deemed to be creditworthy. Attempts were made to interview the loan recipients every two weeks in order to follow their trading activities in detail.[3] Simultaneously there was a focus on the group as a whole to observe whether the co-operative was a creditworthy group, whether it benefited from the loan, and at the same time whether it was capable of adopting technological change of importance to agricultural development.

Data about the co-operative and the loan were collected from the co-operative's account books. To assess the group's ability to adopt technological change, project staff encouraged the women to build a modern maize storage crib. This particular project was chosen as one within the women's means, which answered a community need, and which was in line with the women's main concern—individual trade. As staff assisted in the construction and use of the crib they kept notes on the activities and effects taking place.

Although the several components of the study concerning motherhood and fertility regulation, individual trade and access to credit, and co-operative activity and technological innovation, are described and were carried out as discrete sub-studies, it was expected that they would be inter-related. In working from day to day over a considerable period with the women as co-operative members, it was often noted that an event concerning a child or trade or the co-operative impinged on, or motivated change, in the other areas of the women's lives, and that the women did not expect activities connected with their roles as mother, wives and producers to be compartmentalised. Because of this, some questions were designed to explore areas of overlapping concern and as we shall see, some inter-related issues surfaced on their own. In fact it was our specific intention to examine the complex interface between women's activities and expectations as mothers and as co-operative members and earners.

The Women

Nineteen of the 26 women in the co-operative were currently married and enjoying the status of being 'in their husbands' houses'. Even the six widows were still firmly associated with their late husbands' families. One married woman who did not have any children had left her husband's house and returned to her father's house. During the study period, one woman separated from her husband and went to live with her family of origin. All but eight were in polygynous marriages and more than half were in junior positions.

People from the Ife area tend to spend part of their time on the farm and part in town. None of the women claimed to live in the village full-time, but 15 spent half or more of their time in the village. Women who are relatively free of child-bearing and farm labour because of old age or because there are junior wives to do the work tend to spend more and more time in town until they are finally allowed to 'retire' to the husband's urban residence. In the study we found that seven women lived mainly in town and an additional four lived only in Ife town. Most of the older women who spent a lot of time in the village were widows, who were looking after their children's interests in their late husbands' farms.

It was very difficult to establish the women's precise ages, but it was possible to estimate that eleven respondents were of child-bearing age (40 or below), nine were of an age to consider not bearing any more children (41 to 50), and six were at least 50 years old.

Twenty of the women's husbands were or had been farmers, and this was the basis of their ties with the village. Of the remainder three were government employees, one was a labourer, and one a traditional officer holder. Most of the husbands (14) had not completed primary school. In general the educational achievements of the women were much less than those of the men, although three women had more schooling than their husbands. Only five of the women had completed primary school and none had secondary education.

Perceptions of Motherhood

The most frequently mentioned advantage of having children was security: financial security for old age and assurance of conjugal status in the husband's house. These two advantages (mentioned by 16 women) were often seen as intermeshed in that the older the woman, the greater the probability of her husband dying and leaving her without a home or support. A child ensures her right to live in the father's house and should also provide some financial support. Furthermore, a childless woman has no access to any inheritance from her husband but a mother will receive his wealth indirectly through her children.

However, most of the women who mentioned status in their husbands' families were more concerned with living peacefully from day to day. To them the birth of a child let them 'become someone', where their status had previously been very low. These responses suggest that by marrying the women suffered a loss in status and security which was only redeemable through childbirth. Most said that a barren woman was seen as a person apart, different from the rest, a mere onlooker. A barren woman is alone and her life is meaningless, bringing sorrow to all who know her. There is an assumption that fertility is normal and a barren women 'deviates' or 'turns' towards barrenness. Misuse of the body, including promiscuity and abortion, are often thought to be the major cause of infertility. Life is not viewed as worthwhile without children.

Much of the value of children lies in the future. The women also had a lot to say about the impact of the children on their past and present lives, particularly in relation to their work. The most frequently named benefit of their working was the fact that the profits allowed them to feed and clothe their children. In fact, one of the meanings attached to 'child-care' was the material maintenance made possible by trade. Beyond their basic maintenance, several mothers said they supported their children's progress in school. Some of the women also mentioned that they maintained themselves from their trading profits and others said that the work prevented the shame of poverty, but most seemed to assume they would support themselves. The major advantages were seen in terms of the children and their support.

Perceived Resource Scarcity

Trade is seen as a necessary concomitant to the expenses of child-rearing. It is also one of the areas where resource scarcity is perceived. When asked what they would need in order for their work to progress, all of the women said money to increase the availability of other resources, especially time and energy. Those who wanted to change commodity, for example, wanted to deal in goods with a higher value-bulk ratio, or with a more consolidated source, so that they would use less physical effort and time per unit of capital. Others were interested in bulk buying and selling, either through a shop or across long distances, in order to avoid the tedium of frequent, small, short distance transactions. Still others wanted to invest in storage so as to be able to make one large purchase instead of a series of smaller ones. To some extent the ways in which women developed their work activities as their families increased in size reflected their desire to save time and energy and increase profits. For some, there was a move away from services, such as porterage, to trade. Others added trade to service, and two had been able to change to more valuable commodities by the time their last born was growing up. Diversification allowed women to try something new while sticking to what they were sure of and in a few cases it represented a diminution of capital. Middle-aged women recalled a trend of increasing need for money for child-care, and most of the women felt that their energy and resources had been insufficient for their children's needs.

Less strain was perceived in relation to time available. The majority said that there had been enough time to play with their children. Some attributed this to the long hours they sat down selling goods. Others said that they limited either their daily movements, or the scope of their trading while the children were small. Those who felt pressed for time were the ones who had no shop, or whose trade circuits ranged far from home. The most stressed women in terms of time, money, and energy were those who supported their first children by carrying head loads. Looking at the enjoyment women experienced in caring for their various children, it is clear that the children's health was as important as money in making child-care easy or not. Most women said they did not enjoy one child more than another because they ought not to.

Expectations of Marriage

Half of the women expressed disappointment with their positions as wives. In general, they had not known what to expect. Some had expected to live in town and establish a fine shop to sit in. Due to various misconceptions and misfortunes, they had all found themselves in the village, where they faced the rigours of farm life—some for the first time. For several of the wives, the period of hardship was temporary: some adapted and established rural trade cycles; some 'climbed up' and went back to town. But most were still experiencing disappointment. For a third of the women, the disappointment was due to the effort and trouble involved in child rearing. They had not known it would be difficult. They specifically said that stress had started with the babies.

Of the half of the women who did not express disappointment, some were rural dwellers who said that life was hard but that they had not expected anything better. As one of the older women said, 'In those days, life was hard. We used to carry head loads from Ife to Ondo (40 miles). A wife of nowadays would not expect to do that.' Perhaps not long distance porterage, but the contented farm wives of today evidently expected to perform all the other tasks which have not been mechanised and which are still difficult. These women said they 'couldn't complain'. They did not mention the stress of child rearing. In fact they mentioned children as the expected compensation for what they were experiencing.

The rest of the satisfied group expressed unreserved contentment with their married lives. Life had been even 'more comfortable' than they expected. Their basic expectations were limited to children, health, food, and clothes to wear, with the empasis on children. 'Childbirth is comfort.' 'Children are the profit you reap from your husband's house.' These women said they had found what they wanted, plus enough money. Their level of contentment seems to require more explanation than their humble expectations afforded. One way in which they differed from the other women is that all but one was beyond child-bearing age. In addition, most had adult children. Thus, even though they did not seem to have more capital than the rest, most should have been enjoying the security which is the fruit of child bearing. In fact all but one were living in town. This may have had a mellowing effect on their memories of early child-care. In addition, for the older women, their humble expectations may be explained by their age, their total lack of schooling, and their husbands' lack of education.

Fertility: Experience, Behaviour and Attitudes

All but one of the women had borne children, ranging from two to twelve live births with a mean of 5.92. The mean number of surviving children was only 3.52, however, and in the whole group there were only three women who had not lost a child. As mentioned, there was only one childless woman (although she was not considered barren), and the largest number of women had two living children.

The women's experiences of conception and pregnancy were less problematic than child rearing, but not entirely trouble free. Ten had experienced temporary infertility. They had found the experience frightening, particularly those eleven women who had also suffered miscarriages. Eleven had not had any problem in conceiving and maintaining pregnancy. More than half the women said that they had had no problems during an established pregnancy, and the women did not perceive pregnancy as a condition to be avoided for their own health or comfort. They all reported that they spaced their pregnancies, however, usually for the sake of the last born child. Except for problems of infertility, they reported no difficulties or dissatisfactions with the intervals between pregnancies, and abstinence was the only method used for spacing. Only one woman reported using any other method. She used injections to stop child bearing under pressure from her grown up daughter. Her attitude towards contraception was entirely negative. Only four women showed positive attitudes to modern methods of contraception. Their reasons were: 'Men of nowadays don't leave women alone'; 'too many pregnancies make far too much suffering and even God doesn't want us to suffer'; and 'contraception must be good since it comes from the hospital'.

Others (12) who expressed an opinion were definitely negative in their attitude. Three explained that children are good, children bring prestige, and contraception has side effects, but most refused to discuss the basis of their attitudes. Nine women refused to give any opinions at all. They said that farm people cannot know about such things, or that it does not concern them, or that those who use contraception will know whether it is good or not. Some of this group ridiculed the whole idea of eating things to avoid pregnancy: 'If I know that I don't want to be pregnant, why would I bother to see a man'.

Reasons for negative attitudes became clearer in the light of their lack of knowledge and the sources of their ideas. The following methods were mentioned by a few women: the pill (5); ligation of the tubes (4); injection (depo provera) (3); abortion (3). Four women said they had heard of contraception, but would not give any details as to methods, and nine were adamant as to their ignorance of the whole topic. The primary source of information was said to be hearsay. In preparing the family planning talk, the assumption was made that the women's avoidance of contraception was based on fear and repugnance of permanent infertility and of abortion, which most confused with prevention of pregnancy.

When asked whether they were satisfied with their family sizes or wanted more children, eight women answered in favour of limiting the number of children. Two of them did not want more children at all (one a mother of eight, and the other a mother of five asked to stop by her daughter). The other six wanted more and mentioned their ideal family sizes: four, five, six and ten children. Seven women wanted more children but left the number in the hands of God. This group included two who were currently resting to recover their health and finances. Thus, while spacing was encouraged by this group, limitation appeared ridiculous. The other respondents said that they were too old to have more but were unwilling to consider how many they would have wanted under ideal circumstances, although clearly they would have wanted more, not fewer. When prompted the women were prepared to consider the pros and cons of large and small family sizes, indicating inclinations at least on the part of some towards limitation and a recognition of the strains of parenthood, in addition to a certain fatalistic acceptance of whatever God sent them.

There was a general attitude that money and education for the children were necessary for a couple to be happy with many children. Some women even said that the best marriages had many children and plenty of money, while the worst had many children and no money. For those who came down on the side of limiting the number of children, limited resources were the most prevalent reason and the women were quite specific in spelling out the problems that could arise from unlimited numbers of children. Some of the women who said that few children were better than many realised that they were giving an unconventional answer and made comparisons between the old days and the present. Some of their remarks were pragmatic: costs are higher now due to inflation; in the old days there was no school and children helped produce and sell food. Other comments seem to show a less unquestioning acceptance of God's will. Responses as to how many children 'a woman' should have were consistent with the idea of limiting the number of children because of limited resources. Many said it was an individual choice to be based on the woman's economic power, or that of the husband.

An attempt was made to examine women's activities and expectations regarding child-care. In comparing husbands' and wives' parental roles, more than half the women said that the mother is ultimately responsible for her own children. Reasons given for this were that she is more available and better able to look after her children financially since she has fewer other responsibilities and cares more.[4]

It is interesting that this question on men and women and child-care was interpreted by at least 15 women as a question of responsibility and there was a remarkable acceptance of what women clearly described as men's irresponsibility. The women who said that men were less responsible than women and those who said they had found themselves with unexpected child-care roles included half the women who approved of modern contraception and all but one of the women who had a definite number in mind as an ideal family size.

Twelve of the women had one or more children residing away from them while growing up, mainly with maternal grandmothers and paternal siblings, a practice which appears to be declining but which has been widely prevalent in Yorubaland. The group of women who had not sent out any of their children included three out of the four who had a positive attitude towards modern contraception and all the women who wanted a definite number of children. All but two of the women had enjoyed some kind of help in caring for their children, especially from grand-mothers. A wide range of other relatives was also mentioned, and six women specifically said that their husbands had helped. The two women who said they had never had any help in child-care did have a definite ideal number of children, but disapproved of modern contraception.

All but one woman noted changes in child-care since their own childhood. Most focused on the differences in things fed to or applied to children and babies. In the old days, mothers used readily available materials such as rags for nappies, and leaves for medicine; nowadays, tinned food, patent medicine, hospital care, and proper clothing had become necessities and inflation was making them more expensive all the time. A few of the older women also mentioned that the quality of the contact between mother and baby had changed. Feeding bottles had replaced the breast, schedules had replaced free access, a child had to cry while waiting for his mother to wash her hands before picking him up. The modern mother was never touched by her child's urine—not on her back, her lap, or her bed. The women who mentioned these things seemed to feel that the costs of hygiene were too high.

Women were also asked to compare the amount of help they had given their mothers with the help they receive from their own children. Most said there were definite differences and that the direction of assistance had actually reversed in the space of one generation.

Significantly, many noted that school had altered the parent–child relationship and that as a result the parent had lost status. 'Disobedience is so rampant nowadays that we want to beat them to death. Enlightenment has turned things around.' 'In the old days, children listened to parents. Not now.' When discussing the hopes and expectations they had concerning their children, success at school was specifically mentioned by three-quarters of the women who had school-age children. This was usually seen as basic and instrumental to the hopes mentioned: most hoped that the children would care for their old mothers, raise their mothers' status, and bring good things home.

Trading Activities

Most women traded in two or more commodities, often combinations of locally produced goods and goods from outside the area. After the building of the maize crib most women added maize to their trading items. While most of the women were involved in the distribution of local products, some helped provide the area with materials from other places and a few provided ready-to-eat foods and services.

The amount of capital the women reported having available for trade varied from N12 to N1,000 with a mean of N194. The usual size of investment made by the women again ranged widely, from N18 to N297, with a mean of N64. There was a slight tendency for women with younger children to invest more in their transactions.

When a woman was dealing in a food product, especially a cooked food product, she usually fed herself and her children from her supplies. Most of the women could not account for the amounts of such consumption. Even women who were trading in non-consumable produce counted the feeding of themselves and their children as part of the cost of the trade, on a par with the costs of motor transport or hired labour. In fact, it might be said that the respondents compensated for the lack of cost attributed to their labour by including their own physical maintenance, including health care, in their costing. The concept of profit which was adopted for the subsequent analysis was therefore the women's own concept of surplus after business and maintenance expenses. Using this concept has several advantages: (1) it emphasises that trade is both a productive and a reproductive activity; (2) it allows us to make comparisons on profit which the women themselves would make; and (3) it allows us to reach conclusions as to the women's ability to repay loans which we could not make if their basic maintenance had not been included. A fourth advantage is that by using the women's concept of profit we find the data sufficient for analysis.

Looking now at the gains made by the traders, we see that profit varies even more than available capital or average investment. An average investment of N64.00 brought a mean profit of about N18, but this could vary from a loss of N1 to a gain of more than N100. Profit varied inversely with the traders' ages ($r = -.33$) and to a greater extent with the ages of their youngest children ($r = -.42$). The factor most highly correlated with profit, however, is average size of investment ($r = .92$). Other factors are less strongly related to profit and are almost as much related to size of investment as to the amount of gain. Women making larger investments, for example, were more likely to store produce for longer ($r = .29$), and number of days of storage is positively related to amount of profit ($r = .32$). (Storage time for goods ranged from 1 to 122 days, $\overline{X} = 43$.) Associated with this is the finding that women who invested larger amounts of capital seemed to do so less frequently than those making smaller investments ($r = -.06$). (The number of investments during the year ranged from 3 to 100, $\overline{X} = 13$.)

Most of the women did not go beyond Ife and its surrounding villages, but five traded in the far north, and one traded in Lagos. The local traders all invested less than N80 and made a profit of less than N20 on the average transaction. While the same was true for three of the northern traders, the other two were investing almost twice as much and making N60–100 on the average transaction. The trader who went to Lagos was investing almost N300 and making over N100. It was also found that women who carried out processing as part of their trading activities made more profit than women who did not. Women who processed also invested more in their transactions. It was possible to distinguish two types of processing: that involving the cooking of foods, and a rather fast turnover, and that involving the shelling, peeling or fermenting of produce for later sale. Of the two types, the latter involved both the greater investment and the greater profit.

The women who made the largest investments and earned the greatest profits were those who used hired labour. These were followed by those who made use of relatives and friends as well as hired labour. Traders who relied on family and friends for help made the third largest investments but the least profit, perhaps because of expenses incurred on behalf of their helpers. Compared to them women who had no help with labour and those with partners made more profit, even though their investments were smaller. The women's children did not constitute an important source of labour; only three women mentioned being helped by their children.

The main factors associated with greater profits—larger investments, trade routes, use of labour, and participation in processing—are all factors with implications for physical energy expenditure. Contrary to expectations, mothers of babies and primary school children are at least as vigorous as mothers of adults and secondary school children, and they were more likely to engage in processing than older mothers. Younger mothers accounted for more than half of the women who use no additional labour, and for almost all the women who hired labour. Four of the six women who travelled to Lagos or the north were young mothers, two with young babies. In short, mothers of younger children seem to show more initiative, and to have a greater tendency to engage in practices associated with higher profits.

The Co-operative and Women's Trade

Women who were deemed to be creditworthy by their society were each loaned N60, at an interest rate of 30 per cent for one year. All but four of the loan recipients said that they normally had more than N60 in trading capital. Data on the size of average investments shows, however, that two-thirds of the women invested less than that amount on their average transaction. For them the loan must have made a considerable difference. For five of the women, each investment made was only slightly more than the value of the loan, so it seems probable that the credit had allowed them to expand. Three of the women were operating with more than twice the amount of the loan, and it may well be that the credit was less important to them. The women added the N60 to their existing capital and began to trade with it in July, knowing that in January they would pay half of the interest, N9, and that in June they would pay the other half and repay the capital. In fact, the loan and interest were paid in full. Although some of the women paid a month late, the society as a whole covered its debts. It seems, therefore, that the co-operative can be trusted to handle loans where the amount is only part of the total capital managed.

The modal internal rate of return was about 15 per cent, and only one-third of the traders earned less than this. Loans at an interest rate of 15 per cent should therefore allow the women to maintain themselves and their children, as they have reported doing, and also to repay the loan. Since, upon completing their transactions, the percentage profit was at least 19.6 per cent, one could expect that there would be enough margin beyond the interest to allow for expansion of trade and other expenditures. Meanwhile, the co-operative benefited since the loan was made without interest to the group and the interest paid by individuals was left with the group as a grant. It would, of course, be possible in future for the group to borrow at one interest rate and loan to members at a slightly higher one. The main concern here, though, is with the indirect effects of the loan on capital formation within the co-operative.

It was found that more capital was accumulated through shares, savings, and entry fees during the year of the loan (N68.50) than during the year immediately preceding it (N56.50). However, the increase in capital during the loan year represents a slower rate of increase (51 per cent) than the group experienced during the previous year (72 per cent).

It was expected that the total amount of capital women had accumulated in the co-operative would be related to their investments and profits. This was true to some extent, but the findings suggest that while individual members of the group would gain financially by organising credit for individual enterprises, the gain to the co-operative itself would be slight, and that the growth rate of the co-operative's finances might even be inversely related to the availability of credit from outside sources. In order to counter any such negative trend, it might be necessary for the group to liberalise its savings policy. Originally, members were encouraged to save regularly and allowed to withdraw annually. Thus, there were times of the year when savings did not form an important part of the capital in the credit pool. Women viewed the savings as their individual property, however, and saved as much as possible. Later, government officials insisted that savings be left in the co-operative. This stabilised the credit pool, but members were more reluctant to deposit money with the group. As outside loan sources become more important than internally generated credit, the co-operative may gain more by acting as a rural bank and allowing members access to their own savings. This access would, of course, have to be limited to agreed times so that money loaned out could be made available to the savers.

The Maize Crib

Another of the experimental aspects of the study was to see whether the women could organise themselves sufficiently to adopt improved agricultural technology and to observe the effects of such adoption. The innovation chosen for the experiment was an improved maize storage facility. It was modelled on the low-cost design developed by the International Institute of Tropical Agriculture. The crib cost N60 to build, including cement for the foundation, chicken wire and bamboo for the main body, corrugated sheets for the roof, and the wages of one carpenter. The latter was the only labour cost because, in addition to most of the women, five men volunteered to help with the construction. Use of the crib got off to a slow start due to untimely rains, which kept the early maize crop wet until November. When the dry season crop was mature, women again began to use the crib. They used it individually, each demarcating her own section with old mats. The maize was sprayed by the owners when it was added to the crib. In addition, the whole crib was sprayed on co-operative meeting days. Individual access encouraged more women to use the crib and also allowed them to store for as short a period as they liked. As a result, a total of 4.76 tonnes was kept in the crib for rather short periods. It is hoped that the effectiveness of the crib under normal weather conditions has been demonstrated and that women will be using the crib for longer periods in the future.

The Family Planning Lesson

The remaining intervention was family life education. A gynaecologist, a native of Ife, was invited to give a lecture on family planning in March. The talk was held on a co-operative meeting day and so was very well attended. Women were told to invite their husbands and several men also attended. The men's participation enriched the discussion and their presence prevented the spread of any rumours of a women's conspiracy.

The doctor had been made aware of the major findings of the study on perceptions of motherhood. These, and the lack of medical facilities in the village, guided his emphasis on contraceptive methods such as foams and pessaries which are temporary and local in their effects. His overall presentation of the rationale for family planning was not based on the study findings, however. It had been hoped that such a presentation would emphasise the women's own concerns, such as limited resources and the changing roles of children. While these were mentioned, they were not emphasised, and in fact they shared equal prominence with issues such as eugenics and the population explosion. Participants found these concepts very strange, but interesting, and it seems that presenting them did not detract from the message.

The comments and questions which followed the talk reflected a generally positive response while highlighting two of the major concerns of the group. One such concern centred on the appropriateness of contraception for adolescents. Several voiced the fear that contraception would lead to promiscuity, uncontrollable behaviour, and 'spoiling of the insides'. One woman who shared this fear also spoke very forcefully on the need to keep family size to manageable limits and the advantages of what they had just heard for women who wanted to stop childbearing. She felt very strongly that hygiene and not family planning should be taught to school children. An opposing view was offered by a man who said that contraception could insure a father's investment in his daughter's education—an investment that is often wasted by pregnancy. The doctor then led a discussion on how the behaviour of youths could be guided by parents and how contraception could be introduced in such a way as to be consonant with decent behaviour. Underlying the discussion was the assumption that today's youth would not abstain.

The second issue raised was whether contraception would free a wife from the necessity for chaste behaviour. This was raised by a man who feared that women might misuse the technology and 'carry their husbands' property all around'. The women present laughed openly at his remarks, on two grounds: first, they said that they, not men, were the owners of their own bodies; and, second, they did not know why they should run around looking for sex. As the discussion progressed, it seemed there was a consensus that women were and always had been the owners of their own bodies, and that contraception would not make any difference to their behaviour. As one man put it, a women should be able to protect herself from disease and unwanted pregnancy; even if a woman were adulterous, if she used contraceptives, she would be able to ensure that all pregnancies belonged to her husband. Many women saw men as a barrier to their using contraception, but, as one woman put it, times were becoming so hard that soon no one would need to preach to men. 'When the cassava meal no longer lasts a week, the husband will beg his wife to start using contraception.'

It seems that the talk and discussion did not entirely dispel the idea that contraception means a permanent cessation of pregnancy or that it is used mostly by adolescents under somewhat regrettable cricumstances. On the other hand, the discussion did bring out some areas of change which had not come out in the interviews. It seems that some people did feel that women could be expected to enjoy sex without procreation. Furthermore, there were signs of growing tolerance for pren.arital sexual behaviour in so far as it does not spoil the future of the youth involved.

There were questions as to the availability and prices of the methods displayed. Unfortunately, there was not much reassurance in the answers. Those methods which were most readily available at low cost from the hospital were those which require medical supervision or at least the availability of medical care, should problems develop. Those methods which were safer and more temporary were relatively more expensive and not always available in Ife chemists' shops. No contraceptives were available in the village. This may account, in part, for the fact that there was no known follow-up to the lecture on the part of the participants. No one came to project staff to seek further information or access to medical help. None of the women visited the doctor in his clinic. In fact, after the lecture, the daughter of a prominent co-operative member became pregnant and dropped out of school. Women of child-bearing age did express gratitude for the enlightenment they had received, but it seems that several aspects of thier situation will have to change before they can put their knowledge into practice.

Conclusion

The findings of this study may now be viewed in the light of some of the hypotheses and theories linking economic and demographic change. Kocher (1973, p. 58) using data from several countries, proposed a model of rural development and fertility decline under conditions of equitable income distribution according to which, when increases in agricultural production and income are widely diffused, a great number of individuals will experience changes in the variables which intervene between income and fertility. These intervening variables include: increased survival of children, increased investment in children, rising aspirations for children, higher costs and lower productive value of children, desire for smaller families, and readily available family planning facilities. This study showed that only some of these factors were being experienced by the co-operative women. Mothers did report that they were spending more on child maintenance than they used to and that they were investing more in their children's education. They also complained that their children were not very helpful or productive in the home, in the market or on the farm. The aspirations for their children reported by most of the mothers were high by any standard.

Some of the model's ingredients for fertility decline are missing, however. First, there is no evidence that women's incomes are increasing—either due to developments in the country as a whole, or due to the University's development project, or as a result of actions taken during the present study. Even if some of the women are experiencing improved incomes, it may not be at a level that could affect their fertility behaviour.

Second, while there is evidence that child mortality is lower for younger mothers than for older ones, the survival rate may not be high enough to let mothers plan with assurance. Ware (1975) wrote that the influence of child mortality is felt at the societal level rather than at the individual level. This seemed to be true in the study area, since young mothers were as likely as older ones to reckon with possible mortality in their consideration of ideal family size, although those mothers who had never lost a child were more likely to have a definite ideal family size than the group as a whole.

A third element missing in the study area was family planning facilities. It is possible that some of the women who approved of contraception might have used it if less effort and cost had been required. Furthermore, if both the information and the facilities had been available, it is probable that a cycle of positive experiences and positive attitudes would have been established. Certainly, positive experiences, even second-hand, would be necessary to combat the confusion between prevention of pregnancy, 'spoiling of the insides', and abortion which the women evidently made. This is especially true in a community where enough women had experienced infertility to want to avoid any risk of physical damage. Even the establishment of positive attitudes would probably not have led to reduced fertility, however, since in other Yoruba areas contraceptive use has been found to replace abstinence, usually for the purpose of spacing pregnancies (Dow, 1977). The use of contraception to replace post-partum or even terminal abstinence could even result in increased fertility, since modern contraception is less effective than abstinence.

A fourth element which has not been found in the present study is a desire for smaller families. It is not possible to say that younger women wanted smaller families than older women had wanted because child mortality had placed the whole issue beyond the control of most women, particularly the older ones. The data indicate only that most of the women felt a need to limit family size according to available resources. Since only six women put a numerical value on this limitation, it may be that most of the women were not feeling the pinch of resource scarcity in a way they associated directly with their having too many children. One area of social change which is expected to reduce fertility is the crumbling of the mutual obligation system. The mutual obligation system favours high fertility because it puts a priority on having many children to act as social linkages, it makes it impossible to avoid child-related expenses by limiting one's own fertility, and it provides assistance in caring for one's children. Certainly it was found that the amount of child-care assistance from relatives was declining, and significantly those women who had not sent their children out to be fostered by relatives had more favourable attitudes towards contraception and family limitation. A slight tendency was also observed for those who felt men were less responsible than women and those finding themselves with unexpected child-care responsibilities to have positive attitudes towards family planning.

Changes in the parent–child relationship are also expected to affect fertility. The village women did indicate that they had lost influence over their children because of schooling, but this loss was not apparently associated with any change in attitudes towards family planning. For many women, this loss of influence meant they could not control the behaviour or the labour of their children. Surprisingly, only one woman projected her present lack of control to the future and suggested that her children might disappoint her in her old age. Most of the women still expected to be supported by their children and to be more than repaid for their own expenditures. The very old women were contentedly enjoying such support. In these circumstances with expectations of the net flow of wealth moving from child to parent, fertility can be expected to remain high (Caldwell, 1977b).

To summarise, some of the conditions which are thought to be associated with fertility decline were found in the lives of the co-operative members. Other conditions were not readily apparent. It would seem that before the existing factors—which lead at least some women to desire fewer children than their mothers had, or to wish to plan their births using modern contraceptive methods—can have any impact on the women's fertility behaviour, two major improvements will have to be made. Health care will need to improve to the point where there is less anxiety than was readily apparent about infertility and child mortality, and the women's economic situation will need to improve to the level where they can save and build for the future and thus depend less on their children for support in their old age. There will also need to be more readily available family planning facilities.

Trade was seen as a necessary and natural activity for mothers. Indeed, younger mothers were more active in trade and made more profit than the older women. Profit was most highly correlated with size of investment. Both profit and investment were positively associated with the length of the storage period, the distance goods covered, the processing of produce, and the use of diverse labour sources. Profit and investment also fluctuated due to seasonal changes in the availability of cash from various crops and festivals, and cyclical variations in the availability of trading capital.

The women appeared to be well aware of these factors as they relate to profit. All the women wanted more money for their trades, and most wanted the money for what we found to be economically sound purposes. In this light it would seem that the size of the loan was much too small to allow for the expansion of volume, storage time and distance which the traders were hoping to achieve. The amount loaned seemed especially inadequate in comparison with the sort of loan normally taken by urban traders, only 1 per cent of whom borrowed as little as N125.50 and most of whom borrow over N1,000 (Olufokunbi, 1981).

It was found that the co-operative group was a suitable institution through which to make trading capital available to the women. As a collectivity, and to a lesser extent as individuals, the women were creditworthy. It was found that the interest rate of 30 per cent, which is normally charged on loans made from members' contributions, was too high, and that it should be brought down to 15 per cent in order to suit the women's rates of return.

Under the present policies regulating the accumulation of capital, especially savings, in the co-operative, it is not likely that the co-operative as a whole will benefit in proportion to the progress of individual members. New ·regulations which would make the co-operative function more like a rural bank would help link the growth rate of the group's assets to those of individual traders. As it is, many of the more dynamic women spend a lot of time and energy looking for non-co-operative sources of cash. The returns on such cash never reach the group and in fact are often filtered off to the urban money lender.

The maize crib experiment showed that the group had a very high potential for joint effort and investment. The way in which the provision of labour and materials was organised was very encouraging as was the spirit of co-operation shown by the women's husbands. Although there were some losses in the first year of maize storage, the women did learn how to share the community facilities while carrying out their individual trading activities. The lessons learned and the facility itself should be useful in the future.

One goal of this study was to discover what sort of assistance would benefit the women in the Aganran co-operative and other similar groups, which could be made available through government agencies, rural development projects and self help. The findings point to the need for a review of the government's co-operative registration policy, and the need to grant recognition to groups which are showing an acceptable growth rate, rather than those which are stagnant but large and well-financed. This recommendation has been made earlier (Ladipo, 1981) but is repeated here, as the present study has effectively demonstrated that a small group is capable of handling credit.

Once registered, women's co-operatives could usefully seek bank loans at a relatively low interest rate and then reloan the money to creditworthy individuals at a rate of say 10–15 per cent, depending on the speed at which members decide they want to build up the group's capital. Capital formation in such women's co-operatives could be encouraged through the accumulation of share capital and loan interest, savings being viewed as the property of individuals, and the co-operative as providing a rural banking service. There is, of course, a need for newcomers to the co-operatives and women receiving loans to be interviewed and advised on their marketing. Advice would need to cover such topics as size of investments, seasonality of purchases and sales, storage periods and techniques, processing and use of labour. Since what we now know about trade in the project area was learned from the women themselves, such advice could well be provided through discussions organised by the co-operative members. Realisation of the above policies would have the effect of making the co-operative a more important institution in the women's lives. If such approaches were successful there would be more significant increases in women's incomes than this study was able to discover. Improved income, together with the economic and social changes reportd by the women, might be associated with changing expectations of marriage and motherhood and associated activities, which in the long run could have some impact on fertility.

In this regard a basic need of rural women which this study highlighted is for safer, more temporary, and more readily available forms of contraception which do not require medical supervision for use, when the now prevalent customs of abstinence and conjugal separation start to break down. The study also highlights the need for more readily available medical care.[5] Another concern which surfaced during the group discussion of co-operative members and their husbands was that regarding adolescent sons and daughters. The parents were concerned that they were losing influence over their children and that the youth were consequently engaging in behaviour which could damage both their fertility and their educational careers (as Akuffo describes for southern Ghana in Chapter 9). Programmes relevant to youth, organised through women's co-operatives, which included lectures and discussions on topics such as premarital sex, contraception, changing styles of marriage and the implications of these for parenthood and career opportunities, could perhaps not only help the youth but also help re-establish the influence of mothers over their young and thus enhance their prestige.

Notes

1   The author wishes to express her gratitude to the Employment and Development Department of the ILO for the grant which made this study possible; to the University of Ife for incorporating this project into its ongoing development work; to the Oyo State Ministry of Trade and Co-operatives for its encouragement of this experiment; to Dr. A. Ademowore for his participation in the family planning lesson; to her colleagues in the Isoya Rural Development Project for their assistance and support; and to the women of Aganran village for allowing the clôse study of their lives. The study reported is part of an ongoing experiment in adopting the development process to the needs of women in rural co-operatives. The experiment has taken place in the context of the University of Ife's Isoya Rural Development Project, which was designed as a field laboratory for the teaching and testing of approaches to integrated rural development. The project includes programmes in intermediate technology, home economics, and adult literacy, but the heaviest emphasis has been on agriculture, and one of the project's major achievements has been the introduction of cash cropping of maize to Yoruba cocoa and kola nut farmers.

2   Data for this part of the study were collected by interviewing co-operative members singly, in private, and in Yoruba, using an interview schedule. Interviews were conducted by a university student and by project field staff both of whom were well liked by the women. Interviews were first recorded on tape and later transcribed *verbatim* so that the women's feelings would not be lost in translation prior to analysis. The author developed the interview schedule by (1) discussing concepts of motherhood, fertility, infertility, and birth control with traditional healers, (2) testing and modifying sections of the focused biography guide for the seven roles of women framework (Oppong and Church, 1981)

with the help of several Yoruba mothers, and (3) pretesting questions developed in the first two processes in a village near Aganran. Although it was intended that all of the 30 members of the group should be interviewed about motherhood, due to illness and migration, only 26 were available.

3 Because of the movements of the traders between town and village, among village markets, and even out of the state, it was not always possible to collect data more often than monthly. Even so, the women were apparently able to recollect details of their transactions for longer periods than one month and most of them did this willingly. Only one woman was uncooperative. She took the loan and disappeared until the day repayment was due. Thus, the number of women who provided information on their trades was 24. The author, one undergraduate student of agriculture, and one project staff member collected the data for this part of the study.

4 Remarks to support such assertions included the following: 'A man remembers his responsibility once in a while, a woman does so daily.' 'The father may come and play with the child for a bit, but the mother carries her own thing on the back.' Some men were said not to be interested in what the woman is going through, even when the woman goes into debt to care for a child. It was said that fathers can refuse to help, and that even when a father is willing to help there is competition for his attention. 'Men are polygynous and their favourite children are the successful ones. A woman must work for the success of her children.'

5 Although the State Ministry of Health has planned a rural health scheme that would benefit the study area, it has not been able to implement it. Perhaps in another study, the possibilities of providing community health care through the co-operative could be explored.

7 Catherine Di Domenico, Lee de Cola and Jennifer Leishman

Urban Yoruba Mothers
At Home and At Work

Perhaps no other group experiences the problems and potentialities of socio-economic change in West Africa so intensely as do employed, educated urban women. They seek to raise children, earn incomes, and even to derive personal satisfaction from waged and salaried employment in societies marked by social and ecological upheavals, rapid urbanisation and industrialisation, and, lately, severe economic austerity. This chapter attempts to add to our meagre information about this important group by analysing survey data relating to the work and family life of 676 working mothers with pre-school children in Ibadan and Abeokuta. Records of many hours of individual and group discussions are also used: these portray the subjective attitudes and feelings of the women about their situation and their hopes and fears for the future. Finally, policy recommendations are put forward which might improve the lives of women in this pivotal group and those who depend on them.

The specific crisis addressed here results from the decline in the support networks available to parents of young children as a consequence of the employment of adult family members outside the home and the involvement of older children in full-time compulsory education. Because Yoruba women are the traditional and primary care-givers, this strain particularly impinges on mothers, who may ultimately have to choose between taking a job and leaving children under potentially unsatisfactory supervision or caring for them themselves and forgoing income that is critical to family survival or comfort. The cruel choice is often between inadequate child-care and inadequate income—and sometimes women may suffer both. Our focus is on how the women resolve this dilemma.

To study this problem a sample of working Yoruba women with children under six years of age was studied, clustered by workplace and stratified by type of employment as shown in table 7.1. The women interviewed covered the entire span of the female reproductive period, ranging from 16 to 50 years of age. The mean age of the sample was 30.5 years (median 27 years). Most of the women (70 per cent) were relatively young, aged 25–34 years. Nearly all were or had been married but only three-quarters were living with a husband at the time of the study. Seventeen per cent were married but not living with their spouse, and a further 7.1 per cent were either widowed, divorced or separated. The ages at which the women in the sample had married ranged from 11 to 32 years, with the median age at marriage being 23.1 years. Some of the women surveyed thus married relatively late, one-quarter marrying at the age of 25 or later. In this respect, the sample is atypical, probably because so many were in occupations requiring a fairly high level of education. It is not unusual, however, for Yoruba couples to live apart, especially if the marriage is a polygynous one. A husband may live with a young wife, while his older partner, engaging in her own trade or craft, lives in another household.

Only 27 per cent said their husband had more than one wife. Three-quarters came from polygynous homes. Polygyny is more widely practised by Muslims than by Christians. Relatively more of the Abeokuta women were Muslim, married polygynously, and came from polygynous homes themselves.

Roughly two-thirds of the women had three or fewer living children, while 6.4 per cent had six or more, with the ages of the eldest children ranging up to 30 years. The mean number of children per woman was 3.1 and the mean number of children living at home was 3.0. Apart from adult children living elsewhere, 17 per cent of respondents had children away at boarding school, 9 per cent had a child living with a co-wife, and 11 per cent had children living with other relatives. As remarked above, it is part of traditional Yoruba family practice that children sometimes live with grandparents, aunts or uncles or other kin. It is a way of cementing kinship ties, rendering assistance to relatives, and providing children with sound character training. For the child sent from a rural setting to an urban area, or to a more educated home, it is a way of providing him or her with greater opportunities, often the chance to learn more sophisticated ways or to go to school or to be apprenticed in a craft or trade. The educated and the relatively affluent members of a family are those most likely to be called upon to care for the children of other relations. This in part accounts for the fact that over half of the sample said they had children living with them who were not their own.

Table 7.1   *Percentage distribution of the workplaces of the women*

Workplace	Ibadan	Abeokuta
Government offices	13	9
Para-government offices	4	5
Educational establishments	27	22
Hospitals	6	14
Factories	3	0
Total public sector	54	50
Markets	27	25
Factories	10	15
Banks and insurance offices	8	5
Shops, supermarkets, other businesses	2	6
Total private sector	47	51
TOTAL	101	101
N	470	208

Table 7.2   Percentage distributions of occupations of women and their husbands

Occupation	Women	Their husbands
Farmer	22	1
Trader	22	13
Unskilled	6	1
Semi-skilled	14	7
Clerical and sales	27	19
Skilled	2	10
Semi-professional	15	19
Professional	14	30
Other	—	1
TOTAL	100	101
N	668	609

Occupation

The occupational distribution of the sample is summarised in table 7.2. Just over one quarter of all the women worked in markets, most of them as petty traders. The largest group of manual workers were employed as semi-skilled factory workers (these comprised half of those in the private non-market category); some were engaged in unskilled domestic work, and a number were skilled craftswomen. The largest category of white-collar workers were employed in clerical occupations (including sales). The semi-professional category included women working as primary school teachers. Those involved in secondary and higher education are included in the professional group along with senior nurses, doctors, accountants, and so forth. Women in educational institutions comprised by far the largest group of workers engaged in the modern sector (49 per cent of those in modern sector occupations).

Husbands usually have higher status occupations than their wives but equality tends to increase at the highest levels. Approximately one woman in six had a husband with a lower status occupation, but for the semi-professionals this proportion rose to one in three. Most of their parents were (or had been) engaged in traditional occupations: 71 per cent of their fathers and 92 per cent of their mothers were farmers or traders, mainly on a small scale. Only 12 per cent of their fathers and 3 per cent of their mothers were of semi-professional or professional status.

Only 4 per cent of the women had received no formal schooling. Some 88 per cent were certificate holders of one kind or another (from primary school leaving certificates upwards).

Many of the respondents cherished ambitions for even higher levels of achievement than those they had already attained. Some 42 per cent of them said they were seeking a further educational qualification. Nearly two-thirds of these women aspired to an advanced teaching qualification, a post-secondary technical/commercial/professional qualification, or a university degree. Most of the remainder were seeking either higher secondary qualifications or other secondary or even primary school certificates. These findings suggest a high level of aspiration on the part of many of the women, although the data provide no indication of how realistic their reported aspirations were.

Table 7.3 Percentage distribution of education of women and their husbands

Level of education	Women	Their husbands
None	4	6
Primary	24	9
Modern (practical)	25	9
Secondary	24	26
Teacher training	10	12
Technical college	8	12
University	4	26
TOTAL	99	100
N	656	616

Only 28 per cent were born in the city where they were currently working, and over half of the migrants said that they were born in what they described as a small town or village.

Earnings and Aspirations

The lure of steady, moderate incomes had drawn many women into wage employment in the cities, but many nevertheless looked forward to the day when they would be free to set up their own businesses. They would then be able to please themselves as to hours and types of work, as well as gaining control over the profits of their enterprise and endeavour.

Like women everywhere, they were preoccupied with the high and rising cost of living: all foods, including locally grown produce, had, they claimed, risen tenfold during the 1970s. World Bank (1980) data suggest that prices increased countrywide about fivefold during this period). In addition to expressions of financial anxiety, individual tales of hardship were recorded—of women who were the sole income earners in their households, supporting unemployed husbands as well as children; of working mothers with no one to care for their babies and toddlers. Mothers stressed that it was becoming more and more difficult, at a modest income level, to afford household help. At the same time the higher cost of living made it necessary for mothers to be gainfully employed. A critical factor was the new universal primary education (UPE). As most children went to school, young girls were now only available as housemaids in a part-time capacity. There were still exceptions to be found in 1976, but by 1979 UPE had become both free and compulsory.

Family Relationships

Although men are the socially dominant members of the community, women strive to maintain their economic independence and self-reliance. There is no such thing as sharing incomes unless one of the marriage partners does not have a job. The husbands were largely responsible for paying the rent, providing money for food (including the baby's formula), and paying the children's school fees. The women bought some food and helped to clothe the children. Both wives and husbands had responsibilities in relation to their kin, and some were putting young relatives through secondary school. Few of the husbands gave their wives money to meet their obligations to kin, so wives needed to have their own source of income.

Table 7.4   Occupation level by workplace (in percentages)

Occupation	Workplace				
	Market	Factory	Office	Hospital and educational	Total
Trader	78	—	5	—	21
Unskilled	—	17	—	10	6
Semi-skilled and skilled	22	67	1	5	16
Clerical and sales	—	16	79	13	28
Semi-professional and professional	—	—	15	72	29
Total workforce	100	100	100	100	100
N	161	83	169	221	634

Few men helped in the home and it was up to those women who were working to arrange for the care of their children. If Yoruba women have to stay at home because they are unable to find work, they occupy themselves with trading or craftwork in or near the compound. For most of them being 'only a housewife' is virtually equivalent to idleness and therefore disparaged.

Traditionally, patterns of behaviour between spouses are marked by great deference on the part of the young wife towards her husband and all members of his compound. She must kneel down to him and all others who are senior to her. In their presence she must be extremely reserved and modest in behaviour and appearance, and she must be willing to do the heavy work in the compound. It is only with the birth of her first child that the young wife starts to be treated with more respect. Customarily women are helped with household chores by younger relatives, and by their daughters when they reach an age when they can actively help. Thus the burden of care is often eased over the years as more female children are able to assist the mother. And if a younger co-wife joins the compound, she will then be expected to do much of the heavier work. The older the woman, the more help and respect she receives, and this is increased by the number of her children. However, as groups of women pointed out, this has become more of a problem with the initiation of universal primary education and young girls of school age are now less available to help at home. A further problem is that in the rapidly growing cities, a migrant woman may not have relatives around to help after a child is born.

Many women said that if they had their choice, they would call on their own mothers for help after the birth of a child, as this is a period when help is critically needed. Life in the city is therefore more difficult for a woman if she is a migrant with few family members to whom she can turn. This is especially true for the poor who cannot afford domestic help. While working, a woman may thus have to leave her infant at home with a helper (usually a housemaid or younger sister) who would feed the baby and any older chilren while she is away. Many women were anxious about leaving children with these young and virtually untrained helpers, who may come and go in rapid succession. However they had little choice in the matter, for nurseries and day-care centres are few; those which do exist are privately run and relatively expensive. Many women even had to stop breastfeeding, or continued only intermittently, when they went back to paid employment. While they were away the helpers would give the baby the bottle, and on the mother's return the

Table 7.5 Mean annual earnings and hours worked per day

Workplace	Annual earnings (in naira)	Range (in naira)	Hours per day	Range (in hours)
Market	650	0–2000	9.1	6–12
Factory	1070	500–2000	8.8	8–9
Office	1710	200–4000	8.5	7–9
Hospital and educational	1970	500–4000	7.4	6–8
All workers	1560		8.3	
N	418		634	

breast might be offered as comfort to calm the baby. The women felt a great need for day-care services, established at a reasonable and therefore subsidised cost, and near the mother's workplace. Even the market women felt that their children could benefit from subsidised nursery and day-care facilities.

When asked how many children they would like to have the women in all the groups responded in similar manner, saying, for example, 'As many as God gives me' as 'As many as possible'. Attitudes are changing among younger women, however, especially those with competing work and family responsibilities.

The Women and Their Work

In the cities, as in the villages, are markets where entrepreneurs, mainly women (but a few men), sell products for money or occasionally for items in kind; but whereas in the villages markets may occupy a few hectares and then often only periodically, in Ibadan and Abeokuta the 'markets' are huge, sprawling neighbourhoods of constant activity and elaborate specialisation. In the sense that markets are found in the villages too these institutions are traditional, but the scale and elaborateness of the city markets make them akin more to a modern department store than to a village trading centre. Yet, because the women who work there to a large extent set their own (rather long) hours and may bring their children with them, these workers certainly share many of the characteristics of a traditional labour force.

In the factories, on the other hand, two-thirds of the workers were semi-skilled or fully skilled, yet these women work in a place and under conditions that are not very much under their control. Table 7.5 further shows that these wage earners have incomes substantially higher than those of the market women and tend to work the 8–9 hour day that is nearly universal for factories. While the factory workers do not on average work longer hours than the market women, the latter report an extremely wide range of hours for their workday.

Next up the economic scale are the office employees, who largely describe themselves as clerical and sales workers, along with a few professionals. These wage earners work slightly less than the others, earning 60 per cent more than the factory women and over two and a half times what the market women earn. Yet, just as in the offices of the cities of the more developed world, these workers also have the widest range of earnings, from clerks taking home only a few naira per day to professionals earning salaries nearly comparable to those of their counterparts in the developed world.

Table 7.6   Reasons given for working (percentages)

To contribute to child's maintenance	52
To be able to maintain self and children if something happens to husband	34
To make use of education or training	32
To save money to establish self in trade or business	22
To buy things for self	21
To have an interest outside the home	12
To save for old age	8
To be able to spend money on relatives	7
To pay children's school fees	6

Finally, in the hospitals and educational establishments are found the semi-professional and fully professional workers. Their earnings and working conditions bear little similarity to those of most Nigerians. Their daily hours are least (and for many of the educational workers part-days are the rule) while their earnings are many times those of the workers at the other end of the economic spectrum. These employees are truly modern in a transitional setting.

There is a marked and expected increase in income by skill level. While the market women claim to earn but a few naira per day, the professionals earn often many times this amount while working significantly fewer hours. The economic value of education is powerfully demonstrated. Each additional, or more advanced, certificate means a substantial increase in economic—and certainly social—status. With little or no education a woman cannot expect to support herself and her children without some kind of familial or community assistance, while the women with post-secondary degrees, even in an inflationary economy, can either support themselves alone or at least make quite substantial contributions to their families' total income.

Table 7.6 shows the percentage of women giving each of the pre-coded responses to the question 'What are the reasons why you work?' As expected, financial reasons figured most prominently (accounting for 77 per cent of all the reasons given). Contributing to their children's maintenance and being able to support themselves and their children should they cease to have their husband's support are evidently important considerations for these women.

Significantly, one-fifth of the women said that they worked in order to save money to establish themselves in a trade or business. These were all women in wage employment with relatively low status occupations, who ultimately hoped to achieve self-employed status in the private sector of the economy. This finding suggests that there is a fluidity of employment between the urban office/factory realm and the large urban market. Yet the decline in formal employment opportunities for women during the recent decade of economic contraction has meant that the realisation of such dreams is becoming less attainable.

Although non-financial reasons were given less frequently, the desire to make use of education or training was cited by one-third of the respondents as a reason for working. Indeed, 80 per cent cited at least one non-financial reason. This suggests that the majority of urban Yoruba working women view their jobs as more than an income-generating activity. The reasons given for working and for choosing a particular job vary between occupational categories and between employment sectors. High status workers (skilled and above) are more likely to

Table 7.7   Percentage of workers expressing job dissatisfaction by workplace

Workplace	%
Market	15
Factory	19
Private office	20
Public office	16
Hospital and education	12
Total sample	15
(N)	(575)
Chi-square = 3.10	

give non-financial reasons for working as their first response than are low-status workers.

Since women increasingly experience great difficulty in securing assistance with child-care and other domestic responsibilities, they are often perceived by employers as likely to be less than full-time workers (even though there is no evidence to support this view).

Job Status and Satisfaction

The majority of the wage-earning, as opposed to self-employed, workers believed that women were fairly treated at work in terms of recruitment (71 per cent felt their employer was fair in this area), promotion (a somewhat smaller 58 per cent), and annual leave (67 per cent). Yet 30–40 per cent did have reservations about whether they or other women were treated the same as their male colleagues.

The majority of women in all occupations claimed to be contented with their work (see table 7.7). The dissatisfied 15 per cent earned on average about 20 per cent less than the majority and tended to be concentrated in the middle range of the education spectrum and among those in formal types of employment it was those in the intermediate grade levels who were most likely to be dissatisfied with their status.

Job satisfaction also varies according to the perceived or desired alternatives to the present job. Some respondents aspired to higher status jobs, but by far the most commonly preferred alternative was engaging in trade or one's own business, cited by 73 per cent of the women. Only 13 per cent of the women would have opted for the role of housewife, while a few (5 per cent) would have liked to be full-time students; it was among this last group that job satisfaction was relatively lowest. Indeed 42 per cent said that they were seeking further qualifications.

In addition to their work outside the home, women have to cope with manifold domestic responsibilities. Although the following section deals specifically with the woman's role as mother, it is appropriate to ask here how the problems of reconciling and co-ordinating work and maternal roles influence the women's job satisfaction. First, the welfare and feelings of other members of their families are of critical importance. Because so few of the husbands disapproved of their working (only 4 per cent reported such problems) it is clear that they encountered little explicit resistance from their mates. Yet the number of children a woman has does appear to affect her job satisfaction: the women with one child tended to be slightly less satisfied with their jobs, probably because many of them would prefer to devote more of their time to the exciting process of raising a first child. In this regard it is particularly significant that *all* of the women who reported having been able to breastfeed their last baby for a year or more said they were satisfied with their jobs. The degree of satisfaction with their child-care arrangements also affects the women's job satisfaction: among those with relatives looking after their children, the rate of dissatisfaction was 50 per cent higher.

To balance the focus on job satisfaction, we also asked the women whether they were satisfied with the care their children received. It is significant that over a quarter (27 per cent) of the women said they felt dissatisfied, and it is clear that job satisfaction and difficulties in finding satisfactory child-care arrangements, both together and separately, may influence these feelings. Among the women who were not satisfied with their jobs, for example, over a third (35 per cent) were also not satisfied with their child-care arrangements, and there was a similar proportion among those women who reported that holding a job had caused them 'problems in organising [their] child-care and household activities'. Among the small group of women who were dissatisfied with their jobs and experiencing organisational problems, 44 per cent reported dissatisfaction with their child-care arrangements. Finally, as we would expect, money tends to influence the perception of these problems: the mean annual earnings of the women who were satisfied with their child-care were 12 per cent higher than those who were not satisfied (N1610 as against N1440), and among the office and clerical workers the difference was a substantial 40 per cent.

The middle level urban worker thus appears to experience the greatest difficulty both in finding job satisfaction and in making adequate child-care arrangements. The market traders and casual workers often take one or more of their children with them to the workplace, while the high-status, more affluent women can purchase acceptable child-care services, but for those women who work relatively long, inflexible and unremunerative hours in factories and offices, job satisfaction and adequate child-care arrangements are both harder to find.

Occupational and Familial Conflicts: The Role of Mother

All the women interviewed in the survey were parents who had at least one child under the age of six. All therefore had domestic commitments, and three-quarters of them were living with their husband at the time of the study. A natural question arises: to what extent did their roles as workers outside the home impinge upon and conflict with their roles at home as mothers and wives? It was originally hypothesised that some of the women surveyed would experience problems of role conflict in attempting to combine their economic and domestic, especially maternal, responsibilities, but that women working in the markets would be less likely to experience such problems than those working in more formal and routinised urban workplaces.

Table 7.8 shows that 27 per cent of the women said their job caused such conflicts. The main issue was the care and supervision of young children, mentioned by 42 per cent of these. The two other major areas of strain concerned help in the house (17 per cent) and the lack of time and rest consequent upon the combination of full-time employment and family responsibilities. As expected, only 13 per cent of the 177 women working in the markets reported problems, compared with 33 per cent of the 480 women employed in clerical and sales and 38 per cent of the professional and semi-professional women—thus supporting the premise that such

Table 7.8 Percentage of women reporting that their job causes domestic organisational problems

Job classification	%
Trader	13
Unskilled	28
Semi-skilled and skilled	19
Clerical and sales	33
Semi-professional and professional	38
Total sample	27
(N)	(647)

Table 7.9 Percentage of women satisfied with child-care arrangements

Child-care arrangement	Percentage using this arrangement	Percentage satisfied
Child's grandmother	31	91
Goes with mother to work	12	81
Other relation	11	78
Housemaid or baby nurse	35	69
Neighbour, friend, other	11	56
Total sample	100	77
(N)	(553)	

problems are related to the nature of employment.

As already mentioned, the most commonly cited problem here was making satisfactory arrangements for child-care while the mother was at work. Although most women were satisfied with their arrangements, 27 per cent were not. Among those women reporting problems in reconciling work and family life, 36 per cent mentioned dissatisfaction with child-care arrangements, whereas only 18 per cent of women not reporting problems mentioned such dissatisfaction.

Table 7.9 shows the extent to which mothers were satisfied with the various types of child-care arrangements. The women with the highest incidence of satisfaction were those leaving their children with their own or their husband's mother. Relying on other family members seemed to be less satisfactory. Nor is a baby nurse necessarily the solution. Complaints of barely adequate or unsatisfactory care were legion amongst employers of this type of untrained assistance. The findings also suggest that neighbours and friends do not constitute a popular or satisfactory form of substitute care.

Clearly, then, in relying on a variety of arrangements, mothers are attempting to solve the problem of substitute child-care, but they are not necessarily doing so to their satisfaction. It would seem that the lack of alternatives accounts for the fact that some mothers continue with methods of care which cause them anxiety and distress. In adopting these varied and sometimes unsatisfactory solutions, the women in this study have much in common with working women in other industrialised countries, who must devise child-care arrangements from a range of feasible, affordable, and not always satisfactory systems. What is different about the Nigerian women, however, is the extent to which they make use of older relatives for this purpose, especially grandmothers. This is a traditional pattern, but as urbanisation leads to the separation of kin, working women—especially those in the formal sector—will face greater difficulties in securing happy, let alone enriching, environments for their children.

The women devote a substantial amount of their waking lives to their occupations, an average of 8.5 hours per day, with 51 per cent working five days per week, 39 per cent working six days, and 1 per cent working seven days. It was noted above that some of the women commented on the lack of time available to them. When asked what they did in their leisure (non-work) time the most common activities, in order of importance, were sleeping or resting, spending time with children, and housework.

Only 38 per cent of the women were able to devote their remaining energies to purely personal leisure activities, such as reading, hobbies, or social or community activities. This is often the experience of mothers in industrialised countries where the combined demands of work and domestic and family responsibilities entail constant rush and fatigue. The women in the present study appeared to be highly committed to their occupational role, and the majority of them spent a great deal of time in work related activities. Almost all the women were full-time workers, probably because of the lack of availability of part-time work. It is hardly surprising, therefore, that most of the rest of their time was spent on their families.

Time is thus likely to be a highly valued commodity, particularly when work and family roles are quite separate. When there is an opportunity to work and care for children simultaneously, the problems are perhaps less likely to arise. Significantly, satisfaction with child-care arrangements seemed to be more widespread amongst those who spent long hours with their children: 84 per cent of those spending 12 or more hours per day with their children were satisfied with their children's care, compared with 73 per cent of those spending less than 12 hours per day with them. Futhermore, the findings indicate that satisfaction with child-care is more widespread amongst market women: only 13 per cent were dissatisfied with the arrangements for their children, compared with 19–38 per cent of those in the other types of workplace.

The link is not so much between the employment sector and length of time spent with children, however, as between employment sector and type of child-care arrangement made. While women in the markets frequently care for their own children, women in the modern sector make greater use not only of grandmothers but also of housemaids and baby nurses. This last type of arrangement is often considered unsatisfactory.

All of the women contributed financially toward the upkeep of their families. Over one-third said they contributed towards food, medical expenses, children's school fees and clothes, wages of household help, and leisure activities. Fathers appeared to bear a major share of domestic financial responsibilities, especially rent. For no item did more than half the women report that they were the sole provider. A wide range of items were shared obligations. Women's responsibilities tended to be either more child-centred or, as in the case of leisure, more elastic expenditures.

Women continue to bear responsibility for work in the home and the smooth running of the household, including responsibility for hiring and firing household help. (This was the one area in which less than half reported joint decision-making

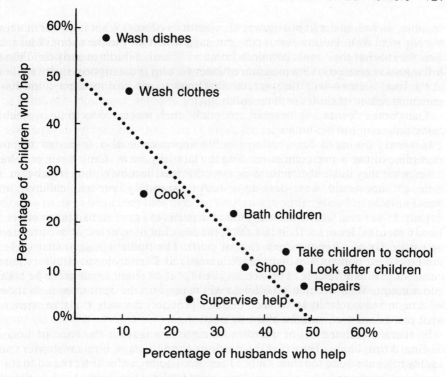

Figure 7.1: Percentage of women reporting assistance from other family members

with their husbands and for which 35 per cent said they made the decision alone.)
With regard to having children, children's education and discipline, gifts to relatives, and financial decision-making in the home, decision-making was reported to
be a joint process in six or seven cases out of every ten.

In the absence of paid household help, women can only look to members of their
own family for assistance with domestic chores and family affairs. Women were
asked to what extent, if any, they received help from their husband or children.
Only 25 per cent of husbands did not take part in domestic work at all. As figure 7.1
shows, the supervision of household help was largely the mother's responsibility:
25 per cent of the husbands assisted in this area and only 4 per cent of the older
children did so. About half got help from other household members, and to some
extent the older children and husbands acted as substitutes (note the negative trend
of the points). Apart from household repairs, the most favoured areas for
participation by husbands included looking after the children, taking them to
school, and doing the shopping. Those tasks regarded as more menial and less
'masculine', such as washing clothes and dishes or cooking food, were correspon-
dingly less popular among husbands, but older children did help.

Many women are thus constrained to spend their leisure time doing housework,
caring for their children, or simply sleeping after their chores are finished and
many spoke of the need for some kind of household help. One third of the suggestions for improving child-care facilities involved having a helper in the home.
Other possible solutions focused on the extension and improvement of child-care

facilities, as well as the improvement of conditions of work (especially for married women workers). Twenty-seven per cent suggested that mothers should give up their jobs so that they could remain at home with their children in early childhood. A few also suggested giving men more money to help them support their families. In the face of financial stringency, it is difficult to see how mothers could have genuine freedom of choice with regard to staying at home, especially if in doing so a woman would be acting contrary to traditional mores concerning women's participation in the labour force.

However, the need for a more flexible approach is also suggested by, for example, women's preferences for longer maternity leave. Only 8 per cent had taken maternity leave of 6 months or more for their last baby, but 18 per cent of them said they would like to have done so. A substantial 46 per cent had taken less than 3 months off work, although only 30 per cent said they liked so short a maternity leave. As these figures indicate, many women (45 per cent) had taken between 3 and 6 months' leave for their last child, the duration of maternity leave preferred by a majority of all respondents (52 per cent). The findings suggest that while a substantial proportion of women prefer a relatively short maternity leave, requirements vary, and a flexible approach is called for if different needs are to be taken into account. What women actually do will depend on the options open to them. With regard to maternity leave, their decision probably depends to a large extent on what provisions are made for them by employers.

Inextricably related to the problem of maternity leave is the issue of breast-feeding. Most women breastfed their infants for periods of time far shorter than has traditionally been the case. Only 15 per cent had breastfed their last child for 6 months or more, and 39 per cent had breastfed for less than 3 months. A variety of reasons were given for the cessation of breastfeeding, including ill-health, insufficient milk, and so forth. But the most common reasons concerned work and personal choice. Some 36 per cent of the women felt they had breastfed for long enough and 25 per cent had stopped because of their work. These findings reflect a change in attitudes towards breastfeeding as well as the changing demands and nature of female labour force participation.

By and large, suggestions for change and improvement were modest and couched in terms of existing patterns of provision. With child-care arrangements, flexibility again seems to be a key element in the women's proposals. Twenty-nine per cent thus suggested shorter working hours or more part-time jobs to enable women to spend more time at home with young children. Another 23 per cent thought some form of financial assistance could make for improved care, and 14 per cent suggested the provision of nursery schools. As reported above, the most popular proposal (given by 33 per cent of women) was to have a helper in the home. The concern with improving household arrangements is further revealed by mothers' preferences regarding child-care: some 21 per cent mentioned a baby nurse or housemaid, while 29 per cent said they would prefer a relative. However, 43 per cent would ideally opt for a nursery or day-care centre with trained personnel.

Indeed, the majority of women (85 per cent) said they would make use of such a facility, provided charges were reasonable. More than half of those who thought they would not make use of a nursery said they already had a preferable alternative (most frequently, their own mother). Others felt it would be too expensive for them, or believed nurseries did not look after children well, and that they themselves could take better care of their children). Many women were in favour of nurseries, however, on the grounds that they provided just the right kind of safe educational environment for pre-school children.

A wide range of child-care arrangements were thus used by the women. Satisfaction with these arrangements tended to decrease with a woman's job level, especially in the industrial/office sectors. Most satisfied were those women who were able to leave their children with grandparents, and even they would generally have preferred to be able to spend more time with them. Many women sought to retain a more formal version of a traditional institution. Whereas their parents and older relatives had once shared the responsibility for child-care (because the women 'worked' at or near their homes), they used, and wished to use more, paid household help, as well as external child-care facilities. Like women elsewhere they also craved more part-time opportunities to earn money in fulfilling employment. In any case their demands certainly point to a growing need for a cadre of specialised child-care workers to take their places in an increasingly ramified economy.

Policy Recommendations and Conclusion

This study thus indicates that the provision of adequate day-care facilities and personnel must be a central element in any successful attempt to reduce the problems and conflicts engendered by the increasing separation of home and work. Community provision attached to clinics and health centres, and large-scale places of employment, could provide basic medical facilities for children as well as adults, thereby reducing the number of working hours lost waiting in hospital queues. Work-based provision of child-care has the advantage of allowing the mother to visit her child during break periods, thereby reducing the extent of separation between mother and child during an 8–10 hour working day. It also facilitates prolonged breastfeeding. There is thus a strong case for increasing the length and flexibility of the period of maternity leave after the birth.

No one denies that women's maternal responsibilities place an added burden on their employers, particularly in the area of leave provision. But the commitment of a dedicated employee, whose job satisfaction has been assured by the provision of means whereby she and others may meet the needs of their children, is a tremendously valuable asset to a firm. To refuse to hire such a woman not only goes against a modern sense of justice but is bad business management as well.

The present maternity leave regulations tend to provide too much time before the birth of a child and too little afterwards. Mothers need to be free to spend as much time as possible with their newborn children during the critical early 'bonding' period when ample breastfeeding and frequent contact is so important.

Work in the modern wage sector tends to be rigidly organised and to be available only in indivisible full-time units. There is a need for more flexibility in working hours and more opportunities for part-time work. Job sharing might provide one solution. Employers might thus consider making use of more part-time workers and respond seriously to women who want to share jobs.

In the modern urban economy organisation is the key to change, and great potential for change lies in the hands of those labour unions with large female memberships or with women's wings (one such wing of the Nigeria Labour Congress was launched in Ibadan in December 1982). The sound of a chorus carries much further than a single voice.

Whatever the attractions of urban living, it is in rural society that work and home usually remain most fully integrated. Although industrial development is largely an urban phenomenon, fostering of rural development may provide a powerful break to urban migration. Nearly three-quarters of the women in the present study were migrants, over half of whom said they had been born in a 'small town' or village. Were such women and their families, particularly the less advantaged (who generally wish to move), encouraged to remain in their home town or village, the problems of child-care which confound mothers in the urban areas might be avoided, or ameliorated, in so far as the wider network of kin could be called upon for help in the home setting. Promotion of rural development and rural industrialisation and other positive inducements (in the way of services, for example) to counteract the lure of the towns would help family members remain together.

No matter how good the conditions at work, it appears that Yoruba women prefer to be self-employed and independent, as they have been for so many generations. They frequently express the wish to support and educate their children on the proceeds of their own trading or business enterprises. Thus, many women in the wage earning sector later opt for self-employment. In so doing, they may be more fulfilled both as mothers and as independent individuals with ambitions for personal achievement and more able to avoid the strains and role conflicts of employed mothers working away from home.

Part III

Population Policies, Family Planning and Family Life Education: Ghanaian Lessons

I do not think it will be possible to understand West African attitudes about family planning unless one understands the significance of parenthood for the individual and kin group in West Africa (Fortes, 1978, p. 23).

It seems to me incontrovertible that many traditional marriage customs and norms relating to the bearing, begetting and rearing of children in West Africa are too vital and deep-rooted to be overlooked let alone fought against, in future population planning (Fortes, 1978, p. 47).

Data for the three analyses in this section come from Ghana in the 1970s, a country in which the majority of both men and women were engaged in agricultural production using traditional, labour intensive methods. A minority were engaged in manufacturing and only 6 per cent of men and 2 per cent of women were engaged in professional, administrative, clerical and similar work, the majority of whom were employed in government service in ministries, hospitals, schools, colleges, and government trading outlets.

During the 1970s political crises, economic stagnation and financial instability were common (Bequele, 1980). The cocoa industry declined, the manufacturing sector did not get off the ground, and the education and health systems, set up in the early sixties after independence to cater for the needs of the total population, were constrained by shortages and the need for serious economies. In addition declining currency values meant that in the mid-seventies and the following years hyper-inflation was a major concern. In 1977, for example, the consumer price index rose by 116 per cent; such inflation was the cause of a rapid decline in the real income of those on fixed wages and salaries, including government employees like those described here. In 1976 local food prices rose by 78 per cent, and the figure was 139 per cent in 1977. Prolonged drought, limitation of food imports and rising government deficits, largely financed by increases in the money supply, were among the factors blamed.

Ghana is one of the few countries of Africa which has a relatively long history of population data collection, and an array of demographic data are readily available, though relatively less has been done in this field in more recent years. The population is currently estimated to be over 13 million and increasing at a rate of about 3.1 per cent per year. The crude birth rate is about 50 per thousand and the average woman bears six to seven children. Ghana's fertility rate is thus among the highest in Africa and in the world. In the past two decades the death rate fell (26 per thousand in 1960; 21 per thousand in 1970; 19 per thousand estimated for 1980). The result of all this is a youthful population, among whom 35 per cent are under seven years and 48 per cent under 15 years. There are considerable differences in fertility levels in different cultural and geographical regions of the country, and striking differences between various socio-economic subgroups (Gaisie, 1979).

During the 1960s the large family system continued to be supported by the high economic value of children, who still shared the work burden on farms and sent remittances to parents as migrants, thus providing security in old age and sickness, as well as social prestige to parents (Caldwell, 1968a). Even at that time, however, the declining labour value of children was already being recorded in areas where there were marked shifts away from subsistence farming to mechanisation and where there were strong pressures for children to attend school. Significantly, it was noted that resistance to pressures for schooling tended to occur in areas in which children's labour inputs in home and farm were still highly valued (e.g. Oppong, 1973 regarding the Muslimised Dagomba in the north). At the same time the economic burden of the large family was beginning to be felt by the urban educated salary earners, who depended upon earned income and entertained high expectations about their children's education and the style of living of their domestic groups (Caldwell, 1968b; Oppong, 1982b). Already in the sixties the small urban élite had shown expectations and behaviour with regard to procreation that were quite different from the traditional pro-natalist cultures from which they originated. Economic constraints as well as changing ideas about familial roles were noted to be prime factors. Widespread education and employment resulted in such a massive migration of workers that by the end of the seventies over 60 per cent of workers were counted as living outside the localities of their birth.

In the 1960s a number of surveys had been carried out which collected data on Knowledge, Attitudes and Practices regarding family planning (Caldwell, 1968a). Among Ghana's educated, knowledge of some contraceptive method other than abstinence or abortion was already quite widespread at that time. In the population at large abstinence was widely known and used by some in a regular 'rhythm' method, as well as longer term conjugal separation to ensure maintenance of traditionally valued birth spacing lengths (Gaisie, 1981). Discussion of family planning was reported to be relatively uncommon among rural populations, but prevalent among a quarter of urban dwellers and among three out of seven of the urban educated. It was found to be most likely in monogamous first marriages (Caldwell, 1968a).

A number of small surveys were carried out in the late sixties to discover what might be some of the familial correlates of comparatively low family size desires and achievements, especially among those educated and employed in urban areas. Caldwell (1968b), in his study of residents of suburban areas, was at pains to note signs of greater separation of the conjugal family from kin, of 'closer', more stable marital ties, and of increasing 'child-consciousness' regarding own offspring. However, systematic data on use of time, energy, or money within and across the boundaries of the conjugal family were lacking at that time. Subsequent sets of data from educated Ghanaians showed interesting correlations between social and spatial mobility, measured in terms of generations of education, occupational status and migration, and changing sex roles and family relationships. The results of some of these studies have recently been outlined and summarised (Oppong, 1985a). In these latter enquiries, three significant dimensions of family role expectations and behaviour were identified and several different component dimensions measured and compared. These included the degree of openness of the conjugal family (its functional boundedness) including maintenance of kin and fostering of children; the jointness or segregation of the conjugal role relationship including for example the extent to which women maintained the family and husbands shared housework and child-care; and conjugal power and modes of decision-making, especially the degree of equality and shared discussion of decisions. These several dimensions were linked on the one hand to social and spatial mobility (which have elsewhere been labelled 'modernisation') and access to education, jobs and incomes, and on the other to family size aspirations and contraceptive innovation, as well as to the availability and allocation of scarce resources in money and time and thus to parental costs.

One salient aspect of women's changing roles which was documented was the effect of spatial separation of productive work and domestic responsibilities, of paid work and child-care. Women in the urban labour force were seen to be subject to strain and tension, both at work and in the home, if they were inadequately supported by domestic substitutes. The ability for them to share domestic tasks was seen to be critical. At the same time, female autonomy and independence within marriage were seen to be at risk where conjugal resources were markedly unequal, with observed effects upon the conjugal balance of power (Oppong, 1982b). It was accordingly decided to carry out a study in which a model incorporating several types of demographic changes, especially relating to mobility, family size and birth control, could be inter-related in terms of intervening changes in family relationships, in such areas as the domestic division of labour, channels of communication and power and decision-making, and access to, and allocation of, finite domestic resources—hence the study reported in Chapter 10, which for a change focuses on males' role within the family.

The Ghana National Family Planning Programme

Ghana was the first African country to develop a comprehensive population policy, which became operational during the 1970s, and to set up a National Family Planning Programme organised by the Ministry of Economic Development with services from the Ministry of Health, the Department of Social Welfare, the Ghana Medical School, and the Planned Parenthood Association of Ghana.

During the seventies the Government of Ghana was concerned to strengthen this programme, which enjoyed considerable international support. These activities led more recently to the incorporation of family life education materials into school curricula. The GNFPP also developed a research and evaluation unit, as it was recognised that more information was needed to improve the planning efficiency and success of the programme. By 1978, however, according to service statistics, still only 4 per cent of Ghanaian women aged 15–44 were using contraceptives (as compared to 7 per cent in Kenya and 50 per cent in Mauritius). Of these, 55 per cent were using the pill, 9 per cent the IUD, and 34 per cent other modern reversible methods. The programme continued to focus upon married women.

In the three chapters which follow we address important aspects of women's and men's roles which are highly pertinent not only to the improved design and execution of the family planning programme and family life education in Ghana but to the region as a whole, for the three essays underline the importance of giving programme attention to the young, to the unmarried, and to males—not only to married women, as if they were the only sector of the population involved in procreation.

The first essay thus focuses upon the image of the family and women's roles as portrayed or assumed in the country's family planning programme. In view of the autonomy and independence of many women, the fatal consequences of early pregnancy for women's education and careers, and the frequency of extra-marital and teenage births, Bleek argues that birth control services should be more readily available to the young and unmarried.

Earlier work had already illustrated how birth control is eagerly sought and practised in pre-marital relationships but hardly practised by married people (Bleek, 1981). As he notes, the far-reaching negative consequences of an early first pregnancy move young people to use desperate methods to prevent childbirth, such as unreliable contraceptives and dangerous abortion techniques (Bleek, 1976a, pp. 210–225). Completion of girls' schooling or training is a major reason for attempting to postpone, prevent or get rid of unwanted early pregnancies. Evidence on the frequency of abortions confirms this. Both Bleek (1981) and Bartle (1978, p. 527), who carried out ethnographic field work in Kwahu towns, are of the impression that for many rural Akan women the first pregnanacy comes too early. Since the timing of the first birth is so critical for girls' training and career development, Bleek argues that availability of family life education and contraceptives for young women in training would be an important factor contributing to their potential status.

This theme is taken up once more with regard to school girls and boys in Chapter 9 by Akuffo, who highlights the need of the young for both family life education and family planning services, this being a need of which medical personnel in the country are fully aware. He also stresses that male as well as female adolescents should benefit from programme interventions. Thus Lamptey et al. (1978), in evaluating male contraceptive acceptance in rural Ghana, noted that the programme did not reach 15–19 year old boys, especially those attending school. As they emphasised, however, this group is active sexually and pregnancies resulting from their relationships with school girls are often terminated in illegal abortions that carry a high risk of mortality (Bleek, 1976a; Ampofo, 1969). They thus concluded that these young men need adequate information about contraceptive methods and a means of ready access to them that they find socially and financially acceptable.

In general, access to family life education materials in Ghana is limited and there are few materials developed for adolescents. The youth have thus been singled out as a vulnerable group in dire need of information and education on family life, sexuality and other population issues. We here touch upon a policy issue of region-wide, even global proportions, as already outlined above.

Most family planning programmes are planned and organised mainly by male administrators and aimed often almost entirely at married women as the target group; population being one area in which women are not treated as marginal. Yet men's own maintenance of the children they beget has on several occasions been noted to be a significant factor encouraging responsible fatherhood and male birth control use. The ease with which fathers in comparison with mothers can evade their parental responsibilities is well-known, and in the case of southern Ghana has been related directly to their lack of interest in either 'family size decision-making' or use of contraceptives (Oppong and Bleek, 1982).

Thus the final chapter in this section is concerned with responsible fatherhood and the part played by males in birth control. The case examined in some detail is that of teachers in Ghana but the lessons are far-reaching in scope. Male partners in sexual relationships may play an important part in the reduction of fertility. They deserve to receive more attention than hitherto in educational and family planning programmes. Moreover, there are interesting and policy-pertinent associations between greater equality in the sexual divisions of labour both inside and outside the home and family size values and contraceptive practices (Oppong, 1984).

8 *Wolf Bleek*

Family and Family Planning in Southern Ghana[1]

Even critics seem to hold a rather optimistic view of family planning as a means of enhancing women's control over their own lives. In this chapter, it will be argued that in Ghana, among the Akan-speaking people of the south, and more specifically in Kwahu, where the data on which this discussion is based were collected, family planning is not 'correctly presented' and as a result does not contribute to women's emancipation, freedom, family well-being and health. It is argued that the main reasons for this failure are the Eurocentric and male-centred bias in the family planning policy, which mistakenly assumes that the reproduction and socialisation of children take place in a well-defined Western-type of conjugal family in which the father/husband is the only or main 'breadwinner' with a dependent wife and children. Data will be discussed to show that in fact the contexts of procreation and socialisation are rather varied in form and changeable depending, to a large extent, on the different and altering economic roles of women and men as well as cultural expectations and environmental constraints. Perhaps three kinds of family organisation could be distinguished: the matrilineage (*abusua*), the conjugal family, and the matrifocal family.

The two contexts which are neglected by family planning organisations will be described, and emphasis will be placed on the often tense relationship between conjugal family and matrilineage. Subsequently, the central position of women in families where husbands play only a marginal part, or no part at all, will be examined.

This chapter is based on anthropological field work conducted in the seventies in Ayere, a rural community of about 4,000 inhabitants, situated on the Kwahu Plateau. The people of the area belong to the Twi-speaking group of the Akan, whose society is characterised by matrilineal descent reckoning. Most Kwahu are peasants growing food crops such as yam, cocoyam, cassava, plantain and vegetables. Many of them, mainly the men, are cocoa farmers and some are traders.

The Kwahu 'Family'

The Kwahu family differs sharply from the Euro-American concept of the conjugal family, which appears to have been the assumed model in the philosophy

of the Ghana family planning programme in the seventies. To begin with, use of the
English term 'family' is confusing in the Ghanaian context. In the Twi language
there is no single term to denote the nuclear or conjugal family. The Twi word
abusua, which is often translated as 'family', refers to the matrilineal descent
group, a group of people who can trace their descent from an ancestress one or
more generations back. *Abusua* can also refer to a much larger group of people, the
matriclan, those who believe themselves related through women to a distant
mythical ancestress. These matriclans, which are spread over the whole of Akan-
land, number not more than eight.

The *abusua*, the matrilineal descent group with a depth of about four
generations, is the most significant social group in Kwahu society. Its important
functions include establishing personal status as royal, commoner or slave and
supporting claims to political office or citizenship as well as to use of lineage land
and houses. Its members form a unified group, sharing rights and responsibilities
relating to people and property. The lineage disposes of dead members, the head
supervising the rites. Beliefs about life after death among the lineage ancestors
indicate its spiritual continuity. Recent developments have caused some cracks in
the lineage structure, but as a whole it still stands. Indeed, the lineage is the great,
permanent and fundamental institution which permeates every aspect of life.
Marriage and conjugal family, on the other hand, have a temporary character and
are subordinate to the lineage. The lineage needs marriage for procreation but it
sees to it that the loyalty of the marriage partners stays with their respective
lineages. When lineage loyalties are endangered, lineage members often try to
disturb the conjugal relationship till divorce has been achieved. If the lineage does
not succeed in restoring the 'right order' by bringing about a cleavage between the
two partners, it holds the trump card—death. It is the lineage who buries its
members. Those who flout the authority of the lineage should know that the
lineage may refuse them this last service. Such a refusal is the greatest shame that
can befall someone. It is also lineage members who inherit each others' property so
that it is not uncommon for a woman who has worked closely with her husband to
be left with virtually nothing when he dies. The matrilineal rule of inheritance pre-
scribes that the man's property goes to the lineage member who is selected as his
heir, usually a younger brother. If, however, a man has received considerable help
from his wife and children, it is possible for him to give a portion of his privately
acquired property to them.

Lineage and conjugal family are therefore in some kind of competition with one
another. The intriguing thing, however, is that most actors in this competitive
game play a double role. As members of a lineage, they try to advance the interests
of their lineage; as members of a conjugal family, they fight the interests of the
lineage (to which they do not belong). On the whole, however, the lineage has the
better cards. In the ensuing discussion we shall see how this competition takes place
on the different fronts of family life.

Marriage has always been something of secondary importance among the Akan,
and especially among the Kwahu. The same applies to the natural outcome of
marriage, the conjugal family. A woman, her husband and their children are of
course distinguished as a group linked by biological ties, but their functioning as a
social group is less clearly recognisable, certainly in comparison with the European
concept of the conjugal family. Households or residential domestic groups cannot
simply be identified with conjugal families. Indeed, various students of Akan
family life have found themselves at a loss when they have had to define a

'household'.[2] The confusion about who constitutes the basic group for domestic interaction of several kinds reflects the fluidity of domestic family arrangements in Kwahu and more generally in Akan society. The biological connection of father, mother and offspring does not necessarily determine the composition of a clearly defined basic social group. The residential factor probably has decisive consequences for many social activities. As a rule the conjugal family is not the most effective social unit. Many decisions are taken on the level of the lineage, some are taken on the conjugal family level, and many again are taken on a still lower level.

It is necessary to distinguish between the residence of marriage partners and that of their children. Marital residence among the Akan is either duo-local (the separate residence of spouses), which seems to have decreased during the past 50 years, or the spouses live together. There is evidence that a married couple tend to live separately when they stay near the wife's lineage home. Continued residence with the respective lineages is preferred, if that is possible without interrupting the basic prerequisites of marriage: regular nocturnal access, and the wife preparing meals for the husband. If the lineage homes of both partners are within reasonable walking distance of each other this can be done. In all other circumstances the spouses have to take up common residence. These other circumstances are mainly of three kinds: migration to an urban centre, a stay in a hamlet or on a farm, and marriage between two people from different home towns. With the increase in geographical mobility, separate conjugal residence will therefore diminish.

Children's residence patterns are also very fluid. The most important factors seem to be conjugal residence, migration, schooling, divorce and fostering.[3] Some children live with both parents, some with their father, and some with their mother and/or her kin, but the residentially intact conjugal family appears to be the exception rather than the rule. Most children grow up in situations which are very varied and changing all the time.[4]

Marriage, Divorce and Non-Marital Relations

The marriage ceremony has little social significance.[5] For girls, reaching physical maturity used to require extensive rituals which marked a woman's physiological ability to become a mother. Social sanctions around sex and pregnancy were linked chiefly to this initiation rite and not to marriage. Sex before initiation was strongly disapproved of and punished, and required a ritual cleansing. Some sources claim that sex and pregnancy before initiation (*Kyiribra*) used to be punishable by death. The sanction which is most commonly remembered by old people is ostracism of the couple in conjunction with sacrifices, purification, and shameful exposure (Sarpong, 1977. pp. 49–52). The implication seems clear: the social condition for sex and pregnancy was not in marriage but socially recognised maturity; put differently, the condition did not lie in the conjugal but in the matrilineal domain.[6] In a certain sense, marriage among the Akan could, and still can, be regarded as superfluous. Children born outside marriage are not labelled illegitimate, as they are full members of their mother's lineage. In fact, there is nothing that can be uniquely obtained through marriage. An elaborate marriage ceremony, the Christian wedding, has developed recently, but it is largely an urban elite affair, mainly because of its costliness, and affects only a small minority of the urban population.

Divorce among the Akan is easy and frequent; it is a normal occurrence which is likely to befall anyone at least once, probably twice. In spite of its normality, however, people are critical of it and prefer the idea of a stable and lifelong marriage.

As already noted, however, marriage must serve the interests of the lineage. Whatever people may say about their preference for stable marriage, in practice lineage stability comes before marriage stability. Security is found in the lineage rather than in marriage, and it would be foolish to invest too much in marriage. In a time of crisis the lineage offers the most, except when one finds a spouse who is well-to-do. Only such a marriage partner can take over from the lineage. In conclusion, divorce often does not change the lives of the people concerned very much for the high degree of conjugal segregation during marriage may come close to a *de facto* separation. As we have seen, there is nothing which can be obtained uniquely through marriage: sex, having children, bringing them up, earning a living, belonging to a social group—nothing belongs exclusively to marriage. Advantages one might expect from marriage, such as loving companionship, romance, shared parenthood and financial support, are seldom realised. It is no wonder that older people say 'they grow tired' of marriage and that young people shy away from it.

Three types of non-marital sexual relationship are distinguishable: free marriage, lover relationships and prostitution. Free marriage (*mpena awadee*) is not customarily ratified (or only partly so) but enjoys normal public recognition. The couple openly behave as partners, for example through sleeping together, the birth of children, and daily cooking by the woman for the man. In fact, there is little outward difference between a customary marriage and a free marriage. In the lineage studied, about 15 per cent of the members had a free marriage partner. A lover relationship differs from a free marriage in so far as it is a secret relationship. When the relationship becomes publicly known it usually breaks up, but it may also develop into a free marriage or customary marriage. The most frequent cause of publicity is an unwanted pregnancy.

The borderline between a lover relationship and prostitution is vague. Most so-called lover relationships have a 'commercial' component, and affection may characterise a relationship categorised as prostitution.[7] Temporary sexual relationships for reward seem to be quite common in Ayere, but in the urban centres with a high influx of unmarried men its occurrence is naturally more prominent and relationships tend to be more purely commercial. Out of a total of 27 adult women below the age of 40 years in the lineage studied, at least six were earning a living from sexual transactions in Accra. They often came back to Ayere and might then stay for several months. Most of them had children left in the care of relatives in Ayere. At home they were called 'the Accra girls', and although some people might look somewhat askance at them, they were not at all outcasts. On the contrary, most people regarded them as successful migrants, especially when they showed off in their best clothes.

One type of non-marital relationship should be mentioned here: the extra-marital relationship, by which I primarily mean a lover relationship between a married man and an unmarried woman. Extra-marital relationships involving married women are less common, though they certainly do occur. The secrecy around them is tighter, however, because 'public opinion' is much more lenient towards men's extra-marital relationships than those of women.

We can distinguish roughly two kinds of male extra-marital relationship. One takes place during the post-partum period, when spouses are supposed to abstain from sexual intercourse. This period lasts about six months in Kwahu (Bleek, 1976b, p. 227).[8] Male informants assured me that it was a normal practice for a man during that period to 'take a *mpena*' (lover) because, as one said, 'a man cannot live without a *mpena*'. This kind of short-lived relationship shades easily into prostitution. Polygynous husbands are of course in a different position.

The second kind is a lover relationship alongside the legal marital relationship. This too is quite normal. Many women suspect their husbands of having lovers. As long as a man can hide the affair, and particularly the identity of the lover, from his wife, no problems arise. When the affair is disclosed, however, the honour of the wife is at stake, and in most cases the man will either have to break off the relationship or marry the lover. So even though extra-marital relationships are quite common, there are strong reasons for keeping them secret.

The existence of non-marital unions is nothing new in Kwahu, but the reluctance of people (especially the young) to enter marriage is certainly a new development. This postponement of marriage appears to be connected with modern education. The completion of one's education is an essential step if one wants to make progress in life, whereas marriage offers few such prospects. Marriage often constitutes a threat to a girl's school career, because a pregnancy and subsequent marriage may well mean the end of education (see Chapter 10 of this volume). A connected factor is the increasing disenchantment with marriage. Two reasons for this are apparent. In the first place the relative economic contribution of men to their marriages has decreased over the last few decades with the worsening of the general economic situation. Women 'profit' less from their marriages than before, and men find it more difficult to satisfy the 'excessive' demands of women in marriage. Meanwhile expectations of marriage have risen. Young people in Kwahu thus have a somewhat paradoxical attitude to marriage: they hope for too much and expect but little.

Mothers, Sisters and Wives

As we have seen, a woman does not sever the bond with her lineage when she marries. The lineage's interest in its female member rather increases at the moment she marries because it is through the marriage that the lineage hopes to augment its number. We have seen that the lineage keeps a watchful eye on the marriage and promptly interferes when it thinks its interests are threatened. Examples of such threats are infertility or low fertility, and the giving of priority to conjugal rather than lineage affairs. The interference may ultimately lead to divorce.

The lasting association of women with their lineage provides them with a strong 'solidarity group' which cuts right through their conjugal bond. Kwahu women do not stand alone in confronting their husbands, but are supported by their lineage. The fact that the lineage is not a '*female* solidarity group' (Sanday, 1974) but a group which, particularly in the formal domain, is dominated by men certainly makes a difference—in that women may not always feel themselves supported in their activities but rather caught between two male dominated loyalty groups. On the other hand, the fact that the lineage's support often has an unconditional character should not be ignored. This primordial support greatly strengthens the woman's autonomy in marital affairs. An exception should be made for marriages in which the husband, because of his solid economic position, is able to wield considerably more power over his wife, whose material position is thus improved while her conjugal autonomy is reduced (e.g. Oppong (1982b).

Among Kwahu couples there is generally a strict sexual division of activities and responsibilities, but variations due to time, place, residence, economic status and probably other less well-defined factors must certainly be taken into account. The participation of fathers in activities regarding their conjugal families may have been more intensive in the past than it is now (Fortes, 1950, p. 268). Paying for children's schooling is still seen as the least equivocal duty of Kwahu fathers, but there is no information available as to how often it is in fact carried out. (A survey in middle and secondary schools and teacher training colleges over the whole country suggests that about 70 per cent of fathers pay school fees—Ghana Teaching Service, p. 15). Observation would indicate that other contributions by husbands to their conjugal family are less common.

The residence factor seems crucial. Where husband and wife do not live together the husband's contribution to running the house tends to decrease or disappear. Because marriage partners often remain near the woman's lineage home, and because divorce occurs frequently, marriages characterised by a lasting co-residence of parents and their children are exceptions. Household arrangements are fluid and flexible and the chances that fathers' participation in conjugal family affairs will diminish are large indeed (e.g. Woodford-Berger, 1981). Again, divorced women who remarry and co-reside with their second husband are usually solely responsible for the children of the first marriage.

Official norms prescribe that husbands should take substantial responsibility in the domestic sphere, but in reality husbands often fail to do so due to factors which alienate them from their conjugal families. At the same time, official norms prescribe considerable role segregation between husbands and wives. Even in the case of co-residence husbands are not supposed to assist their wives with houshold chores because these are regarded as women's and children's work. Men returning from farmwork usually let women carry the loads, and at meals they do not eat with their wives. In many other ways, men publicly show that the men's world differs from that of the women, and that the men's world is superior. Men rarely walk with their wives, and they are not supposed to show affection for them.

These are the rules for public behaviour. In private, things may differ considerably, but what is 'private'? In the rural home-towns, people live together in large living units and there is very little privacy. It rarely happens that a couple is not observed by others. Segregated conjugal roles therefore predominate. When a couple stays together in a farming settlement (*akuraa*), or migrates to an urban centre where no other relatives or co-villages are around, conjugal roles may be more joint.

The most incisive segregation, however, is brought about by, and reflected in, the financial independence of women. Couples hardly ever pool their resources. They may sometimes contribute to a common good, the upkeep of their children, or they may farm together, or the husband may give his wife a sum to start trading, but ultimately their income and property are kept apart carefully. Even in educated urban families, spouses prefer to keep their money separate in order to avoid conflicts (e.g. Oppong, 1982b). This financial arrangement reflects the dominant view of marriage, namely that a husband and wife are not one but two. Within marriage there is no lasting security because the interests of the two partners rarely coincide fully.

Children are deemed essential for a woman's happiness in Akan society. It is not only that children bring companionship and help. Children constitute the meaning of a woman's life. In the Akan view, a woman without children is incomplete, useless. She is, as one school pupil wrote, 'a pen without ink' (Bleek, 1976a, p. 172). A woman without, or with very few, children is even suspected of being a witch (*obayifo*) and killing the children, or of being a prostitute and having a venereal disease, and thus experiences extreme social pressure. It is therefore no surprise that infertility and other problems related to bearing children seem to be the most common reasons for visiting traditional shrines or healing prophets (Field, 1960, pp. 105–106; Bleek, 1976a, p. 180). To become a 'woman', a woman need not be married, but she must have children. Only a *mother* is a true woman. The pitiful plight of the childless woman is expressed in proverbs and songs (e.g. Asare Opoku, 1977, p. 108).

Matrifocal Tendencies

In Kwahu both tradition and recent socio-economic developments promote matrifocal tendencies and female-headed households are common. Tradition emphasises the father's importance and his responsibilities and yet at the same time undermines his position. There can be no doubt, however, that in spite of some paternal role rhetoric, the cultural tradition tends to marginalise fathers with respect to their conjugal families.

Marginalisation of the father/husband does not necessarily imply matrifocality, however, the focus in family affairs can also lie with men in their position as brother or uncle, as may happen in corporate lineage groups. Among the Kwahu, men in the lineage certainly take a dominant position with respect to female members, but this dominance is largely limited to formal and public affairs. In the more informal domestic domain, women run their own affairs. The lineage offers little help with concrete problems regarding bringing up children and daily subsistence. A woman who does not receive sufficient support from her husband has to bear the brunt of it herself, even if she stays with matrikin in the same house. Widowed and divorced women often get no help from their brothers in paying for their children's education or meeting daily expenses. Substantial assistance from the lineage in these matters is rare. This may seem to contradict previous statements stressing the importance of the lineage. The lineage derives its authority not so much from tangible economic services, however, as from its vigorous social sanctions and traditional sentiments of solidarity, which have strongly emotional overtones. Lineage members do, of course, offer each other services, but they are largely of a social character, much less often financial.

There is therefore justification for speaking of a tradition-based matrifocality. But we must at the same time emphasise that recent developments have greatly increased this matrifocal tendency. The three most important factors seem to be the worsening financial position of men due, among other things, to the overall crisis of the Ghanaian economy, the increased mobility of people, and the spread of education.

In the period of subsistence economic production, the contribution by husbands to their conjugal family was probably quite stable and regular. Rules about cooperation and task division in farming by husbands and wives guaranteed a relatively steady support by husbands for their children. The introduction of cocoa and other cash crops, coupled with the ethnocentric bias of the colonial authorities towards men as breadwinners, improved the position of husbands, who became the first to have access to cash money. Those men who profited by the cocoa industry enhanced their role as husbands and fathers. They were able to build houses for their wives and children, they sent their children to school, and they attempted—often successfully—to circumvent a number of matrilineal dictates regarding property and its disposal after death, and social loyalties.

This involvement in the international market had a profound impact on life, in the rural home-towns and villages too, but not everybody was able to profit from it. Socio-economic inequality thus increased, giving some men a position close to a *pater familias* and diminishing the ability of others to fulfil the demands of the conjugal role. When international and internal problems began to affect the cocoa industry and the entire Ghanaian economy, the latter category grew. The fact that more men than women are employed in the formal sector of the economy explains why men have lost the most. Women who, usually against their will, were forced to restrict their activities to subsistence food growing and small-scale informal trading were less affected, at least during the 1970s, by the economic crisis. It is exactly their position outside the formal economy which gives them greater resilience. The result is that many men have lost their superior position vis-à-vis women and are no longer able to support their children. Women increasingly run their families with little or no support from their husbands, and men have therefore become more and more marginal as husbands and fathers.

Increased mobility is another factor contributing to matrifocality. Formerly, spouses who divorced were more likely to remain in each other's vicinity, and as a consequence the observance of paternal obligations was more likely to continue than it is nowadays. At present, men often disappear completely after divorce, or the disappearance itself constitutes a *de facto* separation. In the lineage of Ayere studied, the reasons for 93 divorces were analysed. In nine of them it was simply said that 'the partner travelled and left me behind' (Bleek, 1975a, p. 212). Since in most cases children remain with the mother, women then tend to be burdened with the exclusive maintenance of the children. If a woman remarries, the new husband will most probably contribute nothing to the upkeep of the children who are not his.

Greater mobility does not always increase matrifocality, however; in some instances it may actually reduce it. This happens when mobility involves migration of both husband and wife. In that case, as we have seen before, common conjugal residence is likely, which encourages the participation of the husband in domestic affairs such as financial support and decision-making. But divorce, unemployment, or other economic problems are likely to present themselves one day, and this will then curtail the husband's contribution.

The third factor leading to matrifocality is the importance attached to school education. A school diploma is a *sine qua non* for making 'progress' in life. The higher the diploma, the more one may potentially gain from it. Young people therefore attempt to get as much education as possible and to prevent any premature interruption of their education. A frequent reason for interruption is pregnancy, as Akuffo describes in Chapter 10. The school, however, which makes postponement of child-bearing desirable, at the same time stimulates early sexual contacts. It brings youngsters of both sexes together outside the social control of the lineage and organises activities which seem particularly conducive to love affairs, such as sporting events and 'evening studies'. The school building is itself an important place for rendezvous between youngsters, as sexual activity in the farms or the forest is taboo.

In Kwahu, pregnancy proves to be a common reason for girls leaving school. Male pupils rarely have to interrupt school when they have made a female pupil pregnant. This inequality seems roughly in accordance with the ideas of the pupils themselves, boys in particular, but to a lesser extent, the girls too. Table 8.1

Table 8.1   Opinions about pregnancy and dismissal from school, by school pupils from the whole of Ghana (percentages)

School level		Girls who become pregnant should be removed from school		Boys who cause pregnancy should be removed from school		
		Agree	Disagree	Agree	Disagree	N
Elementary school	M	80.8	19.1	61.4	38.5	291
middle form 3	F	81.3	18.7	75.0	25.0	191
Secondary school	M	74.2	25.8	44.1	55.9	367
form 3	F	79.0	21.0	68.0	32.0	317
Secondary school	M	69.6	30.4	30.2	69.8	172
form 5	F	70.1	29.9	62.7	37.3	167
Teacher training	M	69.6	30.4	20.7	79.3	228
college	F	46.0	54.0	40.8	59.2	98

Source Ghana Teaching Service, 1975, p. 52.

presents the responses of school pupils from the whole of Ghana in a survey organised by the Ministry of Education.

This situation puts many young women in a position where they have to bear the responsibility for a child without the support of a husband.[9] Personal histories collected at the Kwahu town of Ayere show that a woman's first pregnancy tends to be the least desired, and that very often the father of the first child is not the same person as the father of the subsequent children. Frequently, too, the father of the first child disappears. Bartle (1978, p. 527) observed the same in another Kwahu town. Matrifocality, therefore, is particularly common after the birth of a woman's first child.

Matrifocality occurs then in two different situations: it may entail marginality of a husband/father, who is still legally married to the mother of his children, or it may imply complete absence of the father, who has no legal bond with the mother, either because they are divorced or because they never married. Both types of matrifocal families exist in Kwahu.

A last factor leading to matrifocality is the virtual disappearance of widow inheritance. Formerly a man's heir inherited his widow with his property. It meant that he took over the deceased's responsibility and care for his wife and children. It seems that Christian objections to polygyny and, more importantly, financial considerations account for the fact that this old institution of 'widow and orphan security' has largely died out. Widows with children to care for are much more likely to be left on their own now than 50 years ago.

The Consequences for Family Planning

Modern family planning in Ghana began in the early 1960s when the Christian Council set up centres in Accra, Kumasi and Ho to advise married couples on how they could regulate their fertility. In 1967, Ghana became the first black African country to sign the United Nations declaration on population. Family planning became the country's official policy. The content of the declaration had a neo-

Malthusian tenor: the population problem was seen as a significant barrier to development. In the 1969 document (Goverment of Ghana, 1969c, p. 19) it was thus stated:

> A population policy and programme are viewed as integral parts of efforts toward social and economic development, improvement of health and nutrition, elevation of quality and extension of the scope of education, wider employment opportunities, and better development and use of human resources in the interests of a more abundant life.

In 1971 Ghana played host to the first African Population Conference and then Prime Minister Busia said plainly in his opening address:

> The Malthusian theory . . . is now being treated with more respect than was accorded to it some years back. In certain parts of the world the squalor and poverty predicted by Malthus is already in evidence (quoted by Bondestam, 1980, p. 1).

In 1970 the government approved the Ghana National Family Planning Programme, which had as its target the recruitment of about 200,000 contraceptive users within five years, but by 1975 the total number of new acceptors was only 142,000. It was not always clear, however, whether or not so-called 'new acceptors' meant users who continued for some time. In an evaluation of the Family Planning Programme, for example, it is reported that by 1975–76 there were about 53,000 current users and 192 family planning clinics (Armar and David, 1977). Family planning services were more readily available to urban women than to rural women and considerably more used by the former. Two non-governmental organisations, the Christian Council of Ghana and the Planned Parenthood Association also promoted family planning.[10]

In the early seventies the various family planning programmes in Ghana showed little awareness of the complex nature of family organisation and the matrifocal tendency in the rearing of children, in both the economic and the emotional spheres. The approach was almost exclusively oriented to conjugal families as they were believed to exist in Europe or in the ideals of Christian teaching on marriage. The Ghanaian Family Planning Programme thus assumed the marital union to be stable and the only context of reproduction. The widely known incidence of pre-marital and extra-marital sex and pregnancies was ignored. It further neglected certain cultural features of family organisation which are not familiar in the European countries from which it had borrowed its model, but which are quite common in Akan society. The most important of these features are the custom of fostering and the influence of the matrilineage on marriage affairs.

The approach was male-centred in that it was assumed that fathers are heads of their families, breadwinners who take full responsibility for their children. The fact that women often have to support their families alone and under difficult conditions was largely ignored. In an official document stating the government's policy, the impression is given that women in Ghana are housewives who should be encouraged to participate in 'gainful employment' with the help of family planning facilities (Government of Ghana, 1969c, p. 21). This picture clearly applies to many West European countries where extra-domestic work is mainly a man's affair, but certainly not to Ghana where practically all women engage in some kind of work to earn—or to share in earning—a living for their children. In the 1970 population census only 11 per cent of rural women called themselves 'housewives', and the real percentage would probably be still lower if we took 'housewife' to mean only working in the house (Addo and Goody, n.d., p. 20).

What are the consequences of such a Eurocentric and male-centred view of the family? They can be summarised in two points: the most important target population, rural married women, is hardly affected by the family planning programme, while those who need birth control most, the young unmarried women, have very difficult access to it.

Married Women and Family Planning

A pamphlet distributed by the Ghana National Family Planning Programme reads: 'The National Family Planning Programme makes it easier for couples to get the information and services they need to space the frequency of births and/or limit the size of their families when necessary.' On the same page it says: 'Family Planning can help you and your family to a better life.' The pictures show an extremely well dressed couple with three children: they look happy, and one picture allows us a look into their well furnished home, flowers on the table and a television in the centre. The designers of the pamphlet seem to suggest that such prosperity will come to people if they adopt family planning—but more probably people will take it that family planning is for the élite and none of their business. One impression is, however, unequivocal: family planning is for married couples.

In the light of the ambiguous position of marriage and the matrifocal tendency of domestic groups, it will surprise no one that such 'family planning' appeals little to ordinary married women living in rural areas. It will appeal even less to their husbands or sexual partners. A large proportion of women do not find themselves in a marital union which has any similarity with the picture drawn by the family planning organisations. And the remaining women who do have a more or less stable conjugal relationship are well aware of the vicissitudes of married life and the possibility that their marriage may break down in the future. 'Having children', both in the sense of bearing them and in the plain sense of supporting them, is mainly a woman's affair. As we have seen, Akan men often do not really support their children. For them, planning their families is not relevant if they have little to do with the result of the planning (Oppong and Bleek, 1982).

Why do rural Akan women rarely plan the number of their children? The answer is twofold—first because the uncertainty of their situation allows for little planning. The context in which women give birth to children and bring them up is subject to so many vicissitudes and their conjugal situation is so uncertain that their ability to foresee their future is extremely limited. For a woman, it is extremely hard to estimate the pros and cons of having a few or many children. It depends on how long her marriage will last; how many times she will marry; the financial position of her husband(s); what conjugal responsibilities her husband(s) or lover(s) will accept; how many of her children will be staying with her; how many children of others will be put in her care; how much help her lineage will give; how successful she will be in earning her own income; how much help her children will offer; how successful her children will be at school and in achieving a good economic position; how healthy her children will be, and how many of them will survive to adulthood. Of course, some of these uncertainties are universal, but it should be taken into account that in the relatively rich industrialised societies at least the worst of the economic pressures resulting from misfortune have been greatly reduced by social security and insurance measures. In Akan society such measures hardly exist. The greatest unknown there, as in many other Third World societies, is that children can become factors of social insurance as well as factors of social risk. The aggregate 'decision' in such a complex and contradictory situation is most likely inertia. Inertia is also brought about by the strong traditional norm of high fertility. Children are the raison d'être of marriage. Kwahu people engage on the uncertain course of marriage because they want children. So to stop or to limit fertility while married seems contradictory and has a tinge of absurdity.

This leads to the second reason why many married women do not actively plan the number of children they have. Family planning programmes fail to convey a meaningful message to most married women simply because their message does not apply to them. The domestic level reasons for family planning suggested by these organisations refer to a type of family and family life which is often not part of the women's experience. As we have seen, their propaganda makes many incorrect assumptions about family organisation. This inevitably alienates rural women from the purposes and means of family planning and makes them think that family planning is an affair for the urban educated élite but not for them. Their everyday problems hardly appear in family planning propaganda.

Unmarried Women and Family Planning

There is another criticism that is sometimes made of family planning, though it is seldom discussed and appears improbable: that family planning, in the way it is often promoted, actually helps to curtail the freedom and socio-economic perspectives of women. This may sound provocative, because in spite of all criticism it is widely acknowledged that family planning does enhance the control of women over their own lives. How, then, may such a contention be understood in the case of Ghana?

Women in Ghana, particularly rural Akan women, have a great degree of independence. This independence, as we have seen, derives among other things from their involvement in extra-domestic economic activities. It is also true, however, that the economic opportunities of women have been systematically reduced by the fact that they have less access to education, professional training, and formal employment than men (Oppong et al., 1975). Apart from a few famous examples, most women carry out their activities on the margins of economy, in the informal sector. The unequal chances of women in the economy are related to their unequal chances in education. But why do women not have the same opportunities as men to receive education? No doubt this is partly explained by the existence of cultural beliefs in the superiority of men. There is also a more concrete reason, however, which contributes to the imbalance in education between the sexes: women drop out of school because they become pregnant and, more importantly, parents discourage the education of their daughters in anticipation of their dropping out (cf. Bukh, 1979, p. 66; Bleek, 1981; and Chapter 9 below). Education is seen as an investment; if the investment looks too risky, it is left.

It is not only lack of formal education which curtails the career prospects of women. An early pregnancy in itself tends to have unfavourable consequences for a young woman. The fact that she is burdened with a baby at a young age but does not yet have a stable partner—which is the usual pattern—diminishes her chances of finding an attractive marriage partner who will be likely to contribute to the upkeep of her children.

From observations in Ayere it would appear that most first pregnancies are undesired. This admittedly impressionistic statement is supported by the high frequency of induced abortions and still higher frequency of attempted induced

Table 8.2   Marital status and age of lineage members involved in induced abortions (percentages in brackets) (N = 26)

Marital status	Under 25	25–39	Total
Legal marriage	—	3 (27)	3 (12)
Free marriage*	1(7)	3 (27)	4 (15)
Lover relationship*	14 (93)	5 (45)	19 (73)**
Total	15 (100)	11 (99)	26 (100)

*   For definitions see p. 234–235.
** Three unclear cases are excluded.
Source Bleek, 1978b, p. 113.

abortions in the lineage studied (Bleek, 1976a, pp. 210–219). Abortion is induced using dangerous means, and it is generally known that young women frequently die or become sterile as a result of such abortions. Moreover, abortion is against the law and one risks prosecution when performing it, while public opinion strongly disapproves of abortion. The fact that it is practised nonetheless underlines the extremely strong motivation to get rid of an untimely pregnancy. About half of the 19 adult women in the lineage in our study had experienced an induced abortion, and out of the 91 pregnancies of these women, 16 had been terminated by abortion. The most common reason given for abortion was the woman wanting to complete education.

Table 8.2, covering all abortion cases in which male and female members of the lineage were involved, clearly shows that most abortions involve young people in a pre-marital sexual relationship.

The high incidence of abortion outside marriage indicates the need for family planning advice and services for unmarried women. In fact, unmarried youngsters showed a keen interest in contraceptive devices and did use them. In the lineage of Ayere, birth control was practised about five times more frequently outside marriage than in it.[11] The problem, however, was that the family planning organisations did not seem to offer their services to these young people. The effective and safe contraceptives distributed through such organisations hardly reached the unmarried generation. In the lineage we studied, no young people ever visited a family planning representative, although a family planning clinic existed in the nearby town of Nkawkaw and there was a family planning fieldworker in Ayere itself. The only contraceptives which reached the young were condoms and pressurised foams (spermicides), which the government distributes through commercial outlets. The most common methods of birth control used in Ayere were, however, various kinds of obscure pills (e.g. Alophen and Apiol and Steel[12]), which were often wrongly believed to be contraceptives, and to induce abortion.

It is not the birth of many children which deprives an Akan woman of the possibility of finding gainful employment outside her home. A large number of children is in many ways self-supporting. Older children help take care of younger ones and may also assist the mother in external economic activities such as farming and trading, although school attendance has of course diminished this considerably. It is, however, still true that a mother with eight children does not experience significantly greater obstacles to working outside the home than a mother of two.

This applies even to women in salaried state employment who are granted maternity leave, for example, teachers and nurses.

What does, however, diminish a woman's economic prospects is the birth of her *first child*. A family planning programme which is intended to enhance the position of women but delays its action till women are married thereby misses the opportunity to achieve such enhancement. In present day Ghana family planning programmes need to concentrate on the young. The fact that organisations fail to do so contributes to the continuation of sexual inequality in training and employment prospects in Ghanaian society. Ability to control the timing of births, and in particular to postpone the first birth, is a prerequisite if women are to complete their education, contract attractive marriages and engage in profitable economic activities outside the home, and is thus essential for the improvement of the position of women in Akan society.

A final point to be taken into account is that the absence of effective family planning for young women leads both to the use of dubious contraceptives and to undesired pregnancies. Consequently, young women often resort to ineffective and/or highly dangerous abortion techniques, which may result in serious medical complications such as sterility and even death.

Family planning does not seem to have contributed sufficiently to women's emancipation, individual freedom, family well being and health. It therefore seems warranted to call for a more realistic assessment by Ghanaian family planning organisations of the socio-economic contexts of reproduction.[13] If they want to respond to the needs of rural women, they should make their messages more relevant to those women and should make their services much more readily available to young women.

Notes

1   The research for this chapter was made possible by a grant from the Institute of African Studies of the University of Ghana. The first writing up period of the data was sponsored by the Netherlands Foundation for the Advancement of Tropical Research. I am grateful to Dr. C. Oppong, Mrs. M. Dijkema and Mrs. J.J. Kossen, who contributed to the final draft of this article. People and places in the text have been given pseudonyms.

2   The concept of 'household' which fitted the 'familial individualism' (Laslett, 1972, p. 49) of European observers proved problematic in the more fluid and communal Akan society. See, for example, the problems encountered by P. Hill (1963, p. 24) among Akan cocoa farmers; Vercruijsse et al. (1974) among the Fanti; Bartle (1977) among the Kwahu; and Woodford-Berger (1981, p. 32) who worked in Ahafo. For a general discussion of the concept in the Ghanaian literature see Oppong (1976). Meanwhile some researchers have simply ignored the problem, e.g. Dutta-Roy (1969), whose Household Budget Survey does not define this key concept. Others have used varied definitions: Caldwell (1967a, p. 63) remarks that in the 1960 population census, 'the concept of what constitute a house or compound varied sometimes from enumerator to enumerator'.

3   See, for example, Bartle (1977) regarding migration and child dispersal in Obo, and Esther Goody (1978, p. 227; 1982) who, in writing about West Africa in general, notes a striking contradiction in the concept of parenthood. On the one hand, a tremendous emphasis is placed on parent–child relations, which is reflected in the strong desire for

children. On the other hand there is a wide variety of practices delegating parental roles to others. She points out (1978, p. 229) that the explanation must not be sought in the cultural definition of parenthood but in the specific conditions which lead to the delegation of parental roles. Brydon (1979), in her study of a non-Akan community in Ghana, remarks that fostering has increased as a result of the community's incorporation into a wider economy which has led to migration, both of men and women, and a drift away from the stable conjugal family pattern.

4   The situation is beautifully illustrated by the following observation by Bartle (1977, p. 239): 'In the Obo compound where I lived, and many others I visited, the girls would say, lets play *Mame ne mame* (mother and mother) or *Mame ne nana* (mother and grandmother). The adults these children emulated were their mothers and their mothers' sisters (same word in Twi for Mo or Mo-Si: *eno* or *mame*), the most important people to them in their hometown residence unit. Their socialization took place in a matrilineal rather than bilateral kinship system'.

5   During the one and a half years I spent at Ayere I never succeeded in attending such a ceremony. Although I blame myself for the omission, I cannot help blaming also the insignificance and subsequent invisibility of the custom. The ceremony, which mainly consists of the payment of a modest sum of money, the giving of gifts, and a libation, need not be described here. Elaborate descriptions can be found elsewhere (Rattray, 1923, 1927, 1929, pp. 24–27; Fortes, 1950, pp. 278–281).

6   It is therefore somewhat misleading that Sarpong (1977) refers to this ceremony by the English term 'nubility rites', as if the rites were concerned with *nuptiae*, which means both marriage and wedding ceremony. Sarpong's own description strongly suggests that the rites should be seen as 'maturity or maternity rites', allowing a girl to bring forth, to become a mother. It is significant, for example, that after the rites the girl is dressed as a mother (*eno*) (Sarpong, 1977, p. 75).

7   Pellow (1977, p. 208) in her study of women in the capital of Accra, noted: 'no self-respecting woman would remain in a "friendship" without material recompense.'

8   Fortes (1954, p. 265) recorded the same duration in Asante in 1945, but a slightly longer period (eight months) has recently been mentioned by Gaisie (1981, p. 246). Warren (1974, p. 42) reports that among the Bono of Techiman, another Akan group, the abstinence period after a first child lasts at least six months but that 'after succeeding births a 40 day period is deemed sufficient'.

9   It should be noted, though, that making a schoolgirl pregnant may involve another heavy sanction for the man in question. As the pregnancy is believed to have spoiled the girl's education, some parents claim indemnification for the loss suffered. In Kwahu I came across amounts from 50 cedis (£20) to 260 cedis (£104) but much higher sums have been demanded elsewhere. It is rumoured that some parents encourage their school-going daughters to engage in sex in order to secure an attractive sum of money.

10   All these activities were supported with foreign funds, mostly from the United States (David and Armar, 1978). At the same time grants were given to the University of Ghana to establish a teaching department for demography and population research programmes (Bingen, 1972, p. 81). The most ambitious and most expensive programme was without doubt the Danfa Project (1979).

11   In the Final Report of the Danfa Project (1979, pp. 8–37) it says: 'around 66 per cent of married male acceptors reported that they used the contraceptive method only with their wife, 20 per cent said they used it exclusively with another partner, and 12 per cent used it with both their wife and other partners.' I do not think this contradicts my findings at Ayere, for three reasons. In the first place, a survey such as was carried out in the Danfa Project is not suitable for questions about extra-marital relationships. The report makes no mention of unmarried youngsters. I suspect that they have been excluded from the experiment. It is highly unlikely that church authorities, education officers and other defenders of public morality would have permitted school girls to take part in this family planning pilot project. The third reason is that the community

involved in the Danfa Project, by its very status as a *project* constituted an exceptional community. The presence of so many doctors, students, nurses and other personnel and the delivery of so many services made the community sample totally unrepresentative of the Ghanaian population as a whole. The conclusion of the Report (pp. 8–34) that the typical female acceptor of family planning is married, 28 years old, has three to four children, farms, and accepts the pill, is a research artefact and probably, point by point, the reverse of the typical female 'acceptor of birth control' in Ghana as a whole.

12   Alophen, containing phenolphthalein, is a purgative, but is commonly used both as a contraceptive and to induce abortion. It is sold in drugstores. In 1973 it was used as a contraceptive everywhere from rural villages to university campuses. Apiol and Steel is a dubious drug freely obtainable in drugstores. Again, it is used both as a contraceptive and to induce abortion but exactly how it works is unclear. Martindale's Extra Pharmacopoeia reports on Apiol that it is used as an emmenagogue but that its therapeutic value is doubtful. Severe toxic effects, including nephrosis, have resulted from its use.

13   It must be emphasised that the research on which this article is based dates from 1973. Cursory information (e.g. De Nie, 1977, p. 35) suggests that the availability of effective contraceptives among secondary school students subsequently improved somewhat and that dismissal of pregnant pupils from school decreased. Representatives of the National Family Planning Programme further claimed in the late seventies that their organisation was becoming directed towards the unmarried. The only published statement I know is a short letter by the Director of Information and Education of the National Family Planning Programme in *The Mirror*, a Ghanaian weekly, of 30 July 1976. The letter was a reaction to a series of articles by me in which I criticised the Programme for barring unmarried youngsters from their services. The writer, Mr. Henry Ofori, stated, 'It is only the Christian Council of Ghana which limits its family planning services to married couples.' It seems we have to distinguish between a formal and informal policy of the Programme. It may be true that family planning agents seldom or never actively refuse unmarried people, but it is clear that they do not formally conduct a policy directed towards the unmarried. The reluctance of official institutions to take pre-marital pregnancy and contraception seriously is also demonstrated by a report of the Ghana Teaching Service (1975, pp. 51–52). Although pre-marital pregnancy during school training is recognised as a problem, and although around 50 per cent of students think that contraceptives should be made freely available in schools, the curriculum makers have in the past usually tended to avoid this topic altogether.

9   *Felix Odei Akuffo*

Teenage Pregnancies and School Drop-outs

The Relevance of Family Life Education and Vocational Training to Girls' Employment Opportunities

Much attention has been focused on the effects of relatively low levels of education on the status of women in West Africa and elsewhere, and it has been suggested that the incidence of early school leaving affects the full participation of women in social, economic and political development as well as fertility levels. In the case of Ghana, despite the significant traditional economic and political participation of women, there is today a substantial gap between the occupational position and status of women and men in the formal sector of the economy. The high drop-out rates of girls in elementary schools, the disparity in girls' and boys' opportunities in higher education, and the increasing competition for scarce jobs, have restricted women's access to employment, especially in those areas demanding high academic qualifications. A large proportion of women remain economically active, but the sectors in which women participate the most heavily —trading, farming, domestic services, dressmaking and hairdressing—are those which do not require much education, although they may not in fact be particularly poorly paid. In 1970, 61.1 per cent of all Ghanaian women were engaged in some economic activity. Between 1960 and 1970 female employment increased while male employment dropped, though the latter was largely due to the fact that more males over 15 years old remained in school (Government of Ghana, 1972, XXIV).

In this chapter the focus is upon Ghanaian elementary school girls, the reasons why some leave school before completing the course, and the economic and demographic implications in terms of training, employment needs and opportunities, and early child-bearing.

Providing financial support for girls while they attend school and undergo training is an accepted part of familial obligations in Ghana. But girls persistently fail to move on to the same levels of educational and vocational achievement as boys, and a relatively high percentage of girls drop out of the educational system before reaching levels of certification equivalent to those of their male age mates. Both analysis of country-wide statistics and studies of individual schools demonstrate these trends.[1] This situation is leading to a growing sense of concern among educationalists and others, and it is frequently pointed out in discussions of women's roles in Ghana that relatively lower educational qualifications are one of the major causes of the increasing inequality of women vis-à vis men. A number of reasons have been put forward to explain why this should be so, including teenage pregnancies, financial constraints, and relative lack of achievement orientation. In a survey carried out in Asamankese of 125 girls who had dropped out of school, it was found that pregnancy was the major cause of their leaving school prematurely: 45 girls had dropped out because they were pregnant; 25 were force to drop out as a result of financial constraints and another 20 were asked to withdraw by their parents (Akuffo, 1978). Interrelated with these factors are poor academic work, lack of interest in schooling, and the traditional norms concerning sexuality and reproduction which underlie the different attitudes towards the training of girls and boys, and have considerable impact on the social and economic organisation in rural areas.

In both rural and urban areas parents place a lower value on the education of their daughters than on that of their sons. Their negative attitudes are partly attributed to fears that their daughters will become pregnant before completion of school and certification. They may also be explained by the traditional view that a girl's place is in the kitchen and that, whatever the level of her education, she will one day be married and cared for by a man. Parental attitudes are also influenced by lack of financial resources, which often thwarts the efforts of schoolgirls and apparently encourages some girls to seek material support through promiscuity.

In this chapter we shall look in particular at the incidence of teenage pregnancies resulting in girls dropping out of elementary school in a rural community in southern Ghana, examining the various precipitating factors. We shall examine the kind of domestic training schoolgirls receive at home, and their economic and sexual activities, keeping in mind the economic aspects of the latter and the traditional ideals, norms and behaviour patterns, if any, associated with them. We shall also look at the ways in which the individual, the family, and the community react to the social problems caused by the incidence of teenage pregnancies and the attendant premature withdrawal of girls from school, along with the obvious need for more appropriate training of girls to fit them to assume both their occupational and their maternal responsibilities. The discussion is based on data collected in farming villages in the Asamankese district in the eastern region of Ghana, a mainly Akan-speaking area, concerning school children and drop-outs between 6 and 19 years of age. Girls in Asamankese itself, the district headquarters, were also included in the survey: apprentice dressmakers and hairdressers, many of whom were drop-outs from elementary school; girls trading in the large and busy market, and girls living with people other than their parents or living alone in the town without guardians.

The sample of 250 girls studied was carefully selected according to age group and schooling: 125 were in school, and 125 had dropped out. Information was sought through surveys of children and teachers, collection of individual case histories, essays, interviews with knowledgeable informants, observation, and written records.

Home Backgrounds

Rural family life and the system of kinship and marriage in the Akan area show little sign of change from the traditional features of the matrilineal system described above. The husband does not usually stay with his wife or his younger children. The girls and younger boys stay with their mother, who cooks and sends food to the husband each day. When the boys grow older, they often stay with their father or their mother's brother, who then assumes full jural control over them. There is little evidence to suggest that the co-residential conjugal family is very common in the rural setting, or that paternal authority and responsibility have completely eliminated the traditional complementary functions and powers of the mother's brother and other kin.

In all households the routine daily tasks of cooking, washing clothes and household utensils, fetching water and firewood, and caring for children fall mainly on the women, who are helped by the children, especially the girls. These chores are time-consuming, and occupy the women and girls for considerable periods of the day. The performance of these tasks is considered a necessary training for adult life, and they begin as early as the girl is able to speak and obey simple instructions. As she matures and develops to take on and share some of the mother's domestic and economic tasks, the mother gains greater freedom to assume other responsibilities, which may include having more children. Thus, it has always been considered advantageous to have a girl as a first child, and in times past such girls were not sent to school. These household tasks are performed by non-school goers and school-going girls alike. The sharing of tasks between them lies with the mother. Few mothers can afford to spare the services of their school-going daughters, who have therefore to perform domestic tasks as well as meeting the demands of school. From the age of seven or eight, moreover, girls typically begin to help their mothers economically, especially in trading. The economic pursuits of a schoolgirl are seen almost as a duty. Since her financial needs are greater than those of her stay-at-home sisters, she is required to contribute more—even though her time is taken up with schooling.

Mothers who are traders (a typical occupation among Akan women) expect their daughters to accompany them to the market. Girls may also be asked to take goods somewhere to sell, and it is common to see schoolgirls selling on market days when school is in session. Often the aim is to earn money to purchase the things required for school, thus relieving their mothers of some of the financial burden. Other girls are asked to stay at home to care for the baby or prepare meals for the father and brothers and sisters while the mother is at the farm or the market. The task of marketing for the household is also entrusted to the older girl. In the early stages, she often accompanies her mother to the market, learning the art of selection, bargaining, making purchases, and budgeting for a household. In seeing that she performs these task, the mother is preparing her daughter for her adult roles. At the age of 15 or 16, a girl is considered enought to perform a large number of household chores without the close guidance and control of her parents. She is the one who looks after the family when the mother is away on the farm or at the market.

Most girls have their first menses between the ages of 13 and 15. Elaborate puberty rites used to be performed, which marked the sexual maturity of the girl and signalled her coming of age and readiness for marriage and child-bearing. Owing to the social respect which these rites gave girls, they usually became more obedient from about the age of 12 in the hope that their parents would sponsor them for the rites (this tended to restrain the sexual behaviour of pubescent girls). Such elaborate rites are no longer found in the area, but some simple rites are performed for the girl who is courageous enough to tell her mother about the event. These girls are given a ritual meal of mashed yam and eggs. Some parents may add a chicken or a gift of clothing. Advice on boy–girl relationships may be offered, and it is made clear to the girls that they are now mature and have to behave accordingly, especially where sexual behaviour is concerned.

The teenage years are the period when girls' material and financial demands on their parents and guardians increase. It is a time of preparation for adult occupational and familial roles and thus for learning new facts, acquiring new skills, expanding the range of social contacts and activities. Conflicts may arise between the demands of parents for assistance in domestic tasks and trading, the demands of teachers for homework assignments and errands, and the demands of friends for companionship. Parents often become anxious that their schoolgirl daughters may indulge in pre-marital sexual relationships and accordingly try to restrict their movements away from the home, which sometimes results in quarrels and strained relationships between them and their daughters. Some parents, unable to control their daughters' activities as they would wish, try to shift responsibility on to teachers. The inability of parents to control their daughters may be aggravated by the frequent separate residence of the mother and father caused by conjugal separation or divorce, or the parents' absence for farming or business purposes. Another contributory factor may be the parents' reliance on the school as the main agent for training girls, and their inability to fulfil their financial responsibilities towards their daughters. The generation gap may also cause a lack of knowledge and understanding. With regard to the residential patterns of the 125 girls in the survey who had dropped out of school, only 20 per cent were found to be living with both their parents, 32 per cent were with their mother, 8 per cent were with the father, 12 per cent were with relatives, and 24 per cent were with non-relatives. Four per cent were living alone in rented rooms.

School Attendance

The decision to send a girl to school is influenced by a number of social and economic factors, including her position in the family, the number of brothers and sisters she has, and the financial and other resources of mother, father and kin. Given that the traditional expectations of matrikin prevail, there is a continuing stress upon the girl's reproductive role. To ensure that she is prolific, and bears several children for her matrilineage, she must marry at least once and must therefore learn the skills associated with motherhood and marriage, including informal methods of earning money such as farming and trade. Above all she should not be barren—a disaster believed to afflict promiscuous women or those who delay birth too long to accommodate a protracted educational career. Since childbirth is a girl's major goal in life, school is of secondary importance and only accommodated if circumstances permit and resources in terms of money and time are considered adequate. School is considered more important for boys. In large families the tendency is therefore for the girls' education to be sacrificed. The decision may rest largely with the mother, depending on whether she needs her daughter to help in the house and on the farm, and whether she is ready to bear the extra financial and domestic burden.

The decision to send a boy to school does not present so much difficulty to the parents. He has very few domestic responsibilities and the father may even forbid him to engage in what is considered to be women's work. Except when it is absolutely necessary, the boy does not cook, sweep the house, wash cooking utensils or perform other domestic chores. A son's absence from the house is therefore rarely felt.

Financial constraints and school attendance

Participation in the school's academic programmes, and extra-curricular and social activities at home and school, involve what are perceived as great expenses to poor rural parents. School-related expenses include uniforms, footwear, underwear and handkerchiefs; fees for books, desks, school buildings, special lessons such as science, agriculture, and art and crafts, examinations, etc.; and pens, pencils, and equipment for practical lessons. Daily pocket money may also be needed for food, and transport costs if the school is far away.

If the parents' financial resources are limited and they cannot adequately meet these needs, the child's efforts at school may be thwarted. Our survey data show that schoolgirls do indeed have many problems associated with a lack of financial support from their parents. Half encountered some difficulty in getting their school fees paid. Thirty-five per cent had difficulties in paying the government-stipulated book fees, while 60 per cent had problems paying other additional fees and were often sent home to collect them. The majority had inadequate school uniforms and other clothing.

The inability of parents to provide adequate dresses for their daughters for school, for evenings, and for Sunday church services, especially the adolescents, is a major factor encouraging girls to seek other means of obtaining money. Eighty-three per cent of the sample schoolgirls said that at one time or another they had had to buy dresses for themselves. In fact, for the girls in the 16 years and above age group, it is becoming a permanent feature of life. Eleven per cent of the girls in the sample quite often got dresses from their boyfriends, 42 per cent from their mothers, and 22 per cent from their fathers.

Many of the parents bought dresses for their children only at Christmas and when they were confirmed as members of the church. The Muslims gave their children new dresses during religious festivals. Many children were not then provided with dresses until next Christmas or the next festival. The majority of parents were cocoa farmers, and it seems that they depended largely on the proceeds from the sale of cocoa to buy new dresses for their children. This was usually done in the November–December period. While 80 per cent of the parents agreed that a parent should provide school kits, fees and food for a child, 75 per cent of them gave vague answers to the question about who should provide pocket money, underwear and other clothing. The men contend that the women should provide them, the women feel that it is the duty of the men, and in the end the girl is left with nothing. About 70 per cent of mothers claimed that girls between 15 and 19 years were old enough to provide their own clothes and pocket money. Asked about the sources of income for girls of this age, they said, 'but other girls of their age are doing it'.

Case studies collected on these issues indicate that problems with clothing often result in girls withdrawing from school. When parents are unable to meet all the financial and material demands of their daughters, they often use the smallest excuse to ask the girl to drop out of school, especially where there are boys attending school as well. This enables them to concentrate their limited financial resources on the boys. In some cases, too, because the requirements of the girl are overlooked and denied, out of frustration she involves herself in activities that eventually lead to the termination of her schooling.

Another important school expense is pocket money. The need for pocket money arises from a number of factors. Many pupils walk a long way to school, and as they are not home for some of their meals, they need money to buy food. Some pupils leave their homes very early in the morning and need money for breakfast and a snack as well as lunch. Money is also needed for lorry fares and some to meet other expenses.

Pocket money for pupils in elementary schools in the rural areas appears to be extremely inadequate. Over 95 per cent of the respondents—both boys and girls—claimed that the pocket money given them by their parents was always inadequate. Most of the girls received between 1 and 2 cedis for breakfast and lunch which is not enough. This means that many of the girls went to school without food or with insufficient food. This had adverse effects on their work: they were unable to take full part in school activities; their response to lessons became poor; they were liable to become angry and quarrelsome at the least provocation.

As a supplement to what was provided by their parents or guardians, some girls got pocket money from their boyfriends and others augmented it with their own earnings. Twenty-four per cent of the girls (30 out of 125) claimed they got pocket money from their boyfriends or through their own efforts—in ways they did not specify, but which would not exclude getting it from boyfriends. As far as fees are concerned, 40 per cent of the girls had their fees paid by their fathers, and 24 per cent by their mothers while 10 per cent claimed that they were paid by their boyfriends and six (4.8 per cent) provided the money themselves.

Inadequate material support from parents and kin compels girls to seek other sources of income to satisfy their needs. Such attempts to earn extra money may frustrate a girl's educational aspirations through loss of study hours, fatigue, inadequate attention in class and pregnancy. Of particular importance in this regard are trading and sexual activities. Out of the 125 schoolgirls, 80 per cent sold bread, oranges, vegetables, eggs, kerosene, soap, iced water, groundnuts, foodstuffs and other items. Much of their time was taken up by these trading activities. Out of 100 schoolgirl traders, 15 per cent sold in the morning before classes, and 88 per cent sold actively during the weekends; 91 per cent sold at some time almost every day of the week. Half occasionally sold during school hours, especially on market days. The effects on school work are obvious. They had little time for studying and too little sleep, and often went to school late and tired, unable to participate fully in the school programmes. Of the 100 schoolgirl traders 60 per cent agreed that these economic activities interfered with their schooling, and many teachers complained of large numbers of absentees on market days. The earnings from these trading activities are quite substantial, and may offer the girls a solution to their financial problems. They may therefore influence the decision to drop out of school in order to undertake trading as a full-time job.

Earnings from petty trading are not usually used for educational needs such as books, fees and uniforms, but rather for pocket money and clothing. Table 9.1 gives details of the ways in which the girls spent the money they earned.

About 85 per cent of the girls engaging in trade said that their financial and material needs were not completely satisfied through petty trading. In order to meet their needs fully, some girls sought other sources to supplement their earnings,

Table 9.1   Use of earnings from the trading activities of schoolgirls

Use of income	Frequency				
	Never	Occasionally	More than half the time	Always	Previously but not now
Pay fees	81	7	6	5	1
Buy uniform	59	22	11	8	—
Buy clothes	1	11	10	78	—
Pocket money		6	10	84	—
Breakfast	30	38	5	27	—
Lunch	70	10	15	5	—
Supper	90	2	—	8	—
Give it to mother	20	30	14	20	16
Save at the bank	58	23	5	14	—

[N = 100 schoolgirls who trade]

including boyfriends. The majority of these relationships involved covert sexual relationships. Some girls, however, considered the affairs as non-sexual, meant only to broaden their social outlook and improve their academic work. Many of the sexual relationships did not involve deep emotional attachment as some of the boyfriends were older married men (popularly termed 'sugar daddies') (cf. Dinan, 1983).

In such affairs, no marriage is intended. When pregnancy occurs, most of the girls hide it from their parents, and some may be persuaded to terminate it by their boyfriends. Assorted medications and concoctions of herbs and roots, which may prove fatal, are sometimes used. Not all boyfriends are ready and willing to accept responsibility for pregnancies, and there are instances where more than one person is mentioned by the pregnant girl. This also testifies to the girls' ignorance. In other cases the parents may refuse to recognise a man's claim to paternity, regarding him as unfit to father the child because of questionable character or obvious absence of means of caring for the baby and mother.

Seventy of the schoolgirls had boyfriends. Of the remaining 55, 50 were aged between 6 and 15 years. Only five out of the 75 girls above the age of 15 did not have boyfriends. The girls apparently begin to engage in sexual relationships at a very young age. Teenage pregnancy is a predictable outcome of this early sexual experimentation, coupled with little knowledge or total ignorance of contraception. Of the 70 girls with boyfriends, the majority admitted that the most important reason for having boyfriends was financial. A further 36 per cent mentioned the purchase of clothing and other goods. Thirty per cent claimed that their mothers had encouraged them to get a boyfriend, and more than half said that they had boyfriends so as to get a place to sleep. These responses make it clear that the girls' involvement in sexual relationships is not simply aimed at looking for husbands, nor a result of any desire for early motherhood. Nor is it considered as an experiment. It is an attempt to provide for basic needs, and any other outcome is unintended.

The economic aspect of these sexual ties is also revealed by the type of men the girls take as boyfriends. Most of the girls said that their regular boyfriends were men in gainful employment who could offer the necessary financial and material assistance, providing them with regular money for school fees, school uniforms, money for breakfast and lunch, and clothing. Certainly there is peer pressure to have boyfriends, and the majority of both school drop-outs and schoolgirls had learned about sexual relationships from their girlfriends. Given the potential rewards involved, having boyfriends is becoming a modern fashion.

This pre-marital sexual activity on the part of schoolgirls can be associated with the practice of parents residing apart, and the parents' consequent inability to control their children at home. From the various reasons given for having boyfriends, it is also clear that most parents in the rural areas, whether separated or not, fail in their obligations towards their children—both boys and girls. It appears, however, that the girls are hit harder than the boys, especially in financial matters, during the period of adolescence.

The active role played by some mothers in their daughters' sexual activities cannot be overlooked. As stated earlier, 21 (30 per cent) of the 70 schoolgirls in the sample who had boyfriends claimed that their mothers had encouraged them. According to a number of the girls, whenever they went to their mothers to demand anything they were refused. They were told to provide themselves with their meals.

The parental role in sex education is minimal. Hardly any of the girls were told anything factual about sex and reproduction by their parents. When the subject was mentioned, this happened when the girls menstruated for the first time, and had had the courage to inform their mothers or grandmothers of the event. Then they were typically told, 'You are now old, so take good care of yourself, especially in dealing with boys, else you may become pregnant.' Many girls claimed that they never told their mothers when they menstruated for the first time and their mothers never asked. Sex education is not formally taught in schools either, though all the teachers interviewed agreed that it would be useful. The absence of a full-scale puberty rite or even a modified form of it deprives girls of an important ritual opportunity for learning and socialisation. Since most mothers refrain from discussing sex directly with their daughters, and only advise them in vague terms as they approach puberty, most girls become shy about sexual matters and keep their menstruation secret from their mothers. These are clear indications of a breakdown in traditional norms concerning pre-marital sexual relations; there is a failure in parental responsibility, especially maternal responsibility, towards the girls.

A number of factors and pressures propel schoolgirls in rural areas into a position in which they are likely to become pregnant. These include the meagre and inadequate sex education and lack of contraceptive knowledge; the desire for material support from young men; the desire of some mothers to have grandchildren before they die; the idea that a woman is respected only if she has children, and the strong pressure put on an only daughter to have children to continue the family line. Thirty-six per cent of the out-of-school respondents in the survey had dropped out of school because of pregnancy. Information on terminated pregnancies could not be obtained, however, though teachers and parents were of the opinion that schoolgirls often terminate pregnancies when neither they nor their relatives are prepared to take on the extra burden of a baby.[2]

Fears of precocious sexual activity on the part of schoolgirls and of pre-marital pregnancy may precipitate early marriages. Islamic teaching, for example, demands that a girl should not give birth to a baby before she is married. If a parent realises that a girl is sexually mature and fears that she may become pregnant, they may withdraw her from school and give her to a man in marriage. In some cases the girls are betrothed at infancy and the prospective grooms cannot wait for them to complete their courses. Three instances of this were reported by two teachers: two withdrawals in Middle Form 3 and one in Middle Form 2. This phenomenon may be predominant in areas where there is a large Muslim group.

Girls who fail to complete the elementary school course—whether due to pregnancy, financial constraints, or other related factors—do not remain idle. Moreover, according to the majority of the girls who had dropped out of school, their parents did not seem to be disturbed. Some of the girls who had dropped out of school because of early unwanted pregnancies had, however, been treated harshly by their parents and either neglected or forced to marry the man concerned. Girls sometimes return to school after the birth, leaving the baby with their mother. Thus among 40 girls who had changed schools in the upper middle forms, half had done so following pregnancy. Significantly, over half of the school drop-outs said that since they had left school, their parents had not shown much interest in the education of their sisters. Eighty per cent of them, on the other hand, had parents and guardians with positive attitudes towards the education of boys, and boys who had dropped out indicated that their withdrawal from school did not seem to have affected the attitudes of their parents towards the education of their brothers.

The elementary school curricula include, in theory, needlework, dressmaking, home management, cookery, leatherwork, carpentry, carving and handiwork. Except at the most rudimentary level, however, neither girls who drop out nor those who complete the course really acquire any skills which can be utilised for earning a living. There is a lack of connection between what is taught in school and the vocational needs of later life. Leaving school early, therefore, provides parents with the opportunity to equip their children with income-earning skills. To achieve this, the drop-out is often apprenticed to some trade so that she can acquire skills which the formal elementary school course did not provide. A number of informal apprenticeship facilities are available to the girls. Sewing and hairdressing are the main areas. There are also a number of private girls' vocational institutions in the country which provide training in a variety of skills.

The financial obligations of parents whose daughters are in a vocational school or apprenticed to a dressmaker are much heavier than those of girls going to elementary school in terms of fees, course materials, pocket money, and basic personal needs. During the period of apprenticeship, the learner has to be provided with course materials as well as pocket money. Expenditure on trainees in vocational schools is even higher. In a survey of 100 dressmaking apprentices, the majority were being sponsored by one or both parents. This is an indication of the parents' desire to equip their daughters with relevant skills. Ten of the girls were being catered for by the other relatives while another 16 were being sponsored by their husbands.

Some parents see the fact that a girl has dropped out of school as a chance to utilise her services for the benefit of the family or herself. Attempts are made to find employment for such girls. In the farming communities, parents may try to draft girls on to the farm. Many children do not oblige readily, but if the parents persist the children usually give in. Sometimes, the girl is enticed on to the farm with the promise of a later apprenticeship, or money to start trading or to seek subsequent employment in the urban centre. These promises are, in most cases, honoured. If the parents have younger children, the girl may stay at home to look after them while the parents are on the farm. Apart from working for their own parents, the girls may also work on the farms of other people as daily wage labourers. A day's work lasts for about four hours and in addition to the pay of

10–20 cedis the employer provides one meal on the farm. Another source of employment are the shops or market stalls where the parents trade. School leavers can help in making accounts of sales and in recording the names of debtors. It is a common practice for illiterate traders to come back from the shop in the evening and give all the day's sales for checking to the child who has been to school.

There are, however, some who drop out of school with no marketable skills who are unable to find any suitable employment, especially when they do not have parents or guardians to sponsor them in apprenticeship schemes. Others refuse to work with their parents on the farms. Some drift into the urban centres, where they may cause considerable problems. Since they do not possess any skills, they have a difficult time finding employment. Some of these may start hawking one or two items in order to earn a living. Others remain unemployed, and in order to supply their needs they resort to illegal activities. One lucrative avenue for the drop-out girl is prostitution, which may result in other unwanted pregnancies which may in turn lead to attempts at abortion or infant abandonment.[3]

Conclusion

Our study of elementary schoolgirls in the eastern region of Ghana has pointed to several significant findings. There is certainly discrimination by parents against girls in the provision of opportunities and resources for schooling and subsequent training. Boys' education is considered of more importance and given priority. The main future role of girls is considered to be that of mother, and unhappily many become mothers before they are prepared, before they have left school, before they have found an occupation or even a suitable husband. Many girls seem to be thrust at a young age into the multiple activities and responsibilities of adult women—domestic work, earning an income through trade, and motherhood (in addition to attending school). Observation of elementary school curricula and home teaching reveals that they are mostly ill prepared to assume these multiple and sometimes conflicting responsibilities. Vocational training is biased towards certain stereotyped skills, and family life education in general and knowledge of family planning in particular are sadly lacking. Teachers, parents and girls are eager that training and knowledge in these areas should be expanded to help girls cope with the demands of adolescence and adulthood. Given the inability of parents to cope with their growing children's material and financial needs, possibilities for part-time work alongside part-time schooling need to be further explored. This would enable pupils to earn what they need without depending upon illicit relationships which so often lead to unfortunate outcomes.

The value and intrinsic meaningfulness of combining vocational training with family welfare and planning education has been recognised by the Ghana National Council on Women and Development, and current programmes are operating and more are planned which combine these dual elements so as to better equip women in rural areas to cope with their multiple responsibilities as income earners, domestic workers and mothers (see below the chapter by F.A. Dolphyne). We have here provided further evidence to support the contention made by Bleek in the previous chapter that in realistic family welfare and planning programme more attention needs to be given to the young and immature who are least equipped to face the heavy responsibilities of sudden unplanned parenthood.

Notes

1   The educational system in Ghana consists of seven principal stages, as follows: primary, middle, secondary, technical, teacher training, and university. As the figures indicate, there is a steady reduction in the number of females as one gets higher up the educational system. The elementary school consists of primary and middle schools offering 6 year and 4 year courses respectively, and leading to the award of the Middle School Leaving Certificate. Church (1977) revealed that in the 1974–75 academic year females comprised 43.66 per cent of the enrolment in primary schools, 28.23 per cent in middle schools, 35.95 in secondary schools and 11.63 per cent in teacher training, commercial and technical institutions. See also *Women in national development in Ghana* (USAID, 1975). Neither of these sources make clear, however, whether they took into consideration the number of pupils who gained admission to secondary and technical schools before calculating the drop-out rate, and no mention is made of transfers to different schools.

   A more recent detailed study (Akuffo, 1981) tried to remedy this omission in selected communities and schools. In selected schools in a rural community, out of the original 67 girls enrolled in Primary Form 1 in one year, only 16 were in Primary Form 6 at the end of the sixth year. Twenty had dropped out of school by the end of the sixth year; 14 had repeated some classes and so were unable to reach Primary Form 6 at the appropriate time; and nine had transferred to other schools. In the case of the boys, 41 out of 75 originally enrolled in Primary Form 1 were in Primary Form 6 at the end of the sixth year. Eight had dropped out of school, and 15 had transferred to other schools. In the selected middle schools, 64 boys and 76 girls were admitted into Middle Form 1 in the same year, but only 27 boys and 13 girls completed the fourth year, the year of certification. These represented about 42 per cent of the boys and 17 per cent of the girls originally enrolled. Of the girls, 28 had dropped out while seven were in lower forms because of having to repeat some classes. Of the boys, 13 had dropped out of school before the end of the fourth year, eight had sought transfer to other schools, and ten had gained admission to secondary schools. Only two of the girls gained admission to secondary school before the group reached Middle Form 4.

   The same study revealed that in one middle school, of the girls originally enrolled in Middle Form 1 at the same time, only two could complete Middle Form 4 at the end of the fourth year. Fourteen dropped out before the end of the fourth year; four in Middle Form 1 (i.e. the first year), six in Middle Form 3, and four in Middle Form 4. A larger number of boys were able to complete Middle Form 4 at the appropriate time, however: six dropped out before the end of the fourth year. Three of the boys and two of the girls gained admission to secondary schools before the end of the fourth year.

2   According to the head teacher of a middle school, in the 1976–77 academic year eight girls in the school became pregnant and dropped out of school. He said most of the pregnancies occurred in Middle Form 3 and 4. The *Weekly Spectator* carried a news item in its issue of Saturday 10 March 1979, that two schoolgirls in a Bolgatanga middle school had been pregnant for four and five months at the time of publication. The same publication revealed that in the 1977–78 academic year seven girls had to be dismissed from the school for being pregnant.

3   Abortion, child abandonment and prostitution are issues of growing national concern which have led to public debate and documentation in the popular press and by concerned medical and social scientists. See, for example, the *Daily Graphic,* Accra, 16 April 1980, p. 5. Pupils in the study, when asked to suggest reasons for girls dropping out before the end of their course, mentioned as one reason that they wanted to go to Abidjan. Further enquiries revealed that girls from the area go to Abidjan for the purpose of prostitution.

10 Christine Oppong

Responsible Fatherhood and Birth Planning

In most models examining the value and use of household time and family size or fertility related values and behaviour a major focus has been upon women's time and its value, measured for examples in terms of market wages forgone (Goldschmidt-Clermont, 1982 and 1987). In many of the studies focusing on opportunity costs or role incompatibilities, the subject has been the choices and stresses of women, who are compelled either to choose between paid work outside the home and child-bearing and rearing, or to try to assume simultaneously the roles of mother and producer outside the home, with all the associated pressures and strains. Indeed, considerable interest has been shown in the literature of several disciplines in establishing links between female labour force participation outside the home and fertility-related behaviour and attitudes. In different cultural contexts positive, negative and nil relationships have been established. Informative reviews of large segments of this work have recently been undertaken, focusing specially on the 'work'–fertility links or the occupational–maternal role conflicts and opportunity costs (Standing, 1983). There has also been a focus on the maternal role and its potential rewards in relation to women's other roles—conjugal, domestic, kin, community and individual (Oppong, 1983b).

Comparatively less effort has been focused upon male roles in this regard, other than as providers of income—the husband's wage and education being standard items of information used in many economists' models seeking to explain differential fertility and female labour force participation rates. Thus it might well be argued that there is evidence of a sexist bias in this field of studies!

Family Planning Programmes: A Female Focus?

It has also been argued that in the past family planning programmes, like studies of child-care and fertility, have tended to concentrate on mothers, and that fathers and potential fathers have often been overlooked and undervalued in considering parenting and responsibilities and contributions to child-care and maintenance. Reviews of research dealing with the male role in family planning decision-making have concluded that the bulk of studies have concentrated upon women, even prior to the development of the pill and intra-uterine device (e.g. Rosen and Benson, 1982). More recent studies, while recognising a male role, have tended to use female perceptions of this role. One reason for the male role frequently being downplayed appears to be general lack of concern with how decisions are made, which would frequently involve couples. A medical model of the pregnant individual female patient has been used. In addition researchers' unconscious acceptance of sex role stereotypes are recognised as being a factor. Family and children are assumed to be the sphere of women. There is thus an increasingly recognised need to include the male in all studies of family planning decision-making, and there are indications that family planning researchers are becoming increasingly concerned to include the male directly in their studies.

In the past, services have often been tailored to meet the needs of women rather than those of men. Education likewise is frequently focused on women rather than on couples or families, and so may not help to develop favourable male attitudes to family planning. And yet, as has recently been re-emphasised, before the advent of modern contraception birth control was based almost totally on *coitus interruptus* and the condom, both male methods. These methods, together with abortion in the event of failure, were mainly responsible for the demographic transition in Europe, Japan and North America (IPPF, 1981). Indeed male methods are still reckoned to account for one third of the estimated 250 million people of the world currently using contraceptives (Stokes, 1980). Thus many family planning associations and governments do in fact have projects which reach men through the workplace and labour and trade unions, a number of which are currently assisted by the ILO, and there is reputed to be a growing realisation among both trade union leaders and employers of the potential contribution of family planning to their members' and workers' well-being.

Some years ago the experience and findings of the Danfa Family Planning Programme in Ghana illustrated how the male partner in sexual relations may play a considerable role in the reduction of excess fertility among rural African couples (Lamptey et al., 1978). Indeed, literate men were found to be quite prone to adopt modern contraceptive methods. Pool (1970a) had shown earlier elsewhere in Ghana that educated men may in fact have more positive attitudes towards family planning than their wives. The findings of Lamptey et al. (1978) suggested that male acceptance of contraception was at least as effective in preventing pregnancy as female acceptance, perhaps even more so, given the higher continuation and use effectiveness rates. They concluded that at least half of the fertility reduction in the Danfa project area was related to male contraceptive acceptance and on the basis of these findings recommended an increase in family planning services specifically for men.

This chapter is another attempt to rectify the imbalance of interest, focusing upon the parental and domestic roles of men with respect to resources and power, the division of labour, family size and family planning, rather than upon the extra-domestic roles of women.[1] The fathers selected for study were Ghanaian primary school teachers who varied considerably with regard to activities and expectations as parents, husbands and kinsmen. These differences were found to have interesting associations with family size preferences and related behaviour, including aspirations regarding quality of children, the incidence of infant mortality, and family planning practices. In particular, men's activities and responsibilities in the domestic domain were seen to be very relevant to differential and changing fertility aspirations and related behaviour. Implications for research and policy issues are raised.

Fathers and Teachers

The population selected for study comprised a national random probability sample and was relatively homogeneous with regard to educational level and hetero-geneous in other aspects such as social and spatial mobility (generations of educa-tion and migration status) urban-rural residence, and ethnicity. In Ghana, as in other areas of tropical Africa, school teachers are considered by many to be important models for social change, especially in rural areas. In addition, although scattered all over the country, they were relatively easy to contact. They under-stood and sympathised with social survey research, and they were willing to res-pond, since the subject of the questionnaires interested them. The investigation was not designed to cover a massive sample, but rather to study an analytical sam-ple of people and to use the data to illustrate at the individual level important social and demographic change, which might be operative among very different sectors of the total population. The survey data was collected by means of postal ques-tionnaires and supplemented by the recording of focused interviews from a selected sub-sample.

Here we use data from 398 men, married elementary school teachers with one or more children. They ranged in age from 21 to 54, with a mean age of 33 and a modal age of 28. Over 55 per cent were from southern Ghana, of the Akan ethnic group, which comprises over 45 per cent of the total population of Ghana; the remainder include Ewe (20 per cent), Ga (7 per cent), and other minor ethnic groups. Nearly all claimed allegiance to a Christian sect, especially the Presbyterian (20 per cent), Roman Catholic (20 per cent) and Methodist (16 per cent) churches. All were trained teachers, mainly with a Certificate A. Fewer than 6 per cent had attended a secondary school. Two-thirds were born and raised in farm families in rural environments and were first-generation educated migrants to communities within their home regions. Only 21 per cent had educated parents and 11 per cent educated grandparents. Mobility had characterised their occupational careers, nearly half having worked in three or more different communities; clearly as junior civil servants they were subject to transfer to different schools whenever the need arose. At the same time of the study only 12 per cent were living in their home towns, 62 per cent in different towns of their home region, and 26 per cent in different regions. They had become salary earners at the mean age of 21 and had held on average two different jobs, mainly in the teaching profession.

Resources and levels of living

As government employees earning fixed salaries ranging from 500 to 1,000 cedis per annum during a time of chronic inflation, nearly half complained of the very inadequate level of their income. More than one in three assessed their financial situation as declining, and only a small minority (13 per cent) were optimistic about their financial situation in five years' time. Only 5 per cent had been able to make regular savings in the past, and 42 per cent none at all. Scarcely any felt that they had adequate resources put by, while nearly half considered their financial security to be declining. Nearly all considered savings for the future to be extremely important. Open-ended questioning highlighted the fact that many were preoccupied with financial worries, especially the inability to meet the needs and demands of dependants. It is not surprising that subsequently many of these teachers were among those throngs of skilled and unskilled migrant workers who went to Nigeria to seek more remunerative employment. As we note below, most depended upon their wives to assist them in meeting domestic expenses.

Enquiries about the purchase of various consumer durables revealed a paucity of possessions, especially among the young. (Twenty-seven per cent had never purchased a radio, 56 per cent had no sewing machine, 73 per cent did not own a bicycle, 84 per cent had never bought a cooker, and hardly any had a refrigerator (6 per cent). Only 15 per cent had bought land and 9 per cent had bought a house.) Many were in fact living in cramped rented accommodation in the neighbourhood of the schools to which they had been posted, in conditions which varied considerably according to the resources and opportunities available to them through wives, parents and relatives.

Systems of kinship and marriage and residential patterns

Certain features are characteristic of the varied family systems of the ethnic groups from which they came: the persistence of descent groups which hold land, accommodation and other property, remain influential in the arrangement of marriages and funerals, and have some responsibility for the maintenance of members: a lack of functional boundedness of the conjugal family and the associated potentially polygamous nature of males' marriages; the frequent fostering; a sense of spiritual, social and material solidarity among siblings; the salient importance of parenthood and fertility, and the emphasis on filial piety and support to parents and respect for the elderly; and the variety and flexibility of co-residence patterns (Oppong et al., 1978; Oppong (ed.), 1983). In marriage segregation and separation of roles is the norm, with frequent duo-locality and a large measure of autonomy. All these features were seen to persist to some degree among the population selected, both at the level of expectations and in their actual behaviour.

With respect to production, management of resources, and maintenance, members of kin groups and conjugal families have traditionally worked together in different combinations, depending upon culture and task, to provide sustenance and cash for family members. Characteristic features have been the active part played by the young, until the introduction of schooling and even subsequently, and the separation of the long-term financial interests of husbands and wives, in spite of day-to-day co-operation and assistance, both retaining financial links with their kin.

Following the advent of universally available schooling and widespread wage employment, together with the migration and social mobility entailed by these, numerous changes have been witnessed and increasingly the majority disapprove of relatives living together—though they do approve of some financial investment with kin. The issue revealed by this investigation to be fraught with the most ambivalence and conflict was that of inheritance, whether it should be by kin or by spouse and children.

Considerable sums of money were sent to relatives, especially parents, and the majority did approve of giving such financial help to kin. A number of earlier enquiries had shown that wage and salary earners—in contexts in which elderly kin are illiterate, relatively poor, and lacking sources of old age financial support other than children—often have obligations to the relatives who reared them and to the latter's offspring who need educating. Indeed migrants, though spatially separate from relatives, may have considerable financial demands made upon them (e.g. Oppong, 1974a). In this study three out of four were asked by relatives to give financial help, a third receiving many such demands. The majority were helping to support their mothers and one or more brothers and sisters. In 24 per cent of cases the mother was completely dependent on them. Over half had responsibility, mainly partial, for one or more sisters' children, who in fact formed the largest single category of dependants. More than one in three helped to maintain their fathers (though only 6 per cent were entirely dependent) and nearly one in three had responsibility for brothers' children and wife's relatives—again mainly partial. A minority also gave support to dependent sisters of their parents and other relatives. Given the lack of other sources of maintenance such as pensions, these are obligations they would find it difficult, if not impossible, to shirk.

Marriage and conjugal roles

Age at marriage was reported to range from 17 to 41 with a mean age of 24 and a mode of 22, 83 per cent being married by the age of 25. By the time of the study they had been married on average for 10 years (mode 7 years).

Marriage for the majority was monogamous, though potentially polygynous and celebrated according to customary rites. Thirty per cent had married more than once by customary law and 21 per cent had been divorced at some time. Fewer than one in ten marriages had been celebrated in church or under the marriage ordinance which legally precludes polygyny. Most couples lived together, but one in five were living separately at the time of the study, either in different houses in the same community (8 per cent), a customary pattern, or in different communities in the same region.

There is not simply a difference in legal rights and obligations between those married customarily and those married under the ordinance. Men married under the marriage ordinance were more likely to stress the importance of social paternity and to be aware of the difficulties involved in a wife combining a career and parenthood. They were also more likely to favour the inheritance of property within the conjugal family and to approve of a more joint conjugal relationship in terms of co-residence and communication. On the whole they also had a lower· burden of kin dependency and their wives tended to contribute more than average to the domestic finances, all features which, as we shall see below, are interwoven with other kinds of changes taking place in family life. Nearly one in four wives had no schooling; 11 per cent had primary level education, 47 per cent middle schooling, and 8 per cent higher education. Twenty-three per cent had no formal employment outside the home. The majority were working, however: 7 per cent were farmers, 15 per cent who were illiterate were engaged in unskilled activities, 33 per cent in skilled work, 3 per cent clerical staff, 9 per cent semi-professionals (teachers and nurses), 0.3 per cent professionals, and 3 per cent students.

Earlier investigations of familial role prescriptions had revealed diversity, conflict, and lack of congruence and consensus among the mobile and educated (Oppong, 1975). Few norms were observed to be widely supported. In this population the most widely accepted norms regarding conjugal behaviour were co-residence of spouses, shared parental responsibilities, and the allocation of housework to wives. Moderate levels of support were given to conjugal equality, joint housing interests, shared domestic tasks, and maintenance and inheritance of property by spouses. Other issues such as the husband's financial responsibility for the conjugal family, the degree of self-reliance on the part of the wife, and the proportion of her time that should be spent on child-care at home were much more controversial. By and large husbands professed to spend little time on domestic work (76 per cent) while reporting that their wives spent a lot of their time on it (71 per cent).

As in earlier studies of salaried government employees, there was considerable variation in the extent to which husbands and wives shared the task of providing for the material needs of their domestic groups (Oppong, 1982b). But the overall pattern of responsibilities indicates that husbands tend to shoulder certain costs more readily than others, especially educational and housing costs, while wives most frequently contribute towards the costs of children's clothes and food.

Parenthood

Fatherhood does not always follow marriage—for more than one in ten the first child had preceded marriage. For most it had followed soon afterwards. For many, procreation is still seen as a process continuing throughout marriage well into middle and later life. Only 36 per cent perceived themselves as stopping begetting children before the age of 40 and many expected to continue beyond the age of 50, and more than 40 per cent had had children with more than one woman.

The modal number of children for the sample was two with a mean of 3.8. The majority would have liked to have four to six children, and the modal ideal was six. If financial constraints had been removed nearly half would have wanted seven or more. Even if poor the majority would have wanted two children, a number which in normal circumstances was perceived to be too few. The generally acceptable family size therefore ranged between three and six. Thus while the preferred family sizes of this set of educated men was significantly below traditionally valued ideals of six or ten or more, it was still far higher than that of men in parallel professional positions in industrialised countries. Analysis of their perceptions of how many children other people thought they shoud have indicates that wives were perceived as having similar aspirations to themselves, but mothers, fathers, brothers and sisters want them to have significantly more children than they wanted for themselves. This indicates that couples living near to kin may be subject to pressures to produce more children than they might otherwise.

Fathers' reports regarding the amount of time they contributed to child-care varied greatly. The majority helped to buy their clothes but only a minority participate actively in feeding and bathing their little ones. Aspirations regarding children's educational attainment were high. The majority expected some of their children to go to secondary school and a sizeable minority expected them to go to university. Aspirations for sons' education were higher than for daughters'. In accordance with local traditions and migrants' constraints, more than one quarter of their own children were not living with them at the time of the study. In fact, 44 per cent had one or more of their children living elsewhere, while 22 per cent had a child who had been staying away for more than three years. Twelve per cent had one or more children staying with grandparents. Many also had children of kin staying with them. Indeed, some had several children of kin living with them. The majority were their brothers' and sisters' children. Some were their own younger siblings and a few were children of their wives. Child-care and medical intervention is not always adequate to ensure survival, and of the average of 3.8 children born to them, 0.47 had died in childhood.

Fertility Regulation

These fathers came from an educated sector of the population with relatively easy access to family planning services. During the period of study the National Family Planning Programme was active and modern contraceptives available in family planning clinics, medical centres and commercial outlets. The topics of family planning and family size were thus not uncommon, the majority having discussed both of these issues with their wives, a few with relatives. In addition, it appeared to be common to discuss family planning in both neighbourhood and workplace. Indeed it was at that time a topic for nationwide publicity campaigns and advertising.

Twenty per cent reported that they had used some contraceptive method before the first birth, and 33 per cent after the first and second births. Forty-five per cent were currently using some method, while 68 per cent intended to do so in future. Forty-seven per cent of the sample had used contraceptives at some point in their lives. The most commonly used methods of preventing pregnancy reported were abstinence and 'rhythm' methods (38 per cent), use of chemicals (foams, etc.) (34 per cent), contraceptive pills (28 per cent), condoms (24 per cent), and *coitus inter-ruptus* (21 per cent). A few had used douches (4 per cent), diaphragms (3 per cent), abortion (4 per cent), IUDs (3 per cent) and local medicines (3 per cent).

Changing Familial Roles

Differences and changes in the familial roles and relations of these men were apparent which appeared to be related to levels of education, migration and employment, not only of themselves but of their parents and spouses. In southern Ghana, education in the parental and previous generations, with the associated social and spatial mobility and consequent individualism, in terms of property ownership and income-earning and financial security, has already been demonstrated to be an important factor associated with differences in the expectations and obligations attached to kin roles (Oppong, 1982b). Significant variations have also been seen in the extent to which customary expectations and behaviour patterns are maintained—according to the levels of social and spatial mobility, migration and education over three generations. In this study both those with educated forebears and migrants living away from their home towns had a lower kin dependency burden and had fewer in-laws coming to stay.[2] Social and spatial mobility are also associated with diminishing approval of economic solidarity with kin, both through inheritance and through joint investment, increasing disapproval of fostering of children by relatives, and greater conjugal jointness and equality, both in norms and in behaviour.

With regard to parenthood, the more socially and spatially mobile tend to have a greater sense of the importance of individual parental responsibility, and have non-traditional ideas about how many children they want to have and over what period of the lifespan, and a greater readiness to adopt scientific methods of birth control. Approval of fostering of children by kin was also negatively correlated with the extent to which the men themselves had lived with their own fathers at different stages of their childhood, indicating the kinds of life experiences that lead to changing parental role expectations.[3]

Wives' Domestic Resources, Power and Division of Tasks

It has been frequently hypothesised and demonstrated that the more equal the status of wives and husbands (mainly in terms of resources from education, occupation and kin ties) the more likely are they to have an egalitarian conjugal role relationship and a more flexible division of domestic tasks and responsibilities, including the parental (Oppong, 1984, reviews some evidence). Attention has been called to the importance of cultural prescriptions, values and beliefs, the prevalence of sexual stratification, the possibilities for bargaining between husbands and wives, and the relevance of external resources to domestic power (Safilios-Rothschild, 1982a, and 1982b). Ghanaian evidence from several socio-economic settings has shown the pervasiveness of conjugal bargaining and the relevance of resources to power, such as the wife's use of her income for maintenance of conjugal family members (e.g. Oppong, 1970; 1982b).

These couples are found to provide further supportive evidence of the effects of relative resource contributions on the balance of conjugal power and decision-making and the degree of flexibility and equality in the division of domestic tasks. Thus similarity of spouses' resources from education and occupations as indicated by financial contributions is associated with more equality and syncratic decision-making, and the latter tends also to be correlated with more flexible divisions of domestic tasks and parenting. In other words, husbands with wives with more resources, that is higher status, are likely to assume a larger share of domestic and parental activities and responsibilities.

We turn next to the consideration of parental costs and perceptions of role strain.

Paternal Costs and Role Strain

Given on the one hand the low salary levels, the minimal accumulation of capital goods and the relatively low standards of living, and on the other hand high aspirations for themselves and their children, it is not surprising to find that many fathers express great concern about bringing up children. In an analysis of school teachers' assessments of the major causes of problems in their family lives, one in four mentioned the strain of having children. Ten per cent mentioned specifically the costs of education and 8 per cent mentioned lack of time or people to care for their children (Oppong, 1975).

There are several other indicators of role strain, both potential dangers perceived and the reality experienced. Over 60 per cent of the present sample were of the opinion that bringing up children was a great strain on a teacher's income, and many thought it was very difficult for a couple to look after small children when they were both employed. These perceptions of strain were associated with general feelings about lack of resources in money and time and having too many children to care for. In fact, 55 per cent complained at some time of having too many children to care for. Some complained specifically of having nobody suitable to care for the baby, and nearly 90 per cent complained of problems with children's illnesses.

The feeling of fathers that they have too many children to care for increased with age and family size, reaching its peak among men over 35 with the largest family sizes for their age group. Among younger men with average and fewer children, however, there were some who felt the strains of parenthood to a greater extent than their age mates with similar family sizes. These were men who felt they had a relatively greater general insufficiency of money and time.

Among high fertility fathers, several traditional traits were found to be associated with perceptions of having too many children and problems in caring for them, in particular openness of conjugal family functioning (i.e. the persistence of expectations and practices associated with the 'extended' family forms, including fostering of children by relatives) and infant deaths. Those who had lost one or more children (21 per cent had lost one child, 9 per cent two children and 3 per cent more than two) more often complained that they had too many children to care for and nobody suitable to care for their babies. Significantly these fathers were also more likely to send out their children to be fostered by kin, to take in children of their relatives to care for, and to approve generally of openness in sex, procreation and marriage—supporting polygyny and polycoity and having less restrictive views regarding births outside a monogamous marriage, all traditionally acceptable. Their solution to child-care problems appeared to be sharing children with kin. The outcome was unfortunately more infant deaths than among their peers who did not delegate their parental responsibilities. Significantly, more recent medical evidence has related the incidence of *kwashiorkor*, a state of malnutrition, in a Ghanaian hospital to such 'substitute mothering' (Waterson, 1982).

In fact high infant mortality has been associated on a number of occasions with 'extended' family functioning, more traditional marriage forms and higher fertility (cf. Stone, 1977). With increasing closure of the conjugal family and more individualised parenting, however, infant mortality rates have been demonstrated to fall.

Some of the ways have already been indicated whereby fatherhood, for the status-conscious, upwardly-striving and responsible teacher, becomes increasingly costly to him personally, in stark constrast to the experience of his rural forebears for whom more children were the joy and responsibility of the wider kin group providing extra labour for family farms, craft production and trade. This process occurs in several ways as the resources in terms of money and time required from the father for child-rearing increase and inputs from others tend to diminish. At the same time expected levels of achievement for children in terms of grades of schooling are increasing.

Men who indicated a heightened awareness of the possibilities of parental role strain[4] were among those who felt overburdened by kin pressures and demands, men likely to be attempting to distance themselves somewhat from kin, contrary to customary norms and practices. In addition, men who expected to be more involved in domestic tasks and parenting and actually did participate to a greater extent were also more aware of the possibilities of strain. This means that fathers with egalitarian, flexible conjugal relationships were among those for whom child-care was perceived as being most fraught with potential strain.

Men with small families than their contemporaries tended to come from more educated and mobile backgrounds, and in the case of the younger men to have wives with higher levels of education. They also expected more joint and equal conjugal relationships and less close kin ties. They were also more likely to think they personally should bear the costs of child-care and appeared less affluent.

The men who state that they wanted fewer children currently had fewer of their own and fewer dependants. They fostered out and took in the children of kin less, often a pattern of which they disapproved, likewise co-residence of kin. None of their children had died and they more often reported playing with their children. They also had higher educational expectations for their daughters and abhorred the birth of children outside marriage. They thus expected and enacted a more individuated style of parenting, with higher costs and healthier offspring. They also approved of joint conjugal budgeting and disapproved of male sexual prerogatives and dominance. They tended to have married monogamously at a relatively older age an educated wife, with whom they were more likely to discuss such issues as family size. These were also the couples most likely to use

Table 10.1   Number of children spouses would like and relative financial inputs

Wife's input	Husband's input			
	Low		High	
	Husband	Wife	Husband	Wife
Low	4.9	5.5	6.5	6.0
High	5.3	5.4	5.8	5.8

contraception and to have a flexible division of domestic labour (cf. Beckman, 1979).

An examination of husbands' and wives' family size preferences according to their relative inputs into domestic expenditures indicates that the couples with the most flexible and egalitarian relationships were also the ones in which the wives' desired family size was perceived as being the lowest (5.4), as well as similar to her husband's (5.3). The couples with the largest desired family sizes for husbands and wives (6.5 and 6.0) were those with high-contributing husbands and low-contributing wives, those among whom male dominance, inequality of resources and inputs, and approval of conjugal role segregation were most marked. The husbands whose family size desires were lowest (4.9)—and markedly lower than those of their wives—were those where the contributions of both husband and wife were low. These were the men most prone to complain of financial problems and indebtedness. These were also among the husbands who most frequently reported that they used contraception.

Contraception

Those most likely to use contraception included men with low family-size preferences whose wives had similar desires. These couples also envisaged child-bearing as continuing for a shorter period of their life span, and communicated more freely about family size and family planning issues.

For every age and fertility category, mothers and other relatives were perceived as wanting couples to have more children than they themselves wanted. It is thus not surprising that those living away from their home towns and mobile in the past had more positive attitudes to contraception in the future, intended to stop their child-begetting at a younger age, and used contraceptives more frequently.

The most likely users of contraceptives included younger men who had been monogamously married for relatively short periods with educated young wives. Men in their early thirties with relatively many children and men over 35 with relatively few children also scored high as regards family planning and use of contraceptives. In fact the highest scoring group of all was men over 35 with relatively few children. Contraceptive users could be distinguished from others by their greater propensity to save and yet to perceive that what they had saved was inadequate. They also differed from non-users in several aspects of their familial roles and relationships. Greater equality and flexibility in conjugal roles, more marked tendencies towards closure of the conjugal family or a cutting down of obligations and exchanges associated with kin ties, and more individual assumption of parental tasks and responsibilities, were characteristic features.

Table 10.2 Perceptions of parental role strain and use of modern contraceptives, sexual abstinence and practice of coitus interruptus

Perceptions* of parental role strain	% use contraceptives	% practise sexual abstinence	% practise *coitus interruptus*
Low	36	26	10
Medium	51	45	25
High	48	41	23
N	(165)	(140)	(77)

* Score 1, 2, 3 on index of child-care strain

Data on several aspects of the paternal role show that caring for one's own children oneself rather than sending them to kin is associated with contraceptive usage, as are feelings that parental costs and tasks should be individualised and the idea that procreation should not continue past middle age. Those who use contraceptives are also less likely to lose children by death. Finally, those with a more salient anticipation of the strains of having children are more likely to use contraceptives, to abstain from sexual relations, and to practice withdrawal (see table 10.2).

These data provide supportive evidence for hypotheses connecting lower fertility with increases in flows of resources from parents to children and the increasingly individual assumption of the costs of parenting; the dwindling of flows of resources and responsibilities, including child-care and support, between kin, and the increasingly flexible allocation of tasks and equality between spouses.

Figure 10.1 links the changing familial role expectations and family size preferences in a model which illustrates how education, and the related migration and employment levels, and thus social and spatial mobility, are associated with approval of increasing parental individualism, dwindling of kin solidarity, and greater flexibility and jointness in marriage. At the same time these role expectations are themselves linked to lower family size preferences, indicating how changing familial role expectations can mediate between the modernising influences of education, urban migration and salaried employment and family size values.

Figure 10.2 indicates how these same influences are linked to increased fertility regulation through the intervening impact of more individualised, more costly parenting, itself a product of a more flexible division of domestic tasks and cutting down of sharing responsibilities with kin.

Figure 10.3 indicates how perceptions of paternal role strain are affected by the assumption by the husband of more traditionally female tasks and the reduced assumption of parental roles by kin, together with perceptions of inadequate income. All these appear to lead to lower family size preferences and greater conscious regulation of fertility.

Policy Implications

At the beginning of this chapter we raised the issue of the possible sexual bias of family planning programmes and fertility research. Recognition is now growing of the importance of the 'invisible man' and his part in fertility decision-making

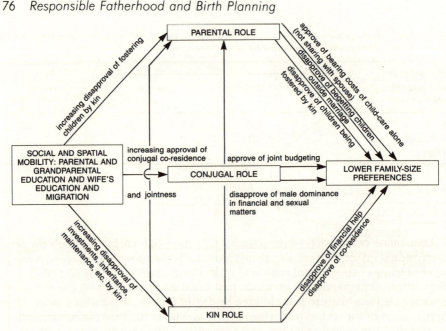

Figure 10.1: Familial roles, changing norms and values, and lower family size preferences.

Source: Oppong (1983c)

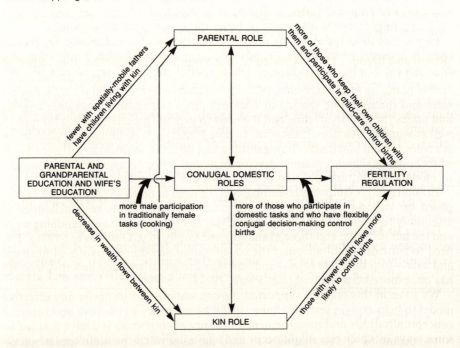

Figure 10.2: Changing familial role behaviours and fertility regulation.

Source: Oppong (1983c)

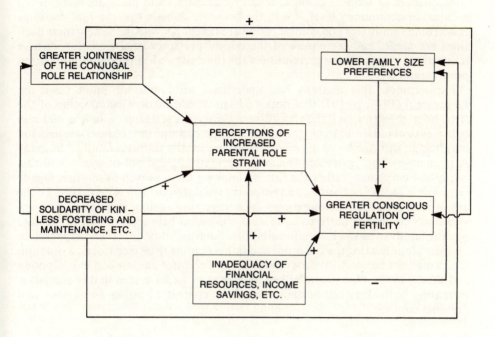

Figure 10.3: Linkages between familial roles, resources, perceptions of parental strain and family size preferences and fertility regulation.

(Rosen and Benson, 1982). This study, like a number of others, has thus indicated the need for a closer consideration of male roles in fertility-related decisions and family planning (e.g. Marciano, 1979). It has also reiterated the significance of sex roles and the equitable sharing of responsibilities and resources between females and males for fertility decline and the need to provide parallel services for men as well as women.[5] An important point to note is that such flexibility and equality of sex roles, and in particular conjugal roles, can occur in societies at different levels of technological and economic development and is not necessarily a concomitant of modernisation, urbanisation or industrialisation (e.g. Howell, 1979).

In addition this study has re-emphasised the need to break the conceptual barrier posed by viewing work as essentially masculine and family responsibilities as essentially feminine and the division of research efforts into those examining work and the labour force and those examining the family (e.g. Gutek et al., 1981). The need to consider simultaneously the occupational and domestic roles of husband and wife—four different roles—and how they are articulated and how they interact has once more been stressed (e.g. Pleck, 1977).

We have in this chapter supported the contention that to devise any effective model to help explain fertility change it will be necessary to improve upon current conceptualisations and measurement of family phenomena. We have pointed to some ways in which this might occur and again indicated the usefulness of small-scale, local, empirical studies of the changing functioning of family systems in conditions of altering resource constraints, highlighting the causes and consequences of familial change. Whatever decisions and plans are made at the national or community level, it is in the domestic domain that the vital decisions concerning family size and contraception are taken. Knowledge of how these decisions are made, and the nature of the critical pressures triggering reproductive innovation, are necessary prerequisites for the design of appropriate population programmes.

Furthermore, this analysis has underlined an important point made by Leibenstein (1977, p. 195) that policy design should involve examination of the 'free-rider' effects, that is the allocation of child costs and responsibilities and who manages to avoid shouldering them. As he notes, certain kinds of family legislation may help to shift the locus of responsibility toward the conjugal family. Or, in the African case of polygyny and frequent free marriage and out-of-wedlock births, one might emphasise rather the fathers, making them as well as mothers legally responsible for their offspring and enforcing child support where necessary. To the extent that economic developments encourage rural–urban migration, they are also likely to change patterns of mutual obligation between kin and to increase nuclear family or individual responsibilities. Such mobility, however, may result in mothers alone bearing the full brunt and fathers opting to be free-riders, a situation which may not be conducive to responsible and planned parenthood (e.g. Oppong and Bleek, 1982). One potential key to change as we have seen in this analysis is increasing individual responsibility within a context of rising aspirations and personal control.

Notes

1   For a fuller discussion of the issues discussed in this paper see Oppong (1983b), the earlier working paper on which this chapter is based.
2   Non-parametric tests of association were used to indicate the strength of correlations.
3   While 82 per cent of those who had had minimal periods of residence with their fathers when children approved of fostering, the figures were 77 per cent for those with intermediate lengths of residence and 67 per cent for those with maximum lengths of residence—differences which are statistically significant ($N = 332: X^2 = 5.6517 P < .05$; $Tau = -0.12331 P < .009; r = -0.1271 P < .01$). Interesting parallel evidence of such changes in expectations came from an earlier study of Ghanaian university students (Oppong, 1975) in which being reared by parents only was negatively correlated with a scale of approval of openness of conjugal family functioning, including fostering. Thus of those who approved of conjugal family closure, 60 per cent had been reared by parents only; at intermediate levels of the scale percentages were 41 per cent, 40 per cent and 36 per cent, while at the open ('extended') end of the scale the percentage reared by own parents only sank to 24 per cent ($N = 653$ male students).
4   The mode of calculating a simple index of such strain is given in the appendix of Oppong (1983b).
5   See pp. 33–35, 'Male and female roles in family planning', in *Challenges and opportunities*, Background, document, International Conference on Family Planning in the 1980s, April 1981, Jakarta, Indonesia.

Part IV

Government Plans and Development Policies

Organisations established to meet the needs of women should be functional, technically competent and should reach rural women. A strategy that should complement the establishment of machineries is the promotion of a women's unit in planning ministries and commissions to feed and monitor national development plans with data on women and to integrate a plan of action in national strategies. The establishment or strengthening of the women's unit in collaboration with member states will be a major preoccupation of OAU and ECA in the second half of the decade (OAU, 1981, p. 112).

The importance of giving special attention to women in the analysis of the reported situation and to measures to be taken in each of these sectors (industry, agriculture and trade, etc.) which have been previously considered is acknowledged. The steps to be taken to solve the problems of African women should not be marginal and separate from the question of overall development (ibid., p. 111).

The areas identified for study in the Plan of Action remain valid particularly in the light of the fact that few national censuses and surveys have been undertaken since 1975. When they are about to commence, it is important to stress to national directors of statistics the need for breakdowns by sex in order to identify areas for action relevant to women, particularly in the sub-theme areas of employment, health and education. Lack of such sex breakdowns has in the past hindered identification of special needs of women (ibid., p. 117)

The aim of incorporating women on an equal basis with men into development planning, as decision-makers, administrators and beneficiaries, has been a recurrent theme of national and international meetings held during the past decade and was repeatedly emphasised as noted above by country delegations during the World Conference to Review and Appraise the Achievements of the UN Decade for Women: Equality, Development and Peace, Nairobi, July 1985. More equitable divisions of labour both inside and outside the home, and more equal access to education, training, employment and income, as well as improved medical facilities and means to control conception, are seen as inextricably associated with this goal.

A variety of evidence and cases have been assembled, however, to illustrate the fact that both development studies and development planning have often remained firmly oriented towards men—men being synonymous with people (Rogers, 1979,

p. 9). This situation seems likely to continue unless there are serious and concerted efforts to counteract it, in spite of the fact that so many special projects have been set up for women in the past few years, in spite of the United Nations having created a decade for women, and in spite of the spate of studies of women's roles.

A major factor contributing to this situation, and already discussed in Part I of this volume, is the persistent reliance on defective quantitative data to provide an 'objective' view of economic development in general and labour force participation in particular, and the stereotypical views of women's roles incorporated into development plans. In addition, a number of myths and misconceptions about the roles of women in the home and outside it are pervasive in many economic and demographic models used by researchers and subsequently by planners. We have already touched upon the inappropriate models of the functioning of domestic groups and the almost total concentration upon women as mothers when the focus is conception, birth and child-care. In contrast, the case studies in this volume have indicated that women in West Africa can in no way be considered dependent and passive home-makers, leaving 'bread-winning' and decision-making to male household heads and husbands. Attention has been drawn to their work in domestic-based production and processing, the parts they play in food production, storage and marketing, and their growing participation in the industrial labour force, in addition to their simultaneous involvement in child-bearing and child-care.

The potential implications of the false myths and stereotypes have already been referred to: the way in which, for instance, rural development programmes have often been aimed almost entirely at men and actually have led to increased work and impoverishment for women agriculturalists (Rogers, 1979, p. 41; Jackson, 1978). External assistance from development agencies may even compound such mistakes, as was noted at the Nairobi World Conference (ibid., 1979, pp. 66–67).

These issues are of great moment to West African governments, within whose territories live peoples of cultures widely known for their traditions of sexual autonomy and equality and among whom the female farming systems and trading complexes, on which their national economies depend for food production and distribution, are of world renown.

In this last section the focus is the government plans and *de facto* policies of three countries in the region and how they treat women's roles. In Chapter 11 the case of Sierra Leone is taken up, and the need to improve women's productivity and incomes. Gaps in government plans, and policies and methods to remedy them, are noted, as well as the persistent lack of relevant data on which to base plans. Chapter 12 takes one country's past national development plan, that of Nigeria, and considers a number of aspects of the plan and related policies in the light of women's multiple activities and responsibilities inside and outside the home. Again the major concerns are women's opportunities for access to income and relevant taxation and property investment possibilities. An interesting aspect of this chapter is that it draws attention to gaps between the perceptions of sex roles evident in the plan and the sex role expectations and activities documented and observed by social scientists within the country. It thus calls attention to the fact that an understanding of the implications of sex roles and varied and changing forms of domestic organisation is basic to the design and implementation of successful policies and programmes and to the need for the greater participation of women and fuller consideration of their interests in policy formulation.

Women's Bureaux

An important means of achieving the goal of sexual equality has been the setting up of appropriate institutional mechanisms. As far back as 1964, the International Labour Conference requested all member States to consider establishing central units for co-ordinating the activities of women workers, and since the International Women's Year in 1975 and the recurrent demands for the integration of women into development, many countries have set up special offices to deal with women's issues. Many bureaux or women's departments have been set up in Ministries of Labour, Social Welfare and Social Security. (Such institutions set up in West African countries have been listed in Appendix I.)

The last chapter of Part IV records in detail the mandate and the activities of one such organisation in the region—the Ghana National Council on Women and Development (GNCWD). The account is given by Florence Dolphyne, who for a decade was first Vice-chairperson and then Chairperson of the council. The major task of the GNCWD is to work with voluntary organisations to ensure that the services of government departments and agencies reach women and to help co-ordinate related activities. The primary need is for income-earning activities and thus for related education, training, credit, improved technologies, etc. At the same time, women's needs related to motherhood, marriage and kinship are recognised and appropriate responses sought, including family life education, marriage guidance, reform of marriage and inheritance laws, etc. The GNCWD provides a worthy example of an institution which has made a valiant effort to base its work on relevant documentation and research. The findings of a number of studies were formally publicised at a conference held in Accra in 1978.

11

Franklyn Lisk and Yvette Stevens

Government Policy and Rural Women's Work in Sierra Leone

According to projections based on the 1974 population census, females currently account for about 51 per cent of the total population of Sierra Leone. Of a total estimated economically active population of about 1.3 million in mid-1984, women, however, accounted for about 460,000 or 35 per cent. A fuller recognition of women's work, in both rural and urban areas, and a more realistic conceptualisation of the labour force, would certainly result in the recording of a higher female participation rate. The economically active population, in terms of available manpower for productive employment, has officially been defined to include:

> ... everyone who is either working (*the employed*) or available for work (*the unemployed*). It excludes young children, the very old, the sick and incapacitated who are unable to work and those who, for some reason or another, are not willing to work at the time, i.e. students and *busy housewives* (Government of Sierra Leone, 1974, para. 2.1, p. 21; authors' emphasis).

The failure to recognise the labour of 'busy housewives' as productive work that contributes directly and indirectly to national output is inconsistent with the realities of the family and the household economy, particularly in the rural areas of the country where women, in addition to their domestic and maternal roles, are also the main source of labour in smallholder agriculture. This to a great extent underlies the insufficient consideration given by policy-makers and planners to the special problems and needs of women as producers, and hence the inadequacy of policy measures and action programmes for raising their employment and income status. It is significant to note that the 1974/75–1978/79 National Development Plan did not make any specific reference to the active part played by rural women in Sierra Leone in the production of both food and export crops, let alone advocate specific policies for improving their working and living conditions. Similarly, the Plan showed almost no recognition of the productive activities of women in the urban informal sector, where they constitute a dominant force in the retailing of basic foodstuffs and essential consumer goods that are indispensable to the vast majority of urban households.

These observations are not intended to give the impression that the planning process in Sierra Leone has entirely bypassed women in their role as producers, since some government policies, especially those in the area of social welfare, have no doubt had positive effects on women's work (ibid., Chapter XVIII). Women have benefited from the expansion in infrastructural, educational and health facilities throughout the country since Independence, certain development programmes and projects in the agricultural sector, though not specifically focused on women, may have contributed to some improvements in their well-being as members of target households. The point that is being stressed in the context of this chapter, however, is the failure of policy-makers and planners to recognise the active part played by women in the production process and to take full account of their special needs in the planning process, which has resulted in

(1) the virtual absence of special programmes for promoting productive employment and income-earning opportunities among women on an equal basis with men;
(2) the failure to effectively translate official policy statements on the status of women into action programmes;
(3) the continuing overt and subtle discriminations against women in various socio-economic spheres based on their historically perceived and predictable roles in society; and
(4) the adoption of policies and programmes as part of the modernisation process that have unintentionally but clearly had negative implications for women's working and living conditions.

This chapter attempts to look at government policies and their effects on women's work, with a view to identifying weaknesses and shortcomings in the approach to planning, policy formulation and implementation, and to indicate reforms and more appropriate directions for policy that would contribute to improvements in the employment and income status of women and to a fuller recognition of their contribution to national development. More specifically, the chapter will examine government policy in relation to the promotion of employment and income-generating activities, agriculture and rural development, industrialisation and the informal sector, and household work.

Employment and Income Policy

According to official statistics, it would appear that the proportion of women in the labour force has been declining, despite the fact that the female component of the population has remained slightly higher than that of males.

Commenting on the growth of the labour force in the intercensal period as depicted in table 11.1, the report of the 1978 ILO/JASPA Employment Advisory Mission noted:

What is surprising is that the number of females in the labour force showed almost no increase over the whole period. The number of working females declined considerably and the numbers not working increased by as much. The decline in the number of working females is indicated to be in agriculture which could not be true as by all accounts the majority of women in rural areas work (ILO/JASPA, 1981, p. 15).

Because of conceptual and definitional biases regarding the status of women's work, the figures are likely to represent some underestimation of the extent of

Table 11.1   Labour force in 1963 and 1974 (000s)

Work status	1963						1974					
	Male		Female		Total		Male		Female		Total	
	No.	%	No.	%	No.	%	No.	%	No.	%	No.	%
Working	576	95.4	331	99.1	907	96.7	705	91.7	262	72.8	967	87.4
Not working	28	4.6	3	0.9	31	3.3	66	8.3	73	27.2	139	12.6
Total	604	100.0	334	100.0	938	100.0	771	100.0	335	100.0	1106	100.0

Source Population Census, 1963 and 1974.

female participation in the labour force but it is difficult to understand how their participation rate, according to official statistics, could actually have declined from 45 to 32 per cent for the period under review. What could possibly have occurred is a significant decline in the proportion of women 'actively looking for wage employment'; those not 'actively looking' would then not be counted as part of the economically active population. With the labour market becoming more competitive over time, many women who perceive their employment chances as poor, due mainly to lower educational levels or lack of skills traditionally associated with men, voluntarily exclude themselves from labour force statistics by claiming *not* to be actively looking for wage employment when asked about their work status. Furthermore, the definition of 'working' relates mainly to those engaged in wage employment, thereby contributing to the incidence of undercounting of women as compared with men, since proportionately more women than men are engaged in non-wage employment in the urban informal sector.

But even if the proportion of women in the labour force did remain constant during the intercensal period, and their participation rate was in fact higher than the official statistics indicate, women are likely to have been disadvantaged as compared with men in terms of earnings and access to better-paid jobs. In this regard, it should be noted that the incidence of underemployment, both visible and disguised, must have been higher among women than men because many more women are engaged in low-productivity and poorly paid jobs or work long hours in unpaid house and farm work. Given that in Sierra Leone earnings tend to be higher in formal wage sector employment than in those activities traditionally undertaken by women outside the formal sector, and that the number of women in wage employment declined in the intercensal period, the average earnings of women in the labour force must also have dropped substantially.

Although no comparable official statistics are available for the period after 1974, there is little reason to believe that the situation as regards the employment and income status of women has improved. The difficult economic circumstances of the country since the mid-1970s have served to depress the employment market further, thereby making it even harder for women, who tend to have lower educational levels than men, to obtain gainful employment in the formal sector. In the rural areas, stagnation in agricultural production in recent years (Bank of Sierra Leone, *Annual Reports*)—due mainly to the decline in world commodity prices and export demand during the recession and the adverse internal terms of trade for food-crop producers—have led to increased underemployment, lower incomes and falling standards of living among female (as well as male) producers. Similarly, overall economic stagnation and the process of modernisation have tended to diminish female employment opportunities in traditional small-scale production and urban informal sector activities; women are now facing increasing competition from men, who would otherwise have been employed in the wage sector, in such traditionally female-dominated activities as petty trading, food processing, market gardening and handicrafts.

In view of the precarious situation facing women in the employment market, and the continuing decline in their total earnings as noted above, it is therefore of great concern that the 1974/75–1978/79 National Development Plan did not include any specific measures for promoting income-generating activities among women within the framework of its manpower and employment policy (Government of Sierra Leone, 1974, para. 2.3, pp. 26–28). This situation again reflects biases in the conceptualisation and definition of the labour force, as a result of which the employment status of the majority of women is not fully recognised by planning officials. Whereas the Plan identified certain other vulnerable groups such as youth and migrant workers in relation to the nature and magnitude of the employment problem, and accordingly formulated specific policy measures for ameliorating their situation, there have been no such special measures for women as a numerically significant though disadvantaged group in the labour force.

Among the variety of solutions put forward in the Plan for reducing unemployment and underemployment, almost the only ones that relate to women—and even then not in terms of specific policies aimed at women as a target group—were those pertaining to family planning as a means of 'reducing excessive growth of the labour force' (ibid., para. 2.2, p. 26) as a long-term solution, and to the modification of the Rural Training Institute at Kenema 'to include both the farmer and his wife with emphasis on demonstrating improved farm practices' (ibid., para. 2.2, p. 27). The only other references to women in the Plan with implications for their employment and income status were in the context of the 'expansion of maternal and child health services' (ibid., Chapter XVII, para. 1.2, p. 257) and programmes 'to improve and expand services and institutions dealing with . . . women's work', along with juvenile delinquency, crime prevention and old age welfare in the social welfare sector (ibid., Chapter XVIII, p. 273).

If in diagnosing the causes of unemployment and underemployment the Plan had shown sufficient awareness of the problems and needs of women, it is possible that the solutions proposed would also have included specific measures for raising employment and income levels among women, who do after all make up a substantial proportion of the total labour force. Yet it is difficult, if not impossible, for policy-makers and planners to focus sharply on women's problems and needs in the absence of relevant data and information for the periodic monitoring of the working and living conditions of women. In Sierra Leone, the main sources of data for planning purposes, for example, relating to employment status, wage rates, consumption, nutritional status of individuals are particularly weak with respect to disaggregation by sex; nor are there longitudinal micro-level studies on women as required for measurement both of their participation in the labour force and of their contribution to the household economy. Furthermore, concepts and definitions of factors affecting the composition and operation of the labour market appear to be strongly influenced by male attitudes towards and perceptions of women's work, leading to a lack of recognition by (male) policy-makers of the important contribution and potential of women as producers in the labour force.

The Outline of the 1981/82–1985/86 National Development Plan does, however, represent an improvement on the previous plan in so far as it identifies an important role for women—as a gender-specific group—in the overall development process and includes specific measures for improving their socio-economic status (Government of Sierra Leone, 1981). Inspired by the various declarations on women's status in the Lagos Plan of Action (OAU, 1981), the Programme of Action adopted by the UN Women's Decade Conference (Copenhagen, 1980) and the International Development Strategy for the Third UN Development Decade, the *Outline* takes cognisance of 'the need not only to expand and integrate the role of women in development, but . . . more importantly [that] women must not be denied the fruits of their labour and should be rewarded commensurately with the contributions made by them to the development process' (ibid., Chapter 2, para. 2.66, p. 42).

Furthermore, the *Outline* makes reference to the employment status of women as well as indicating broad areas for appropriate policy interventions:

> During this plan period, Government expects to improve the status of women in the rural sector by providing education and training for agriculture and related crafts, industries and services. Above all, Government will take steps to ensure more appropriate economic and social recognition of women's important contribution to the rural economy by increasing their earning opportunities and increasing their levels of income . . .
>
> In the urban areas, Government will continue to provide education and training to enable women to move into more diversified fields and to take up more highly skilled and better paid rungs in the occupational ladder (ibid., Chapter 3, paras. 3.50 and 3.51, pp. 79–80).

In terms of specific policy measures to promote income-earning opportunities for women and to improve their socio-economic status, the *Outline* makes reference to the development of agricultural extension services for women farmers; facilitating their access to credit, fertilisers and other agricultural inputs; providing price incentives and marketing channels for women producers; facilitating the establishment of agro-based industries; promoting the introduction of appropriate technologies; increasing the availability of water supplies and energy for domestic use; encouraging wider participation of women in the decision-making process; improving the health and nutritional status of women; and implementing functional adult education programmes (ibid., Chapter 2, para. 2.68).

Whether or not these measures will be translated into effective action programmes still remains to be seen. This will depend, however, first and foremost on the prevailing resource situation, and secondly on the priorities accorded to women's programmes in the new National Development Plan. In the current situation of severe budgetary constraints, women's claims on increasingly scarce resources may be jeopardised by the attitudes and prejudices of a male-dominated decision-making machinery within the planning system. Without adequate representation of women's interests on key decision-making bodies at all levels, it will be extremely difficult to achieve changes in the pattern of resource allocation that are commensurate with the urgent need to improve the employment and income status of women. The absence in Sierra Leone of concrete mechanisms and institutions within the administration (as do exist in a number of other African countries) for planning and co-ordinating action programmes for women—i.e. assessing their needs, securing and channelling public resources to women's activities—weighs heavily against the prospect of achieving desirable changes in the allocation of resources.

Another factor that might impinge on the ability of government to translate policy statements on women's employment into action programmes concerns the current unsatisfactory state of data and information pertaining to women's participation in the labour force. As mentioned earlier, the system for the collection and presentation of official statistics in Sierra Leone (intended for use by planners) has so far virtually failed to recognise women as a separate category in the labour force. As a consequence, there is hardly any baseline information on the basis of which policy-makers and planners can make decisions and formulate coherent policies and concrete programmes for improving the status of women in line with laudatory statements made in the *Outline*. This weakness is in fact recognised in the document itself:

> Planners need more detailed knowledge of the degree of women's access to and participation in certain critical elements of the development process. Consequently steps will be taken during the Plan period to collect information and analyse such factors as agricultural production resources and their control; employment and income generating activities; health and nutrition; women and rural development and access to policy-making and programming for rural services (ibid., Chapter 2, para. 2.67, p. 42)

While the steps outlined above for improving the data base constitute appropriate action for a better understanding of women's needs and problems by planners, they are not likely to have an immediate impact on project selection and implementation for the current plan period, given the time lag involved in the collection, processing and analysis of data. Indeed, since the Outline was prepared there is no evidence of official action in relation to the collection of information on the working and living conditions of women, in order to strengthen the data base for planning purposes.

Agriculture and Rural Development Policies

Women in Sierra Leone undoubtedly play an active part in rural production. They are primarily responsible for activities such as planting and harvesting on family rice farms and on their husbands' cash crop farms. They are also fully responsible for growing food crops for subsistence consumption throughout the year. In addition, rural women are actively engaged in food processing: basic items of the typical Sierra Leonean diet such as vegetable oils (palm oil, palm kernel oil and coconut oil), cassava products (foofoo and gari) and smoked fish are mainly produced by the female members of rural households. Other processing activities in which they are involved include tie-dyeing of cloth (gara) and soap-making. To supplement household money incomes further, rural women also participate in petty trading. Above all, they have to combine their role as producers with their domestic roles as housewives and mothers of large families as well as with certain communal obligations traditional to rural societies in Sierra Leone.[1] Table 11.2 summarises the division of labour by sex in rural Sierra Leone.

Although adequate data on the contribution made by women to the rural economy are not available, it is obvious from table 11.2 that a significant proportion of the gross national agricultural product of Sierra Leone is the result of women's work. Yet, as a distinct segment of the rural labour force separate from men, women have received minimal focus in rural development planning. The failure of planners to recognise fully the value of women's work has led to the failure to give adequate consideration to women's problems and needs in the formulation of government policies.

Table 11.2   Men's and women's work

Men	Women	Both
Cut, burn bush	Plant cassava and sweet	Scare birds
Hoe swamp for planting	potatoes*	Harvest rice
Hoe mounds for cassava and	Transplant rice seedlings	Build houses
sweet potatoes*	Weed upland farms	Make fish nets
Broadcast seed*	Harvest vegetables	Distil spirits
Hoe seeds into land*	Plant kitchen gardens	Market
Plant rice nurseries	Thresh rice	Make medicines
Fence farms	Parboil rice	
Set traps in fences	Hull rice	
Make farm shelters	Dry and preserve crops	
Cut palm fruits	Make dry season gardens	
Build boats	in swamp	
Fish at sea	Farm groundnuts*	
Tap palm wine	Collect wild food and	
Tailoring	medicine*	
Blacksmithing	Make vegetable oil	
	Care for young and old	
	Keep compounds clean	
	Make mats and baskets	
	Fish in rivers	
	Dry fish	
	Make salt	
	Cook	

* Other sexes may do this.
Source MacCormack (1982).

It is usually assumed by policy-makers and planners that men are the heads and breadwinners of rural households, and hence that any assistance or benefits directed to them or to the household as the basic production unit would automatically filter through to their womenfolk. This is not always the case, however. Women are *de facto* household heads where their husbands have deserted them, have migrated to urban and mining areas, or are sick and disabled. Furthermore, the idea of benefits trickling down to women is hardly supported by the evidence from rural Sierra Leone. In traditional rural societies, women are not regarded as co-owners of the family farm in their own right, but in a subordinate role as unpaid family workers making a contribution to the household economy. Moreover, this contribution is expected of them as part of their household duties as housewives. Most key decisions are taken by male household heads, and in this connection social and cultural factors interact to restrict severely any spreading to women of the benefits of rural development projects. One reason why extension work has so far had very little impact on agricultural production at the household level has been the failure of such programmes to address women as well as men.

Income-generating Activities of Rural Women

Farming

According to the latest population census figures, about 75 per cent of the economically active population of Sierra Leone live in the rural areas, where they are engaged predominantly in small-scale subsistence farming. Farming as an occupation is generally carried out on a smallholder basis, with the household as the basic unit of production. Within the household, women are the main source of (unpaid) family labour with respect to the production of both cash and food crops.

The cultivation of rice in Sierra Leone is based on two types of farming practices, namely swamp and upland rice cultivation. Swamp rice farming provides much the higher yields (Government of Sierra Leone, 1974; Spencer, 1974).[2] Swamp rice farming is much more labour-intensive, however (Spencer, 1976), and the rice is grown in pure stands, while upland rice is grown in a mixed cropping system which includes cultivation by women of crops such as millet, maize, cassava and sorghum during off-peak farming periods. Upland rice farming thus makes it possible for women to fulfil simultaneously their prescribed roles as unpaid family labourers in rice cultivation and as cultivators of other foods crops for both family consumption and marketing. Furthermore, in so far as the growing of other food crops is based on the use of idle patches of land on the family rice farm, upland farming saves women the additional burden of clearing virgin land for family food crop production.[3]

In the 1974/75–1978/79 National Development Plan, priority was given to integrated agricultural development as a strategy for rural development. In the first phase of the country's Integrated Agricultural Development Projects (IADP), inland valley swamp rice farming was promoted because of its higher yields even under conditions of low technology. Loans and subsidies provided under these projects have resulted in a switch from upland rice farming (which had been producing 64 per cent of all rice in the country) to swamp farming. Table 11.3 shows the variation of acreage under upland and swamp rice farming for participating and non-participating households in one IADP village.

While it is true that increased yields could lead to higher incomes for rural families, IADPs have had negative implications for women farm workers. First, women have to work increased hours planting and harvesting on the family farms and, second, they cannot combine rice production with other food crop production as they do with upland farming.

In Spencer's survey, it was observed that the workload of women from first year participating households was 4 per cent higher than that of women from non-participating households; the corresponding increase in women's workload in second

Table 11.3   Switch from upland to swamp rice farming in households in Beduma village

	Non-participants	First year participants	Second year participants
Upland rice	1.8	1.1	0.7
Swamp rice	0.3	2.5	3.0

Source Spencer (1976).

year participating households was even higher at 10 per cent. Although according to this survey men's total workload increased more than women's (93 per cent and 40 per cent respectively), it is to be observed that women's increased workload is in operations which are recurrent, while men's increased work is in land clearing and preparation, activities which will decrease considerably after the first few years of cultivation.

Another factor worth noting is that these IADPs are highly subsidised at this stage. A closer look at such projects (Spencer and Byerlee, 1977) revealed that when unsubsidised prices[4] are applied the computed returns to labour of improved rice cultivation will not be much higher than for upland cultivation. The gross margins per hour of family labour for unsubsidised costs were calculated to be Le 0.06 for upland farming,[5] Le 0.13 for traditional swamp farming, and Le 0.09 for improved swamp farming.

The results of the above study would therefore seem to suggest that improved swamp rice farming is unprofitable from the national standpoint; it might also be affecting women's work by increasing the amount of time they spend cultivating rice and so decreasing their production of other food crops.

Another government policy which has affected rural women's work has been in the area of mechanisation. Subsidised tractor hire schemes have been run by the government for a number of years, and the 1974–79 National Development Plan outlined government measures to 'encourage' the adoption by farmers of 'privately owned tractors suited to local conditions'. Tractorisation, while reducing the amount of labour needed for land preparation—a male task—has led to an increase in the labour required for planting and harvesting. Although it can be argued that mechanisation can be extended to these female operations too, it should be noted that mechanised weeding and harvesting would mean giving up intercropping, thus making it difficult for women to combine rice cultivation with other food crop production. Planting would also have to be done in rows, a difficult and time-consuming task for women who have not received the required training.

Food processing
Fish: Fish constitutes a major source of protein in Sierra Leone. It is estimated that 66 per cent of all animal protein consumed by the population comes from fish. Byerlee and King (1977) noted that expenditure on fish and fish products ranked second only to that on rice in total consumption expenditures for a sample of 250 rural households. Annual per capita fish consumption is estimated at 11 kilogrammes. Prior to 1974, over 70 per cent of the total fish landed in the country were attributed to small-scale fishermen using canoes (Government of Sierra Leone, 1974).

In the seaside villages of Sierra Leone fishing and fish processing are the main economic activities. In these villages, there is a definite sexual division of labour, with the men catching the fish and the women processing it (salting, sun-drying and smoking).[6] The processing and marketing of fish is the main source of income for many women in the seaside villages. It is, however, interesting to note that while some women obtain raw fish for processing from their kinsmen free of charge, for a majority of women their supply of fish has to be bought, even from their husbands.

The participation of women in the fishing industry has traditionally been linked to production by small-scale fishermen. Government policy, as it affects this sector of the industry, is therefore relevant to the livelihood of women engaged in the processing and marketing of fish.

During the Second World War when there was a severe shortage of fish in the country, the colonial government embarked on the promotion of trawler fishing. Naval ships were detached from military operations to operate trawls in order to relieve the shortage of fish in Freetown. Since then the emphasis of government policy has been on the promotion of large-scale fishing, often to the detriment of small-scale fishermen. According to current government policy, large-scale fishing enterprises enjoy significant tax concessions, paying only 10 per cent duty on trawl equipment, or importing trawls duty-free in the case of those companies that enjoy 'infant industry' development status. Import duties on nets, motors and other equipment utilised by small-scale fishermen, on the other hand, are levied at a rate of 36.5 per cent (Linsenmeyer, 1976). Certain large-scale fishing companies also enjoy tax holidays which give them exemption from company tax and duties on packaging materials or entitle them to reduced duties on equipment, fuel and lubricants.

Of the Le 7.5 million allocated to the fisheries sector in the 1974–79 National Development Plan, only 6.7 per cent was allocated to small-scale fisheries. The rest was earmarked for building a fleet of trawlers, for purse seiners, and for provision of port and handling facilities. The massive government support given to large-scale fishing is apparently linked to its potential as a foreign exchange earner. Yet, this has also had the effect of reducing domestic supply and increasing prices for local consumers. A more serious consequence has been the diversification of large-scale fishing industries into processing and even retailing, thereby depriving many coastal rural women of a source of livelihood. The economies of scale enjoyed by large-scale fishing makes it more competitive than small-scale fishing. But this, advantage is not passed on to women fish processors or to consumers in terms of lower prices, but is used instead to create a monopoly situation, or at least a cartel, in which the large companies can control supply and prices. Being progressively cut off from the processing part of their activities, women fish retailers, who now buy processed fish from large-scale concerns, are left with reduced profit margins. Furthermore, even in the area of retailing they are now facing increasing competition from large companies, who can afford to undercut their prices.

While it is acknowledged that the expansion of small-scale fishing is still a viable strategy for increasing fish production and providing a livelihood for coastal families,[7] official efforts to promote such development have been minimal. There is an acute shortage of trained fisheries extension workers at all levels. A Fisheries Loans and Credit Scheme, which was set up to assist small-scale fishermen, was abandoned after seven years due to default in repayment by borrowers (Government of Sierra Leone, 1974). Yet, cognisance was not taken of the fact that default was mainly due to the increasing unfair competition that small-scale fishermen were experiencing from the large fishing companies. Similarly, an engine repair scheme set up by the Government for the benefit of small-scale fishermen was terminated because of 'extreme difficulty in obtaining spare parts' (Government of Sierra Leone, 1974).

A recent survey of fishing villages in the Western Area revealed one important implication for women fish processors of the lack of support by government for small-scale fishing (Date-Bah et al., 1984). Rural fishermen are finding it increasingly difficult to buy equipment. In addition, trawlers plying very close to the coast damage the nets of small-scale fishermen, thus reducing their catches.

Women processors who depend on these catches are thus deprived of fish for processing.

As regards the alternative for rural women of purchasing their supply of fish for processing from large-scale firms, there are reasons in addition to those already mentioned why this is an unattractive proposition. First, since these large-scale fishing companies have their market outlet in the towns, it would involve women travelling to the towns to buy the fish, which would then have to be transported to the rural areas with obvious cost implications. Secondly, large companies tend to sell their stock in large quantities and most small-scale processors cannot afford to make such bulk purchases. Thirdly, the women do not usually have the contacts which are sometimes required for obtaining their supplies from large-scale companies, especially when demand exceeds supply.

The government policy of promoting large-scale fishing has thus had adverse effects on rural women. There is the threat that unless small-scale fishermen can be assisted, such women will lose their source of income to large-scale processing enterprises linked to large-scale fishing companies. The 1981 ILO survey of rural women in Sierra Leone revealed that in the four sample villages covered, about one-quarter of women fish processors were affected by lack of supply (Date-Bah et al., 1984).

Palm oil production: Palm oil constitutes a major food component for most of the population of Sierra Leone. The processing of palm oil is based mainly on the fruits of the wild palm rather than on the produce of cultivated palms grown in plantations. While traditionally it is the men who harvest the palm fruits in the forest, in most rural communities women play an active role in the processing of the fruit. Apart from their participation with men in the processing of palm oil, women are exclusively involved in the processing of the kernels. These are usually given to them by their menfolk as a reward for assisting in palm oil processing, and the processing of palm kernel oil is therefore an important source of income for the women.

Traditional methods of palm oil production are characterised by low extraction efficiency, and since the colonial period, the government has pursued a policy of mechanised, large-scale mill production in an attempt to increase oil production. Efforts at setting up large-scale oil plantations to supply mills have largely failed, however, and today the mechanised palm oil industry depends almost entirely on the exploitation of wild palm trees for its supply of fruits. As a consequence, traditional rural producers of palm oil have to compete with the palm oil industry for their supply of palm fruits (i.e. from the wild palm). In addition, since some farmers sell their palm fruits to the Produce Marketing Board,[8] the palm kernels (an important by-product of palm oil processing) are lost to the women, thus depriving them of a valuable source of income. The kernels recovered by the mills are now sold to a large palm kernel processing plant which produces oil and other products for export. In the rural survey conducted in Sierra Leone, 21 per cent of the female processors complained of the lack of palm kernels for their processing activities (Date-Bah et al., 1984).

Other non-farm rural activities

Many rural households (and husbands) depend on women members to provide supplementary incomes through such non-farm activities as handicrafts, tie-dyeing of cloth, and itinerant marketing of foodstuffs and basic consumer goods. According to a survey of three chiefdoms in the Moyamba District, Southern Province, it was found that the average monthly earnings of women from such activities were higher than those of their menfolk engaged in farming. Female household heads might sometimes have to rely on non-farm activities as their main source of income, because of certain restrictions on access to land, such as where inheritance is by custom patrilineal or where decisions on the acquisition and use of land are traditionally biased in favour of men. Within polygynous households, junior wives might also have to rely almost exclusively on cash incomes from non-farm activities to meet their personal and social obligations since they cannot expect to be adequately catered for from the household income pool.

The main problem facing rural women engaged in non-farm activities such as petty trading and itinerant marketing is lack of capital. In most cases such women have to depend on their husbands to provide the capital necessary to launch them into 'business'. But it should be pointed out that the provision of capital by husbands, while based on trust, is often regarded as an investment on which a return in terms of a share in profits or a substantial contribution to the running of the household is expected. Wives might, for example, be expected to meet the costs of school fees and uniforms from their trading activities, as well as purchasing household goods. A wife who fails to fulfil those expectations after being provided with capital by her husband could be regarded as a liability and lose favour with him.

Rural women also obtain capital for their businesses through their membership in thrift and credit co-operative societies. Such societies are generally unable to meet their members' demand for credit, however, because of their very limited financial resources. Most societies have to depend mainly on savings by their membership for their own capital, and these tend to be not forthcoming or insubstantial. A few women's co-operatives have benefited from loans provided by the government-sponsored National Co-operative Bank, but in spite of their very good repayment record the Bank has been unable to continue or expand its lending scheme due to lack of funds.

Although commercial banks have expanded their operations progressively into rural areas in recent years, women are still seriously disadvantaged in terms of access to credit from such banks. The main reason for this is the lack of security, stemming from the low income status of the majority of rural women as well as their subordinate role within the household. One might also suspect that the attitudes of bank managers, who are usually men, are an additional factor working against the interests of women in this regard. As a last resort women can turn to the traditional money-lenders operating in some rural areas, but most of them cannot afford the exorbitantly high interest rates—sometimes over 25 per cent—usually demanded.

Nor do rural women stand any chance of obtaining loans from the National Development Bank, which was set up by the government specifically to provide capital for small and medium-sized indigenous businesses. The Development Bank has set a minimum limit of Le 7,500 for loans to potential entrepreneurs with viable projects, and as the scale of operation of their businesses is nowhere near this minimum rural women are effectively excluded from consideration for loans. The Credit Guarantee Scheme operated by the central bank, the Bank of Sierra Leone, could ideally benefit small-scale businesses such as those operated by rural women. The problem of lack of security, however, coupled with dwindling resources at the disposal of the scheme, has made it virtually impossible for women to benefit from it.

In view of the difficulties encountered by rural women in obtaining credit for business purposes, the policy statement in the *Outline* of the 1981/82–1985/86 National Development Plan about making it easier for women to get access to credit facilities is most encouraging. How this policy will be given operational significance is not elaborated in the document, but it is obvious that it would require first and foremost measures by the government within its own financial institutions, such as the National Co-operative Bank, the National Development Bank, and the Sierra Leone Commercial Bank, to eliminate the restrictions on borrowing by individual women and their organisations. This would have a demonstration effect on private sector lending institutions, which could play an important part in supplementing the public sector resources available for credit schemes. Unless suitable credit schemes are made available to women, they will not realise their full potential as contributors to and beneficiaries of the process of rural development.

The Urban Sector and Modernisation Policies

Women in the urban sector have undoubtedly benefited more from the development process in Sierra Leone since Independence than their rural counterparts. This is not surprising in view of the urban bias in development planning which in Sierra Leone, as in many other African countries, has meant a concentration of resources and investments in urban centres to the disadvantage of rural areas, where about three-quarters of the population live and work. Imbalances between urban and rural areas in the provision of infrastructural facilities (roads, water supplies, etc.), social services (health, education, etc.) and commercial services have led to a relatively better quality of life for urban women. Similarly, the access to domestic labour-saving devices enjoyed by better-off urban women is still a distant dream for women in poor rural households.

As far as the participation of urban women in decision-making within the development process is concerned, the situation in Sierra Leone, as compared to many African countries, could be regarded as progressive in the sense that women have attained important positions in public life. Since Independence women have served as cabinet ministers, high court judges, head of the medical services, permanent secretaries and university professors, and today women are to be found in the professions and in the middle and higher levels of the civil service. In the rural areas, on the other hand, although women have been elected as paramount chiefs, the vast majority of women are still extremely disadvantaged vis-à-vis men in traditional societies where customs and social values condemn them to a subordinate position.

The advances made by women in urban Sierra Leone should not be taken to imply that they have equal opportunities with men, however, or that they are not discriminated against on the basis of sex. Firstly, the situation mentioned above is applicable to only a very small fraction of the urban female labour force. Furthermore, the process of modernisation, and some of the policies adopted by the government in pursuit of modernisation, have had a negative impact on women's employment status and well-being.[9]

Industrialisation has long been regarded by the government as a cornerstone of its development strategy, and special measures have been adopted to promote industrial development. One of the benefits of industrialisation frequently cited by the government is the creation of employment opportunities. Yet, because the process of industrialisation has largely involved the use of relatively capital-intensive technologies, the employment gains have so far been limited. Meanwhile, the spread of education has increased substantially the number of female entrants into the labour force seeking wage employment. Most of these have failed to secure jobs in industry, where there is a clear preference for male workers, even with respect to those activities which could be performed efficiently by women. The male bias in recruitment, and the fact that overall very few jobs are created annually in the industrial sector, have contrived to reduce substantially the employment opportunities open to women in the urban sector. At the same time, many young women with formal education who fail to find wage jobs in government, the commercial services or industry are somewhat reluctant to engage in self-employed activities in the informal sector because they consider it incompatible with their level of education. These factors may have contributed to the higher level of unemployment among women than men in the urban labour force, judging from the imbalances in numbers employed between men and women in wage employment as recorded in the census statistics.

The education system has, by and large, overlooked the special needs of women in terms of employment opportunities. While in principle there is no discrimination against girls with respect to access to formal education, girls have traditionally been expected to engage in certain low-paid occupations and household duties. Strongly held views about the types of jobs suitable for women in a sex-based stratified employment market have thus influenced investment in education by parents to favour boys where a choice has to be made for financial reasons. The education of young girls is also affected by teenage pregnancy, leading to a higher drop-out rate among girls. Young females with incomplete or inferior formal education cannot, therefore, compete with young men for the better paid jobs in the modern sector and tend to be employed in less skilled, lower level jobs in the civil service and the private sector (e.g. as filing clerks and shop assistants).

The recent shift of emphasis away from academic-oriented curricula towards vocational and technical training within the educational system has done little to eliminate the discrimination against girls. The types of training that are emphasised still reflect a strong bias towards vocations which are traditionally regarded as males preserves. In general, there is a bias in resource allocation in favour of training in fields such as motor vehicle repairing, carpentry, machine operating, etc. Vocational training for girls is usually perceived by policy-makers in terms of training in secretarial duties and home economics in preparation for their prescribed roles as the subordinates of men both at work and at home. The provision of equal training opportunities for young women in such fields as engineering, computer and data systems, management, etc., would make it easier for women to compete with men in a changing urban labour market. Improved access of females to education and training opportunities that are currently dominated by males would also help to remove traditional biases among male decision-makers about the capability of women to do certain types of work in the modern sector.

Many urban women for a variety of reasons are self-employed in the informal sector, largely as petty traders and sellers of cooked food. In this regard they play an important part in providing urban consumers with easier access to essential goods and services, both through their stalls being located conveniently near to offices and residential areas and through their long opening hours. Operating in the informal sector they also offer cheaper subsitutes and a wider variety of basic consumer goods than could otherwise be afforded by lower-income groups, and

Table 11.4   Distribution of female entrepreneurs in informal sector by main activity

Activity	No.	%
Food and tobacco	22	8.9
Textiles and manufacturing	3	1.2
Wearing apparel	12	4.9
Leather manufacturing	1	0.4
Footwear manufacturing	1	0.4
Furniture manufacturing	3	1.2
Metal product manufacturing	1	0.4
Retail trade	155	62.8
Repairing trade	1	0.4
Restaurants and cafés	43	17.4
Professional services*	5	2.0
Total	247	100.0

Note * Education, health, social services.
Source Fowler, (1978), Appendix, table 10.

they are more willing than the big stores to offer goods on credit or arrange payments by instalment for clients who cannot afford to buy on a ready cash basis.

An ILO-sponsored sample survey of the urban (Freetown) informal sector was undertaken in 1977, and the distribution of female entrepreneurs in the sector by main activity is shown in table 11.4.

The survey revealed that more than two-thirds of the female entrepreneurs interviewed were engaged in business primarily to supplement the earnings of husbands working in the wage sector, and were therefore expected to make a substantial contribution to the running of the home from their activities.

While, overall, government policy towards the informal sector has not been obstructive (as is the case in some other African countries, where the sector is officially discouraged), compared to modern sector businesses and modern industry the informal sector in Sierra Leone has not received much official support and encouragement for its development and expansion. The sector nevertheless has remained buoyant, even in the current difficult economic circumstances of the country, and continues to provide many urban women with a much needed source of income. Intervention by government to strengthen its linkages with the formal sector has taken the form of assistance mainly to those activities that are dominated by men—e.g. tailoring, metal work, repairing services, woodwork. Male entrepreneurs engaged in those activities have, for example, benefited from government contracts, and some have even obtained loans from government-sponsored financial institutions. No such assistance has been extended to women petty traders, food sellers or restaurateurs.

As far as access to credit is concerned, the informal sector as a whole is seriously affected by this. Because of the nature and the relatively small size of their businesses, however, women have fewer chances of obtaining credit even from those institutions that are willing to lend to the sector. They are effectively caught in a vacious circle, since lack of capital prevents them expanding their businesses, and as long as their businesses remain small they cannot obtain loans from the banking system. Desperate for credit but with no access to established credit institutions, some women traders turn to back-street money-lenders, who operate on the basis of extortionate rates of interest and tight repayment schedules. This has sometimes led to women having to sell their personal possessions to pay off debts, or even to the collapse of their businesses and the loss of their livelihood.

More recently, the severe shortage of foreign exchange in the country has had serious effects on some of the larger female-owned businesses which usually import their goods directly from abroad. The government policy of restricting import licences to a limited range of 'essential goods' (e.g. spare parts, oil, medical supplies), and allocating available foreign exchange only to certain formal sector businesses, has made it more difficult for women traders in the urban informal sector to obtain supplies to operate their businesses. As a consequence of this, many women's businesses have either become insolvent or substantially reduced in terms of the scale of their operations.

Household work

Women's household activities have not suffered directly as a result of government policies. Indirect effects can be observed or predicted, however. In addition, the absence of government policy and action on certain issues has consequences for women's work at home.

First, many of the implications of government policy discussed in the preceding sections are bound to affect women's household activities. In the rural areas, the increased time spent by women cultivating rice as a result of the introduction of the IADP scheme must leave them less time to fulfil their prescribed domestic and maternal roles in the home. Reduced incomes from their non-domestic activities and decreased production of subsistence food crops due to the impact of modernisation on rural societies would also adversely affect the ability of women to meet their family and communal obligations.

Secondly, the lack of government policy in certain areas has affected women's fulfilment in their domestic and maternal roles. The absence of a domestic energy policy in the country, for example, has meant that

1 rural women have to travel increasingly longer distances to fetch firewood, as nearby forests get depleted;
2 some rural women have to resort to purchasing firewood from their meagre earnings;
3 urban women have to pay higher prices for firewood as supplies become scarcer.

The absence of an energy policy may also have contributed to the neglect of research and development work on improved cooking methods and alternative sources of new and renewable energy aimed at conserving energy at the household level, which would have considerable benefits for women. The traditional three-stone method, which is used for cooking in the majority of Sierra Leone households, has a heat efficiency of less than 10 per cent. Improved wood stoves could therefore contribute significantly to energy conservation at the household level, as well as to a saving in the amount of time spent on cooking. Similarly, the inadequate provision of water supply schemes in rural areas has meant that women have to travel long distances, especially in the dry season, to fetch water, which is at some cost to their health as well as leaving them with less time for other household chores.

Conclusion and Policy Issues

This review of the impact of government policy on women's work in Sierra Leone has highlighted a number of important issues which should be addressed by policy-makers and planners in order to improve significantly the employment and overall socio-economic status of women throughout the country. Given that it is now the declared policy of the government 'to expand and integrate the role of women in development . . . [and] to improve their productivity through skill development' (Government of Sierra Leone, 1981, Chapter 2, para. 2.66, p. 42) it is appropriate by way of conclusion to explore feasible means for achieving this objective within a tolerable period. In attempting to do so, however, one should not lose sight of the socio-cultural factors underlying the production structure in the key economic sectors and their relationship with the development goals of the government. In addition, the importance of the attitudes and perceptions of decision-makers about the role of women in society and their contribution to the development process should be stressed in relation to the scope and possibilities for introducing desirable changes.

One issue that stands out from this review is the lack of data and information about women's working and living conditions in Sierra Leone. As already mentioned, in itself this is a major obstacle to effective planning for improvement in the status of women in both rural and urban areas. Without a better understanding by policy-makers and planners of women's problems and needs as producers, house-wives and mothers, it is difficult for them to

(1) modify concepts and perceptions as required for a fuller recognition of women's actual and potential contribution to national development;
(2) formulate appropriate policies for improving the status of women through equality of opportunities with men in society;
(3) plan and implement specific programmes and projects that focus on women as a target group; and
(4) monitor and evaluate on a continuing basis the impact of such programmes on the status and well-being of women.

The current dearth of data on women could be tackled, as recommended by the ILO and other UN agencies, by a reorganisation of the statistical system to allow for more meaningful disaggregation of occupational structures and employment status by sex. This would fill the existing gap concerning macro-level information on the female economically active population and changes in it over time, and, in addition, serve as a useful baseline for the periodic monitoring of factors such as employment status, earnings, consumption, expenditures, and nutritional status. Such information would help to reveal the existence and degree of sex-based discrimination regarding access to education and training opportunities, wage employment and other income-earning activities. Perhaps more importantly, it would contribute to a more realistic conceptualisation of work, employment and underemployment in relation to female participation in the labour force. At the micro-level, special surveys and socio-economic studies should be undertaken to shed light on the participation of women in the labour force in various non-formal sector economic activities, as well as their contribution to the household economy. Such studies would, for example, provide explanations for the higher concentration of women in low-paid jobs, wage differentials between male and female workers, higher drop-out rates among female pupils, higher incidence of broken careers among women, etc.

While it is necessary for planning purposes to identify women as a separate and distinct population group, there is, however, a danger that the identification of women as a 'disadvantaged' group for special action could be misconstrued by policy-makers as an indication of women's inability to undertake certain types of economic activity or of their inferior status vis-à-vis men, when in fact the problem is one of sex discrimination. This sort of thinking has sometimes given rise to the grouping of women for planning purposes with disadvantaged groups in society such as the physically and mentally handicapped, the aged, or even criminals and other delinquents. With the emphasis of government policy on the participation and full integration of women into the development process, policy-makers and planners should first of all focus attention on the nature and feasibility of institutional changes that would enable women, who make up over half the total population, to have a greater say in the formulation and implementation of specific government policies and programmes that affect their well-being. The adequate representation of women on decision-making bodies at all levels would help to ensure that their problems and needs were in the first instance correctly perceived and identified, and that the types of special programmes directed at them as a target group were relevant to their felt needs.

The existence of a special Women's Bureau within the government administrative structure could help to bring women's problems and needs into sharper focus in the planning process. Such a mechanism, however, would operate effectively only if it had at its disposal adequate information to support its claims on developmental resources against other competing interests as well as the necessary authority to influence public sector decision-making. The functions of a Women's Bureau in the administrative structure should thus transcend those of an advisory body on government policy pertaining to women to include control over resources and the planning, implementation and monitoring of women's projects. Apart from being the focal point for women's activities in the administrative structure, the Bureau should have direct links with women's groups and organisations at the local level, as well as with external agencies and non-governmental organisations (NGOs) concerned with the promotion of women's well-being in the country. Over time, the Bureau should envisage the establishment of district-level offices as a means of facilitating its promotional and development activities at the local level.

With specific reference to the situation of women in rural areas, it is important that for planning purposes they should be viewed in the total context of rural development, rather than in relation to those activities with which they are traditionally associated. Given that the government has adopted an integrated approach to rural development, the formulation of programmes and projects must take account of the potential of female human resources in relation to the entire range of economic activities in the sector—e.g. food and cash crop production, processing activities, rural industrialisation, marketing, etc. Women should be recognised as an important segment of the rural labour force in terms of their actual contribution to rural production and household livelihood. The recognition by policy-makers and planners of the vital role women play in rural production could in itself help to break down the cultural and societal barriers underlying the existing discrimination against women with respect to the distribution of benefits from the development process, as well as changing the way in which their menfolk see women only in terms of their traditionally prescribed roles.

While taking steps to increase the participation of rural women in the development process and their share in the benefits therefrom, policy-makers and planners should not overlook the domestic role of women. In this connection, women should be regarded as a target group to benefit from special programmes aimed at reducing their work burden. In the rural areas, the reduction of women's work burden on the farm would leave them with more disposable time, perhaps to undertake more creative activities or join adult literacy classes. Research and development activities by government institutions in the field of technology should be aimed particularly at the introduction of tools and equipment that would lighten the burden of women's work both on the farm and at home. The provision of certain services and facilities already enjoyed by urban women but virtually absent in rural societies could also make a significant difference to the burden of rural women's work at home. As has already been seen, rural women would benefit greatly from the provision of conveniently located water supplies, while the expansion of family welfare programmes and maternal and child health care facilities in rural areas would improve their health and nutritional status and make them better able to cope with necessary domestic work.

The main issue to be tackled in urban areas concerns the disadvantaged situation of women in the employment market vis-à-vis men. To the extent that the problem is due to differentials in educational attainment between men and women, a solution could be sought through measures designed to facilitate the access of women to education and training opportunities in fields currently dominated by men. This would have the effect of increasing the employment chances of women, especially with respect to better paid jobs.

This is not, however, the only, or even the main, factor underlying the higher unemployment rate among women and the higher concentration of women in low-paid jobs. Male attitudes concerning the prescribed roles of women play an important part in the decisions made by fathers and teachers about the type of education to be pursued by a girl, which in turn determines her place and opportunities in the urban labour force. Prejudices on the part of (male) employers about the productivity and capability of female workers similarly reduce their chances of getting better paid jobs. In view of the socio-cultural forces working against women in the urban labour market, government policy with respect to training for certain occupations should be deliberately biased to favour women until such time as the sex balance is redressed. Women should also be given more opportunities to continue educational and working careers which have been interrupted by pregnancy, such as through the provision of subsidised crèches and day-care centres for infants.

The problems of women in the urban informal sector, as already outlined, suggest that one of the critical issues concerns the adoption of policy measures to support and protect the interests of female entrepreneurs in the sector. The government should have a vested interest in this since the sector acts effectively as a bulwark against female (and male) unemployment at a time when job opportunities in the modern sector are shrinking rapidly. The main constraining factor operating against the interests of women petty traders in the sector is lack of access to credit for trade purposes. Government-sponsored financial institutions should be encouraged to give loans to women traders with the potential to succeed in business even when they cannot provide the usual collateral. Such a move would also have the effect of enhancing the status and prestige of self-employment in the urban informal sector, thus making it a more viable alternative to wage employment. Greater offical recognition and support for the informal sector would help to diminish the reluctance among unemployed female school-leavers to seek a livelihood in the sector.

Finally, an important conclusion from this study concerns the general contribution of women's work to national development. Because of the particular way the labour force is conceptualised and defined, there has not been a full appreciation and recognition of this contribution among policy-makers, and there has been a tendency to perceive it in terms of certain prescribed roles and weaknesses vis-à-vis men. This in turn has contributed to the disparate treatment of even those women who are productive in the labour force, such as smallholder farmers and retail traders, who are nevertheless routinely grouped with disabled and older workers in terms of productivity and contribution to national output. Women are also subjected to wage discrimination, which is often linked to occupational segregation and distorted segmentation of the labour market. Even in their prescribed subordinate roles vis-à-vis men, women contribute much more to national output than they are usually given credit for. The important role of rural women in agricultural production—as the primary source of labour—is thus largely unnoticed and unrecognised by planners and policy-makers concerned with rural development programmes as is reflected in the general exclusion of women as a target group from any active participation or share in the benefits of so many rural development projects.

Whether or not the active part played by women in the development process in Sierra Leone is fully recognised for planning purposes will depend mainly on how policy-makers perceive the characteristics of women in the total labour force. This will have considerable implications for the formulation of appropriate policies and the design and implementation of development programmes and projects that address the special problems and needs of women. The issues highlighted in this concluding section; though certainly not exhaustive in terms of solutions to women's problems in Sierra Leone, deserve special attention by policy-makers and planners if the status of women is to be improved in accordance with recently declared government policy.

Notes

1   For example, most women in rural Sierra Leone are members of the 'Bondo', a female secret society.
2   Estimated yields for swamp rice are 2,829 kilogrammes per acre as compared to 1,330 kilogrammes per acre for upland rice.
3   Clearing of land has been a major problem for female farmers.
4   Current subsidy level is estimated at 67 per cent for fertilisers.
5   This figure does not take into account other food crops grown simultaneously in rice farms by women, although the time spent in farming does include time spent in the cultivation of such crops.
6   Linsenmeyer (1976) estimated that over 76 per cent of all labour involved in rural fish processing was female.

7 Production costs of small-scale fishing are much lower than those for large-scale fishing (Linsenmeyer, 1976).
8 Under the IADP farmers receiving loans for oil palm development are required to market their palm fruits to mills acceptable to the Project.
9 Even in the rural areas, modernisation has tended to diminish female employment opportunities in agriculture and traditional small-scale production as revealed by one empirical study in the region (William Steel, 'Female and small-scale employment under modernisation in Ghana', in *Economic Development and Cultural Change*, Vol. 30, No. 1 (October, 1981), pp. 153–167.

12   *Eleanor R. Fapohunda*

Urban Women's Roles and Nigerian Government Development Strategies

In the guidelines of its development plan, the former Nigerian Government emphasised for the first time that development fundamentally entails the growth of human potential and initiative rather than the increased production of material things (Federal Republic of Nigeria, *Guidelines for the Fourth National Development Plan, 1981–85,* 1981, pp. 20–21). To develop initiative, the government stressed that development planning should be broadly based, that wide segments of the community should be involved in plan conceptualisation and implementation and in the imaginative solution of organisational problems. Moreover, the direction and approach of its development strategy should not be determined by foreign ideas but grounded in indigenous aspirations and institutions.

The purpose of this chapter is to consider the evolution and appropriateness of the government policies enunciated in that plan in the light of the realities of household organisation and women's economic activities, as well as in terms of its stated goals of maximising the growth of human potential. Although the plan is now of little more than historical value, it does nevertheless serve our present goal in that it highlights a number of potential pitfalls to be avoided by future planners.

The analysis will focus on plans and policies in four areas:

(a) employment generation and vocational training,
(b) child-care policies,
(c) taxation, and
(d) housing and land ownership policies.

The first two policy areas concern the availability and feasibility of women's income generating activities. The second two deal with women's control and use of financial resources generated from these activities.

In order to compare perceptions of sex roles as evidenced by government pronouncements with the role expectations and activities documented by social scientists, two modes of conceptualising the familial roles of men and women are used here. The first concerns the relative jointness or segregation of the conjugal role relationship—the extent to which husbands and wives share their family tasks and responsibilities. The second concerns the extent to which individuals share their familial rights, duties and activities with kin, thus estimating the extent to which individuals act alone in domestic and parental roles (Oppong, 1982b).

These two concepts and appropriate indicators are used in conjunction with analyses of survey evidence from Lagos, Nigeria's main metropolitan centre,[1] to categorise role expectations and practices with regard to four domestic activities: management of financial resources; financial provision for household needs; child-rearing, and domestic chores. This analysis will provide the background for the subsequent evaluation of specific government policies in the areas indicated above.

Sex Roles and Household Structure in Lagos

The results of a sample survey of 1,600 Lagos women conducted in 1973 (Lucas, 1976) suggest that the majority of women in Lagos are workers with family financial responsibilities. According to this survey, the labour force participation rate was about 60 per cent among married women aged 15–39 years. Participation rates were above average (70 per cent) among wives in polygynous marriages who constituted 21 per cent of the sample (ibid., pp. 183, 177, 182). It is important to point out that many Lagos women are either *de jure* or *de facto* heads of household. Over 9 per cent of the married women in the 1973 Lagos sample survey were living apart from their husbands, and this proportion becomes significantly larger when considering only wives in polygynous marriages (ibid., p. 178).

Even when spouses live together, working women assume a considerable responsibility for expenditure on food and children. In a 1975 survey of 824 working mothers (Fapohunda and Fapohunda, 1976, p. 123); 19 per cent claimed they paid for more than half the family food, while over 34 per cent said that they paid for more than half of their children's clothes. Less than 50 per cent of the husbands were totally responsible for items such as food, children's clothes and medical expenses. On the other hand, over 80 per cent of the women did not contribute anything towards house rent or the purchase of household consumer durables such as furniture, television or radio, and refrigerator.

The financial commitments of working women are not limited to the needs of their conjugal families, but extend also to their kin. Indeed, each spouse will have separate and distinct financial responsibilities to kin. Fifty per cent of the Lagos working mothers sampled in 1975, for example, sent gifts of money to their parents and about 27 per cent sent gifts to other relatives (ibid., p. 50). About 15 per cent of these women also helped pay the school fees of younger relatives. The average amount given to relatives was N168 a year, which is a sizeable amount considering that their average monthly income was N97. Asked why they helped their relatives, 598 simply said that it was customary, and only 123 considered specific future reciprocal benefits (ibid., p. 127).

Management of financial resources

Within conjugal families spouses manage their personal financial resources separately. They do not pool their incomes or have joint bank accounts and they rarely jointly hold assets such as land or houses. A study of spouses of workers at various levels at the University of Lagos (Karanja-Diejemaoh, 1978) found practically no pooling of income. The women generally wanted to maintain separate funds because of potential polygyny and inheritance procedures. In a 1980 study of 226 households[2] in three different socio-economic neighbourhoods of Lagos, 240 wives were asked whether they owned farmland or houses with their husbands or their kin. Only two wives claimed that they owned farmland jointly with their husbands, while 44 claimed that they jointly owned such property with their kin. Moreover, 70 wives owned houses jointly with their kin, while only 18 claimed joint ownership with spouses.

Domestic chores and child-rearing activities are primarily the separate responsibility of wives. Indeed, 23 per cent of the Lagos working mothers interviewed in 1975 claimed that their husbands did nothing in the home (Fapohunda and Fapohunda, 1976, p. 123). About half went shopping but very few did anything else.

Relatives do help, however: 45 per cent of the working mothers claimed that relatives helped them in housework and child-rearing. The child of a Lagos couple may even live with kin outside the city as was the case for 6 per cent of the working mothers (ibid., p. 24). Relatives living with couples in Lagos also play a significant part in child-care. In fact, 41 per cent of working mothers reported that the relatives living with them cared for their youngest child while they worked.

In Lagos homes, the division of labour with regard to domestic activities can thus be described as follows:

(a) management of financial resources—separate from spouse and often together with kin
(b) financial provision for household needs—jointly with spouse and little or no help from kin
(c) domestic chores—wife without husband but with help from kin
(d) child-rearing—wife without husband but with help from kin.

Government Policies and Programmes

We have noted the high level of economic activity among Lagos women and indicated that for many their earnings are important for their own and their families' well-being. In a real sense, the welfare of innumerable Lagos children is directly connected with their mothers' ability to earn an independent income. In the past, however, Nigerian policy-makers have not sufficiently considered women as an important segment of the labour force. In the past the Nigerian government, in drawing up its manpower programmes, has not regarded women as a distinct category of human resource separate from men, thereby not fully recognising the realities of family support systems in Nigeria. Projects especially designed for women have thus been oriented towards social welfare rather than economic development. In the National Development Plans, the only specific references to women have occurred in the sections on social welfare. Women have been included along with children, beggars, destitutes and the handicapped.

The employment situation for women in Lagos is similar to that in other urban areas of Nigeria. Most women are self-employed sales or service workers in the traditional sector. Although the number employed in the modern sector has been increasing, women are still a small minority. Women constituted 15.1 per cent of public employees and 10.4 per cent in the private sector according to a labour force sample survey conducted in urban areas in 1974 (Federal Republic of Nigeria, 1979, p. 21). At the same time, 56 per cent of working urban women were sales workers (ibid., p. 79). Within the modern sector, a disproportionate number of women are employed in a limited number of occupations. Among senior and intermediate level occupations in 1977, women were 36 per cent of librarians and archivists; 37 per cent of confidential secretaries and stenographers; 84 per cent of dieticians and nutritionists; 80 per cent of nurses; and 53 per cent of pharmaceutical assistants (Federal Republic of Nigeria, 1980, pp. 23–26).

In the modern sector, significant labour shortages occur in certain high wage, scientific and technical positions at both senior and intermediate levels. In 1977, there were 40–50 per cent vacancies for architects, surveyors, engineers, medical doctors, and engineering technicians (Federal Republic of Nigeria, *Guideline of the Fourth National Development Plan*, p. 89). Historically these occupations have had few female practitioners. In 1977, for example, only 5 per cent of architects were women, only 4 per cent of surveyors and only 3.28 per cent of civil engineering technicians (Federal Republic of Nigeria, 1980, pp. 23–26).

Although historically the number of females going to secondary school and university has been increasing, there seems to have been no substantial change in the percentage of women trained in the scientific and technical professions. In 1970, for example, only 12.6 per cent of University of Lagos graduates were women, as compared with 19.3 per cent in 1980.[3] Yet the percentage of women who graduated in science and medicine actually declined between 1975 and 1980. No woman graduated in engineering or environmental design in those years.

As a result of recent rapid expansion of the school system and the limited growth of the modern sector,[4] there will be, during the next decade, increased competition for junior and intermediate clerical jobs in the modern sector. At the same time, there will be significant shortages of intermediate and low level categories of technical manpower (various types of technician, artisan and craftsman), agricultural manpower, teaching personnel, etc. (ibid., p. 60). Many of the skills which will be most marketable are in areas which popularly have not been considered appropriate for women and/or which historically have not been of much interest to them.

To direct individuals into these areas of shortage, the former Federal Government proposed 'to promote career guidance in schools through the compilation and dissemination of information on the choice of career and labour market trends' (Federal Republic of Nigeria, *Guidelines for the Fourth National Development Plan 1981–85*, 1981, p. 63).

Both the Federal Government and Lagos State Government planned increased vocational counselling for primary and post-primary students; yet neither took into account the fact that a substantial proportion of these students would be women or considered whether the counsellors would encourage these women to prepare for existing women's jobs or encourage them to think about good economic opportunities beyond traditional expectations. In 1977, for example, women were only 1.54 per cent of refrigeration-air conditioner technicians and 0.27 per cent of plumbers (Federal Republic of Nigeria, 1980, pp. 23–26). The counsellors probably should have undergone special training designed to reinforce the idea that women should have equal opportunities in training as well as to break down their own individual prejudices concerning the unsuitability of certain jobs for women.

Thus, although the *Guidelines for the Fourth National Development Plan 1981–85*, 1981, p. 86), stated that because of 'the size of the female population in the total population and the potential role of women in national development,

Government will promote a more active involvement of women of child-bearing age (15–49) in social and economic affairs', the actual content of the plan showed little recognition of the importance of women's income-generating activities both for national development and for family welfare.

Child-care policies
In the case of Lagos women, mothering/domestic roles and occupational roles are so intimately related that government policies that affect one set of activities affect the other. As seen earlier, child-rearing and domestic chores continue to be the primary responsibility of wives. With rising levels of education, more Lagos women are engaged in wage employment which has fixed working hours and requires them to spend significant amounts of time away from home. In the past, female relatives, particularly grandmothers, helped share child-rearing responsibilities, while mothers engaged in income-generating activities. But aged mothers are unwilling to come to or remain in Lagos for long periods to take care of their grandchildren as housing space is cramped and urban life seems to them strange and isolated. In addition, the children of poorer rural relatives used sometimes to be sent to live in the homes of their Lagos kin, where they helped with the care of the relatives' children, while often receiving some educational or vocational training. With the expansion of free or relatively inexpensive educational facilities by the government, however, rural children no longer need to come to the city for schooling.

Thus while the demand for paid domestic help is growing, the actual supply of such indigenous labour may be contracting due to expanding educational opportunities. Because of the relatively high wages paid to domestics, Nigerian housemaids were formerly being replaced by young, often illegal migrants from nearby West African countries, but this practice has been stopped since 1983.[5] Working Lagos mothers are therefore turning increasingly to commercial institutions outside their homes to take care of their pre-school children from the age of six months. These businesses, proliferating rapidly, vary widely in physical facilities, personnel and cost. For about N30 per month, a child can go to a modern, well-equipped day-care/nursery school designed to nurture intellectual and physical development. For about N10 per month the child can go to a small room with mats where he will be watched by an untrained 'child minder'. It is not surprising, therefore, that the child-care arrangements of a working mother vary with her education and occupation.[6]

The implications of the growing child-care problems in Lagos, as in other urban areas, are widespread. Problems associated with the availability and cost of child-care, given the sexual division of domestic labour, and the unequal burdens shouldered by working women in terms of housework and child-care, are bound to affect the types of employment in which women can effectively participate. Family relations and marital stability are also adversely affected when mothers are burdened with conflicts between their occupational and child-care responsibilities. In addition, children who lack appropriate and consistent supervision are exposed to physical injuries and prone to undesirable behaviour.

Significantly the *Guidelines for the Fourth Development Plan, 1981–85* (1981) stated:

> Government in collaboration with the National Council of Women's Societies and related bodies will explore ways and means of putting on a sound basis the establishment

of Baby Day Care Centres at strategic points. We can no longer pretend not to appreciate the changing role of women, particularly in our urban centres and the impact of this phenomenon on the upbringing of our children (Federal Republic of Nigeria, p. 88).

Although the Government recognised the growing child-care problem it saw its role as 'largely promotional and regulatory' (ibid., p. 88).

In contrast, the National Council of Women's Societies advocated that the Federal Government should provide a universal programme of day-care/nursery centres for pre-school children (Starrett, 1981, p. 16). The Council has argued that when the majority of mothers are illiterate or poorly educated the mental and physical development of their children may be disadvantaged. The position of the council raises a further fundamental issue. Can there be equality of educational opportunity, an avowed government policy objective, if there are differential pre-school learning environments? The Implementation Committee for the National Policy on Education (Federal Government of Nigeria, 1978, p. 10) suggested that individuals, private voluntary organisations, employers of labour, and communities could establish pre-primary schools. Furthermore, the Committee commented that 'large employers of labour should see it as a social responsibility to establish pre-primary schools for the benefit of their workers' families' and recommended that 'this should be an obligation enforceable by law' (ibid., p. 10).

Although the Federal Government of the day did not act on this latter suggestion, it provides a significant example of disunified policy thinking. The committee did not consider whether such a recommendation would have an unfavourable impact on women's employment by causing differential labour costs by sex, nor whether employees would have the means to pay for such a programme if the employer passed the costs on to them.[7] Nor was there any consideration as to whether the general public should assume some of the confidential burdens of such a programme by allowing employers to deduct expenditure on day-care from their income tax as a business expense.

As yet, neither the Federal Government nor Lagos State has a cohesive and well-articulated child-care policy which outlines the scope and direction of government action in a society in which few women see that they have an option not to engage in income-generating activities. The development of such a policy may first require a strengthening of women's collective voice and the development of sympathetic government policy agencies.

Taxation policies

In a development context, government policy planners do not perceive a taxation system as being merely the machinery for government revenue collection. Rather, the tax system is seen as an effective instrument for encouraging investments, through incentives and rebates, in various income-generating activities, thereby hastening the desired economic transformation. In addition, the tax system can result in a more equal distribution of wealth and income both among individuals and among socio-economic groups. In designing policies which would encourage a redistribution for equity purposes, tax designers need to consider adequately not only the forms of income generation and wealth-holding, but also the structure of families in relation to these.[8]

Since 1975, Nigerian income tax management has been unified throughout the

Federation and is based on the British progressive tax system. Colonial administrators brought basic British taxation principles to the colony and incorporated them in such legislation as the Income Tax Ordinance of 1940.[9] Under this system, a progressive tax schedule is applied to all chargeable income, which is defined as total assessable income minus tax reliefs. The basic tax reliefs in 1980–81 included the following:

(a) personal allowance;
(b) wife's allowance: a man who is married either legally or by native law and custom is entitled to an additional relief of N300 for one wife;
(c) child allowance: this is an allowance for each child under 16 years or receiving full-time education in a recognised educational establishment or articled or indentured in a trade or profession. A man can claim an allowance for a maximum of four children. A widow can claim for children borne by her for her late husband;
(d) dependent relative allowance: a husband or wife who has a taxable income can claim a N400 allowance for a dependent relative, if the relative's income is less than N600.

It should be noted that a husband can claim a wife's allowance even if his wife is gainfully employed and a separate tax payer. Moreover, a woman who is married, but not a widow, can only claim child allowance with her husband's written consent. An unmarried mother is not entitled to any child allowance (Akande, 1986, p. 73).

Behind this system of tax relief is the implicit idea that the husband is the principal if not sole income earner who is separately responsible for the financial needs of his wife and children. Only in the case of a husband's death does the widow assume financial responsibility for the children. There is no recognition that in southern Nigerian families substantial numbers of married women are financially independent and jointly responsible for their families' financial maintenance, nor that women may sometimes be heads of households because of illness, migration, separation, or the functioning of a polygynous marriage in an urban context. The present tax relief system, far from promoting equity, is thus actually contributing to income inequalities by sex. This is especially significant as spouses maintain separate financial management of their resources.

In the past the effects of the tax relief system on individual income distribution by marital status and sex have been limited, as most women engaged in self-employed work in the traditional sector had low incomes and were not easily taxed. But these effects will become more substantial as more women are educated and take up wage employment. In addition, the Lagos State Government, faced with the problem of declining federal revenue allocations, is trying to reduce the incidence of tax evasion by requiring a three-year tax clearance certificate to be produced in all transactions with ministries, parastatals and local government in the state. The production of tax clearance certificates is now required for the issuance of various licences as well as for the acquisition, sale or transfer of property. As a result, increasing numbers of self-employed women will be forced to pay taxes, but will not be eligible for the same tax reliefs as men.

Under the Nigerian tax system, another important consideration is the deductions from assessable income. Deductions are 'all outgoings and expenses or any part thereof wholly and exclusively incurred by an individual during the period in the production of the income' (Ashaye, 1981, p. 25). In determining the tax liability of an individual who owns and rents out a residential property, for example, the yearly mortgage interest payments would be deducted from the gross rent. Under existing tax law, however, individuals are not permitted to deduct domestic or private expenses (ibid., p. 25). Working mothers who are primarily responsible for the care of children cannot therefore deduct expenses arising from the need to employ someone to look after their children while they engage in income-generating activities.

Until recently this was not a significant problem as many women, because of the nature of their work, could supervise their children while engaging in income-generating activities. In other situations relatives, often aged mothers or adolescents, helped take care of children. A tax-liable working mother could then claim a dependent relative allowance for these individuals. Such tax treatment was thus in harmony with the structure of family organisation. With economic development, however, an increasing number of Lagos working mothers are forced to seek paid institutional child-care. Under present tax laws such expenses are not deductible as expenses related to income-generating activities, nor are they covered by traditional tax reliefs, such as for dependent relatives. The present tax system is therefore deficient as an instrument for encouraging economic development with equity, since its application leads to differential tax payments by sex. This failure is linked to an incorrect concept of indigenous family organisation, which does not recognise the financial obligations of women. As more women have taxable wage incomes and as family organisation is changing, the existing tax legislation is thus becoming increasingly unfair to working mothers.

Another important issue is landowning and housing policies. In Nigeria, particularly in urban areas, land and residential home ownership are the principal forms of investment for an individual, apart from business activities (Umoh, 1979, p. 175). At Nigeria's stage of development the capital market, although growing, is still relatively small in size, and participation is limited to a small section of the population. In addition, the rapid population growth rate of urban areas such as Lagos, due to rural–urban migration, constantly increases the demand for land and housing units, forcing market prices continuously upward and thereby increasing the rate of return on such investments.

In southern Nigeria, land ownership was not traditionally vested in an individual but rather in the kinship group (Jegede, 1981, p. 8). Individual members of the family had the right to use the land for agricultural and housing purposes and were entitled to ownership of any improvements on the land as well as to the fruits of their agricultural pursuits. The use of the land could be inherited within the descent group, but the land itself could not be sold to strangers as it was to provide for the well-being of present and future generations of descendants. As the commercial value of land gradually increased, however, especially in urban areas, such land began to be sold to non-family members. Although the Lagos State Government registered the sale of land, protracted litigation often arose concerning which family actually owned the land or whether the elders of the family had acted in good faith in selling the land.

To deal with the problems of insecure land title and poorly planned developments, the Lagos State Government began to lease land in planned low or medium density reserves to individuals for housing purposes as well as directly building houses. These state government programmes offered new, relatively secure investment opportunities for women, especially middle and upper class women.

Traditionally, however, it was not expected that a married women cohabiting with her spouse would acquire individually owned residential property except by inheritance from her lineage (Akande, 1986, p. 49). Under customary laws, wives were not regarded as members of their husband's lineage and could not therefore inherit his property. Under more modern interpretations of customary law, a married women can acquire houses by purchase, but she must prove conclusively that no consideration, either directly or indirectly was furnished by her husband if she wishes to claim it as her exclusive property.

In reaction to the apparent corruption involved in the allocation of state lands, a new Lagos State Military Government announced in October 1975 that one family could lease only one plot of land in Victoria Island and South West Ikoyi: 'Husband and wife are treated as one person and will not be allowed to hold more than one plot at Victoria Island' *(Daily Times*, 8 October 1975, p. 1). The new government, in the British legal tradition, viewed the spouses as one legal person and implicitly assumed joint family financial management. But, as shown earlier, husbands and wives do not usually pool their money nor do they jointly invest it. Moreover, there may be more than one wife, either in the present or in the future.

Under public pressure, the Lagos State Military Government was forced to reverse its land policy in less than a month. On 28 October 1975, it announced that leasing restrictions in other government reservations would apply to individuals rather than families *(Daily Times*, 28 October 1975, p. 1). However, the military government did not return the plots seized in carrying out the previous policy. In the case of leasing by both spouses it was the wife's plot that had been seized. The implications of the policy reversal became wider as all urban lands were vested in the State Governors by the Federal Land Decree of 1978. Significantly, with the return of civilian rule in 1979, the elected Lagos State Governor reaffirmed that a wife would be treated as a separate legal entity for land allocation purposes ('Address at the opening of the EKO court building', 28 July 1980, in *365 days of LKJ speeches of the New Order*). Current Lagos State policy thus gives both sexes equal opportunities for land ownership and is in harmony with practices of separate financial management by spouses.

Conclusion

This chapter has been concerned with the extent to which government has in the past predicated policies and plans on a realistic conception of domestic roles. With respect to employment and vocational training policies as well as child-care policies, it was suggested that government in the past has not adequately considered the roles of women and the structure of families before planning and initiating policies. Concerning taxation and land ownership, certain programmes instituted by government were seen to be based on a foreign conception of family organisation that deviated considerably from Nigerian reality.

The discussion of the above four cases suggests that if government on all levels is to be concerned with the optimum actualisation of human resources, and with economic development accompanied by a more equal distribution of wealth, the implications of sex roles and domestic organisation need to be reckoned with before policies and programmes can be designed and implemented.

In the past, planners and policy-makers have been mainly male. A greater participation by women in policy formulation in the future might help to raise awareness of the repercussions of policies for women and their roles. If government wants to design policies and programmes which encourage women to play an important part in the development process, both as workers of the highest calibre and as investors, it must base its policies on the realities of women's roles in the family and in the labour force.

Notes

1   Lagos is the main financial, industrial and currently administrative centre of the country. It is, also, the most important urban centre in Lagos State.
2   Research project of author.
3   Information obtained from the Planning Unit of the Vice-Chancellor's Office, University of Lagos.
4   As a result of the Universal Primary Education Scheme started in 1976 by the Federal Military Government, primary school enrolment doubled between 1975–76 and 1979–80 (Federal Republic of Nigeria, *Fourth National Development Plan, 1981–85*, p. 225). Between 1975 and 1981 secondary school enrolment more than trebled, rising from 704,917 to 2,226,124. In the Fourth National Plan, 1981–85, it is estimated that wage employment will grow at 5 per cent per annum (ibid., p. 424). But, as the plan document points out, 'this is definitely small in view of the high demand for wage jobs which is expected to be higher in the future because of the rapid expansion of our educational system and the usual preference of school leavers for wage employment' (ibid., p. 424).
5   In 1983, the Federal Government announced that all illegal migrants from nearby West Africa countries must leave the country by a specified date or face prosecution.
6   Bamisaiye and Oyediran (1981), interviewing female staff at the Lagos University Teaching Hospital/College of Medicine, found that 64 per cent of the senior staff women sent their pre-school children who resided in Lagos to day-care/nursery schools. The corresponding percentages for intermediate staff and junior staff were 28 per cent and 8 per cent respectively. In contrast, 22 per cent of the children of the lowest paid women were sent to 'baby minders' and only 5 per cent of the intermediate women's children. One quarter of the pre-school children of junior staff women lived outside Lagos (probably with relatives), while the number of intermediate or senior staff children who lived outside Lagos was extremely small.
7   A. Bamisaiye and M.A. Oyediran (1981, p. 13) point out that the lower paid female staff who form the majority of women employed at the University of Lagos Teaching Hospital and College of Medicine could only benefit from a crèche/day nursery at the hospital premises if it were heavily subsidised.
8   Susan Greenhalgh (1982), for example, suggests that government's perception of the extent of income inequality may be affected by whether information is collected by the standard recipient unit, the household, or by the ethnographic income unit, the extended family.
9   For a brief history of the Nigeria taxation system, see S.A. Rabin (1981).

13 *Florence Abena Dolphyne*

The Ghana National Council on Women and Development
An Example of Concerted Action

Following the celebration of the International Women's Year in 1975, and its focus on the need to integrate women into national development at all levels, the Government of Ghana demonstrated its commitment to the objectives of the International Women's Year by setting up the National Council on Women and Development (NCWD) as the national machinery to advise government on all issues affecting the full participation of women in national development, and to initiate programmes to ensure that the objectives of the International Women's Year are achieved in Ghana.

In order to reach women as a special target group, the NCWD works with and through existing women's voluntary organisations. Most women in Ghana belong to a voluntary organisation, either in the church or at their workplace, whether it be the market, a factory or an office. The NCWD's major task is to ensure that the services of existing government departments and agencies reach women. It therefore co-ordinates the activities of those government departments, the programmes and services of which are relevant to the needs of women. In order to ensure effective co-ordination, the NEC Decree 322 that set up the NCWD named ten relevant government ministries whose principal secretaries serve on the Board of the NCWD. These include the Ministries of Agriculture, Health, Social Welfare and Community Development, and Finance and Economic Planning, where the Manpower Board is located. The Board of the NCWD formulates policies for implementation by the staff of the National and Regional Secretariats, all of whom are public servants.

Since its primary function was to be an advisory body to the government, the NCWD initiated research into various aspects of the life of Ghanaian women to ensure that any advice to the government was based on facts. It also organised a series of seminars, consultations and public discussions throughout the country to identify the needs of Ghanaian women regarding training, income generation, employment, health and family welfare. From the consultations and public discussions, it become clear that for rural and urban women alike, the ability to earn more money was of primary concern so that they might be better able to feed and clothe themselves and their children, especially in the light of the high and rising cost of living. In Ghanaian society few women or children are entirely dependent upon their husbands, kin or fathers. The majority of women provide much of what they and their children need, many as household heads—separated wives, divorcees, or polygynous wives. It is thus not surprising that income-earning activities are so important to them.

Related to the need for income is the need for education and vocational/professional training. The NCWD identified a need to change the attitudes of parents and to make them realise that given the same opportunities their daughters will do as well as their sons in school and benefit from higher education, for the low level of women's participation in higher education in Ghana is partly due to the low level of parental aspirations for daughters as compared to sons. Moreover, the vocational institutes for girls, many of which are privately owned, concentrate on only three main traditional subjects—catering, hairdressing and dressmaking. The government-owned technical institutes and polytechnics which take in both boys and girls also make the girls do these 'female' subjects, while the boys concentrate on more technical subjects such as electronics, electrical and mechanical engineering, metalwork, etc. There is therefore a need to train girls for less traditionally 'feminine' occupations and to give them a chance to study more technical subjects. Such changes in vocational training programmes would also help to make parents realise that there is no basic difference in the training potential of their sons and daughters.

The NCWD identified another problem regarding the education of girls in the rural areas, that is a lack of female teachers, not only to teach needlework and cookery, but also to give them the basic principles of family life education—for the incidence of precocious pregnancies among girls in such schools is quite high, giving ample evidence of the pressing need for such courses.

NCWD research also documented the lack of women on the country's decision-making bodies at all levels. Moreover, few hold positions of seniority and authority in the medical and educational fields, or in the civil service, which many women enter.

With regard to the law, it was noted that certain customary laws and practices are detrimental to women, including the marriage of girls under age without their consent, polygyny, and the inheritance laws.

The main activities of the NCWD since its establishment have been in the areas of self-employment, and the introduction of simple and appropriate technology to reduce labour and increase productivity; extensive research to identify the priority needs of women; counselling, and in particular career guidance, for schoolgirls; and using research findings as the basis for advising government and government agencies on the needs of women as regards education, health, employment, family welfare, agriculture, and legislation. The NCWD has identified three target groups for its programme. These are:

(i)   rural women and those living in the poor areas of the urban centres;
(ii) school-leavers and drop-outs; and
(iii) working women, including the professionally trained.

Different programmes are worked out to meet the special needs of the women in the three categories.

Consciousness-raising

The first major task of the NCWD was to create awareness among the Ghanaian public of the plight of women. It launched a programme of education to eradicate prejudices through public lectures and symposia and through discussions on radio and television in English and in the Ghanaian languages. One of the results of this educational programme was the healthy debate that went on in schools and in the newspapers about women's capabilities and their roles in society. The cynicism with which people greeted the launching of the International Women's Year in Ghana soon gave way to sober reflection and an understanding of the issues that the programmes for the Year were designed to highlight. These issues are still being discussed in the media and in other public forums, and every year the week within which 21 April falls (the date the NCWD was inaugurated) is celebrated as Women's Week and the concerns of women and the programmes of the NCWD are published.

Income Generation

For the majority of Ghanaian women in the rural areas and in the poor areas of the urban centres, their primary concern is for employment, in particular self-employment, for many of them are too preoccupied with finding money to feed and clothe themselves and their children to worry about whether they are men's equal in this male-dominated society. The NCWD's response to this preoccupation was to try to help women to provide some of the basic needs of the family. It thus embarked on a series of workshops in all the regional capitals at which new skills were taught and old ones were taught using improved methods that saved labour and increased productivity. These workshops were residential and each lasted eight days. The women who participated in them were invited from different women's associations, the aim being that they would go back and pass on the knowledge to other women in their groups. Some of the skills taught were soap-making, oil extraction, bead-making, pottery, mat and basket weaving from different materials, and handicrafts.

Throughout Ghana there are women engaged in farming, but the farms of most women are too small to attract financial assistance from the banks, or even to attract the attention of the Ministry of Agriculture's extension officers. The NCWD therefore introduced a new system of co-operative farming and revolving credit schemes for the small-scale women farmers. Women are also widely engaged in food processing of one type of another. Like the women farmers, groups of women engaged in the same type of food processing are encouraged by the NCWD to come together to form co-operatives, where people come together in order to get access to certain services and facilities and thereby maximise their profits, while at the same time continuing to work on their own and controlling their own individual profits. Women bakers, for example, will come together to purchase a flour kneading machine. Women who process oil from palm fruits, palm kernel, coconuts, groundnuts and shea nuts have been taught improved methods of oil processing which saves them time and labour and also gives them higher yields.

One important advance has been in the processing of cassava (manioc) into *gari*—a food item made from grated cassava, pressed dry of sap, fermented, and dehydrated by roasting. This is one food item that needs no cooking and which can be kept for months without going bad. In recent years it has become a staple food for many people throughout the country. Cassava is grown in all regions of Ghana apart from the Upper Region, and gari processing has traditionally been a woman's activity. The traditional methods of processing are, however, laborious, time-consuming and wasteful. In recent years simple equipment has been manufactured locally to reduce the time and labour involved. These are mechanised graters, a press for extracting excess starchy water from the cassava dough, and an improved roasting pan for roasting large quantities of gari at a time. All the pieces of equipment, except the graters, are hand-operated. The graters are operated by a small diesel engine. Gari processing co-operatives have been formed and production substantially increased. Other traditional activities that the NCWD has helped to upgrade are fish curing and soap-making.

Beads are worn as ornaments by many Ghanaian women, and bead-making is an old skill which the NCWD is teaching to younger people. The beads are made by melting broken bottles and casting them in moulds. Again the women are encouraged to come together so that they can be helped more easily to learn new techniques and obtain raw materials. Mat and basket weaving is another craft that is widespread throughout the country. This, too, has been fostered and improved by NCWD workshops.

Whenever the income-earning activities of a new women's group or co-operative become well established, it is given publicity so that other women who are interested in the same activity can learn from the group and start one for themselves. The bigger projects, started with funds from international sources, have become models that other groups are expected to learn from and copy.

Education and Training

Each income-earning project has built around it an educational programme on sanitation, nutrition, child-care, family planning and family life education, civic rights and responsibilities. These are non-formal educational programmes which the NCWD runs with the help of the staff of the Public Health Unit of the Ministry of Health, the Ministry of Education, the Department of Social Welfare and Community Development, the Home Extension Unit of the Ministry of Agriculture, and the Ghana Planned Parenthood Federation. Meetings are organised for the women's groups at which lectures, discussions and demonstrations are held on relevant subjects. The response to these meetings has been very encouraging.

Where a project includes the construction of a building, as in a gari factory or a mat and basket weaving centre, the building is used as a common service centre for training young girls, especially school-leavers and drop-outs, in a number of skills such as soap-making, food processing and bead-making. The common service centre is also used as the meeting place for the lectures, discussions and demonstrations. The NCWD plans to have at least one such common service centre in each region so that residential courses can be organised to train young girls in various skills.

One of the long-term plans of the NCWD is to embark on functional literacy programmes for illiterate women. In addition, the NCWD has from time to time made recommendations to the government on issues affecting the education and training of girls, especially as regards making the educational programme relevant to the employment needs of young girls and diversifying vocational training programmes for girls to include non-traditional courses. Action has been taken on some of these recommendations, and it is hoped that more funds will be made available so that the impact of the changes in the training programmes for school-leavers will be felt throughout the country.

The NCWD has also been engaged in counselling and career guidance for school girls. Lectures are organised for girls in their schools on the job openings and training facilities that are available in the country. Both teachers and students have been very enthusiastic about these lectures. The NCWD has helped one voluntary women's organisation to update its publication 'Careers for girls' in which the careers available to secondary school-leavers and the qualifications and training required are discussed. Individual women and young girls have also been helped by the NCWD counselling officers in solving their personal and other problems. It is planned to expand the scope of the career and vocational guidance programme and to link it with family life education and marriage guidance counselling, especially for young girls in vocational training and apprenticeship courses.

One-day seminars are held from time to time in all the regions to educate women workers on how to combine the responsibilities of running a home and working in an office or factory. The problems of working mothers are discussed at these seminars, to which people in management are invited. The suggestions made have formed the basis for some of the NCWD's recommendations to government about the need for adequate child-care facilities near all workplaces, the provision of training for house-helps, the institution of part-time work for nursing mothers, and the improvement of maternity benefits for working women. (At present women are entitled to three month's maternity leave with full salary, and after that one hour a day off work to feed the baby for one year.) Working women are also informed at these seminars of existing facilities for further training, and encouraged to take advantage of them so that they can improve their work output and thereby earn promotion to positions of greater responsibility.

In accordance with its mandate as an advisory body to government on all issues affecting the full integration of women in national development at all levels, the NCWD has from time to time presented recommendations to the government based on its research findings and on the results of discussions at consultations, seminars and symposia it has organised. Recommendations have been made relating to education, agriculture, marketing, health, including family health, traditions and customs, employment and the diversification of income-generating skills, child-care and legislation affecting women.

Conclusion

Before the setting up of the National Council on Women and Development in 1975, women's issues had been handled piecemeal by individual government departments such as the Department of Social Welfare and Community Development, or by voluntary women's organisations. This was, and in some cases still is, the position in many other countries, whether developed or developing. One of the United Nations objectives in calling on member States to set up national machinery for the integration of women in national development was to eliminate the notion that women's issues should only be handled on a non-governmental basis by concerned individuals or by women's non-governmental organisations (NGOs).

The Ghana experience since the setting up of the NCWD has shown that a great deal can be achieved in a relatively short time as regards the integration of women in national development if there is a government body that is solely responsible for ensuring that such integration occurs. The fact that the NCWD has government support has created confidence in it on the part of Ghanaian women, nor would the programmes have been so successful without the co-operation of individual women and women's organisations throughout Ghana. This has also made it possible for the NCWD to attract grants from international agencies which have earmarked funds for women's projects during 1976–85, the United Nations Decade for Women and beyond.

Appendix I

Offices of Women's Affairs in West Africa*

Burkina Faso	Service de la promotion féminine founded 1978 under Ministry of Social Affairs and Women's Welfare. Function: to promote the establishment of governmental and private machinery for streamlining policies on women to encourage the involvement of women in national development.
Côte d'Ivoire	Ministère de la condition féminine, founded 1976. Function: to promote the economic, social and cultural advancement of women and to involve them more actively in development.
Gabon	Direction de la promotion féminine founded 1974 under Ministry of Health, Population, Social Affairs and Women's Welfare. Function: to promote and encourage any activities likely to accelerate the integration of women in development.
Ghana	The National Council on Women and Development, founded 1975. Function: to advise government, to examine women's contributions, to devise programmes, etc.
Guinea Bissau	Comissão Feminina das Mulheres, under Ministry of Labour and Social Security. Function: education, co-ordination and mobilisation of women.
Niger	Direction de promotion de la femme, founded 1981 under Ministry of Youth, Sports and Culture.
Nigeria	Social Development division, founded 1974 as part of Ministry of Social Development, Youth and Sports. Function: to co-ordinate women's activities throughout the country.
Senegal	Secrétariat d'Etat à la Condition féminine, founded 1978. Function: to implement the government's policy for women in all fields in which they are involved, to review legislation, etc.
Togo	Ministère des affaires sociales et de la promotion féminine founded 1977.

*Source: ILO (1983): *Directory of governmental bodies dealing with women workers' questions* (ILO/W.4/1983/ Rev. 1).

Function: to improve the status of women and to enable them to play their part as community members.

Burkina Faso   Direction de la condition féminine, under the Ministry of Social Affairs and Women's Welfare founded 1978.

Function: to assure full equality of access to education, vocational training and employment.

Bibliography

Abu, K. 1983. 'The separateness of spouses: Conjugal resources in an Ashanti town', in Oppong, C. (ed.): *Female and male in West Africa*. London, George Allen and Unwin.

Acsadi, G.T. et al. 1972. *Surveys of fertility, family and family planning in Nigeria*. University of Ife, IPMS Publication No. 2.

Addo, N.O.; Goody, J.R. n.d. *Siblings in Ghana*. Legon, University of Ghana Population Studies No. 7.

Adeokun, L.A. 1974. 'Aspects of the population geography of the western area, Sierra Leone'. University of Durham, Ph.D. thesis.

——1983. 'Marital sexuality and birth spacing among the Yoruba', in Oppong, C. (ed.): *Female and male in West Africa*. London, George Allen and Unwin.

Adeokun, L.A.; Adepoju, A; Ilori, F.A.; Adewuyi, A.A.; Ebigbola, J.A. 1984. *The Ife labour market: A Nigerian case study*. Geneva, ILO; World Employment Programme research working paper; restricted.

Adepoju, A. 1974. 'Rural–urban socio-economic links: The example of migrants in south-western Nigeria', in Amin, S. (ed.): *Modern migrations in western Africa*. London, Oxford University Press, pp. 127–37.

——1977a. 'Rationality and fertility in the traditional Yoruba society, south-west Nigeria', in Caldwell, J.C. (ed.): *The persistence of high fertility*, pp. 123–151. Canberra, Australian National University.

——1977b. 'Migration and development in tropical Africa: Some research priorities', in *African Affairs*, Vol. 79, No. 303, April.

——1981. 'Migration, household structure and productive activities in rural areas (Nigeria)', in Chojnacka, H., Olusanya, P.O. and Ojo, F. (eds.): *Population and economic development in Nigeria in the 1980s*. New York, United Nations.

Akande, J.O. 1986. 'Women's rights in property in Nigerian law'. Dissertation submitted for the L.L.M. degree, Lagos University.

Akerele, A. 1979. *Women workers in Ghana, Kenya, Zambia: A comparative analysis of women's employment in the modern wage sector*. UNECA, ATRCW/Ford Foundation, Research Series No. ATRCW/SDD/RES02.

Akingba, J.B. 1974. 'Some aspects of pregnancy and abortion in some Nigerian adolescents'. Paper presented at WHO Meeting on Pregnancy and Abortion in Adolescents, Geneva.

Akuffo, F.O. 1978. 'High wastage in women's education: The case of the rural elementary school girls'. Paper presented at a National Council on Women and Development Seminar, Ghana, Sept.

——1981. 'High wastage in women's education: The case of the rural elementary school girl'. Unpublished M.A. thesis. Legon, Institute of African Studies, University of Ghana.

Ampofo, D.A. 1969. 'Causes of maternal death and comments, Maternity

Hospital, Accra 1963–67', in *West African Medical Journal*, June, Vol. 18, pp. 75–81.

Anker, R 1980. *Research on women's roles and demographic change: Survey questionnaires for households, women, men and communities with background explanations*. Geneva, ILO.

——1983a. *The effect on reported levels of female labour force participation in developing countries of questionnaire design, sex of interviewer and sex/proxy status of respondent: Description of a methodological field experiment*. Geneva, ILO; mimeographed World Employment Programme research working paper.

——1983b. 'Female labour force participation in developing countries: A critique of current definitions and data collection methods', in *International Labour Review* (Geneva, ILO), Nov–Dec, Vol. 122, No. 6.

Anker, R.; Buvinic, M.; Youssef, N.H. (eds.). 1982. *Interactions between women's roles and population trends in the Third World*. London, Croom Helm.

Anker, R.; Hein, C. (eds.). 1985. *Sex inequalities in urban employment in the Third World*. London, Macmillan.

Armar, A.A.; David, A.S. 1977. *Country profiles: Ghana*. New York, Population Council.

Arowolo, O.O. 1982. *Research on population, communication and implications for population policies in West Africa*, Vol. I, *The Population Situation*, UNESCO Population Communication, technical document No. 7.

Asare Opoku, K. 1977. 'Procreation in Africa: Traditional and modern' in Pobee, J.S. (ed.): *Religion, morality and population dynamics*. Legon, University of Ghana PDP.

Ashaye, M.T. 1981. *Nigerian income tax guide (1981 assessment year)*. Lagos, Skyway Press.

Badoe, Y.M. 1983. 'Rice and dependencies', in *West Africa*, 24 Oct., p. 2452.

Bamisaiye, A.; Oyediran, M.A. 1981. 'Female labour force participation and the care of pre-school children: A survey of mothers employed at Luth'. Unpublished paper presented at the National Workshop on Working Mothers and Early Childhood Education in Nigeria, 13–16 Sept. 1981, Nigerian Institute of Social and Economic Research, Ibadan.

Bank of Sierra Leone. *Annual reports*. Various issues, 1975–82. Freetown.

Bartle, P.F.W. 1977. 'Urban migration and rural identity: An ethnography of a Kwahu community'. Ph.D. thesis. Legon, University of Ghana.

——1978. 'Conjugal relations, migration and fertility in an Akan community' in Oppong, C., et al. (eds.), *Marriage, fertility and parenthood in West Africa*. Canberra, Australian National University Press.

Bashir, M.K. 1972. 'The economic activities of secluded married women in Kurawa and Lallokin Lemu, Kano City'. B.Sc. dissertation. Zaria, Department of Sociology, Ahmadu Bello University.

Beckman, L.J. 1979. 'The relationship between sex roles, fertility and family size preferences', in *Psychology of Women Quarterly*, Fall, Vol. 4, No. 1, pp. 43–60.

Benería, L. 1981. 'Conceptualizing the labour force: The underestimation of women's economic activities', in Nelson, N. (ed.): *African women in the development process*, pp. 10–28. London, NJ, Frank Cass.

——1982. 'Accounting for women's work', in Beneria, L. (ed.): *Women and development. The sexual division of labor in rural societies*. New York, Praeger.

——(ed.). 1982. *Women and development. The sexual division of labour in rural societies*. New York, Praeger.

Ben-Porath, Y. (ed.) 1982a. 'Income distribution and the family', in *Population and Development Review* (New York, Population Council), Supplement to Volume 8.

——1982b. 'Individuals, families and income distribution', in *Population and Development Review* (New York, Population Council), Supplement to Volume 8.

Bequele, A. 1980. *Poverty, inequality and stagnation: The Ghanaian experience*. Geneva, ILO; mimeographed World Employment Programme research working paper.

Bingen, J. 1972. 'Myth and reality of US population assistance to Africa, with an overview of the Ghanaian situation', in *Ufahamu*, Vol. 3, No. 2, pp. 75–96.

Bleek, W. 1975a. *Marriage, inheritance and witchcraft: A case study of a rural Ghanaian family*. Leyden, Africa Study Centre.

——1975b. 'Appearance and reality. The ambiguous position of women in Kwahu, Ghana', in Kloos, P. and van der Voen, K.W. (eds.): *Rule and reality. Essays in honour of Andre J.F. Kobbon*. Amsterdam, University of Amsterdam.

——1976a. *Sexual relationships and birth control in Ghana: A case study of a rural town*. Amsterdam, Anthropological-Sociological Centre.

——1976b. 'Spacing of children, sexual abstinence and breastfeeding in rural Ghana', in *Social Science and Medicine*, Vol. 10, pp. 225–230.

——1978a. 'Parents and children in a Ghanaian lineage', in *Family welfare and planning*, Legon Family Research Papers No. 4. Legon, Institute of African Studies, University of Ghana.

——1978b. 'Induced abortion in a Ghanaian family', in *African Studies Review*, Vol. 21, pp. 103–20.

——1981. 'The unexpected repression: How family planning discriminates against women in Ghana', in *Review of Ethnology* (pub. E. Stiglmayr), Vol. 7, No. 25.

Bodrova, V.; Anker, R. (eds.). 1985. *Working women in socialist countries: The fertility connection*. Geneva, ILO.

Bondestam, L. 1980. 'The political ideology of population control', in Bondestam, L. and Bergström, S. (eds.): *Poverty and population control*. London, Academic Press.

Bongaarts, J. 1978. 'A framework for analyzing the proximate determinants of fertility', in *Population and Development Review*, Vol. 4, No. 1, pp. 105–132.

Boserup, E. 1970. *Women's role in economic development*. London, George Allen and Unwin.

Brydon, L. 1979. 'Women at work: Some changes in family structure in Amedzofe-Avatime, Ghana', in *Africa*, Vol. 49, No. 2, pp. 97–111.

Bukh, J. 1979. *Village women in Ghana*. Uppsala, Scandinavian Institute of Arican Studies.

Bulatao, R.A. 1980. 'The transition in the value of children and the fertility transition'. Paper read at Seminar on Determinants of Fertility Trends: Major Themes and New Directions for Research, Bad Homburg, April. Liège, IUSSP.

Burfisher, M.E.; Horenstein, N.R. 1985. 'Sex roles and development effects on the Nigerian Tiv farm household', in *Rural Africana*, No. 21, Winter, pp. 31–49.

Byerlee, D.; King, R. 1977. 'Factor intensity of rural consumption patterns in Sierra Leone'. African Rural Economy Working Paper. East Lansing, Michigan, Department of Agricultural Economics, Michigan State University.

Caldwell, J.C. 1967a. 'Population: General characteristics', in Birmingham, W. et al.: *A study of contemporary Ghana. Volume 2: Some aspects of social structure*. London, George Allen and Unwin.

——1967b. 'Fertility attitudes in three economically contrasting rural regions of Ghana', in *Economic Development and Cultural Change*, Vol. 15, pp. 217–238.

——1968a. *Population growth and family change in Africa: The new urban elite in Ghana*. Canberra, Australian National University Press.

——1968b. 'The control of family size in tropical Africa', in *Demography*. Vol. 5, No. 2, pp. 598–619.

——(ed.). 1977a. *The persistence of high fertility: Population prospects in the Third World*, Changing African Family Series, Monograph 3. Canberra, Australia National University Press.

——1977b. 'Towards a restatement of demographic transition theory', in Caldwell, J.C. (ed.): *The persistence of high fertility*. Canberra, Australian National University Press.

——1977c. 'The economic rationality of high fertility: An investigation illustrated with Nigerian survey data', in *Population Studies*, Vol. 31, No. 1, pp. 5–27.

——1980. 'The wealth flows theory of fertility decline'. Paper presented at Seminar on Determinants of Fertility Trends: Major Theories and New Directions for Research, Bad Homburg, April. Liège, IUSSP.

——1982. *Theory of fertility decline*. London, Academic Press.

Caplan, P. 1981. 'Development policies in Tanzania—Some implications for women', in N. Nelson (ed.): *African women in the development process*. London, Frank Cass.

Chui, J.; UNFPA. 1978. *Policies and programmes on adolescent fertility in developing countries: An integrated approach*. New York, UNFPA.

Church, K. 1977. *Female participation in public institutions of education between 1960 and 1975 in Ghana*. National Council on Women and Development.

Coale, A.J. 1969. 'The decline of fertility in Europe from the French Revolution to World War II', in Behrman et al. (eds.): *Fertility and family planning*. Ann Arbor, University of Michigan.

Cochrane, S.H. 1979. *Fertility and education: What do we really know?* Baltimore, Johns Hopkins University Press.

Corvalen, H. 1978. 'Unwanted pregnancies. A proposed programme of control in Africa', in Sai, F. (ed.): *A strategy for abortion management*. Report of an IPPF Africa Regional Workshop, pp. 31–43. London, IPPF.

Danfa Project. 1979. *The Danfa comprehensive rural health and family planning project, Ghana*, final report. Accra, University of Ghana Medical School.

Darabi, K.F. et al. 1979. 'Forum: A perspective on adolescent fertility in developing countries', in *Studies in Family Planning*, Vol. 10, No. 10, pp. 300–303.

Date-Bah, E., et al. 1984. *Technological change: Basic needs and the condition of rural women*, project report. Geneva, ILO.

David, A.S.; Armar, A.A. 1978. 'Foreign aid in population programmes: The Ghanaian experience'. Conference paper. Legon, Population Dynamics Programme.

Debo Akande, J.O. 1979. *Law and the status of women in Nigeria*. Economic

Commission for Africa, African Training and Research Centre for Women.

De Nie, F. 1977. 'Verslad van mijn onderzoekservaringen inzake 'Afrikanisatie' van enkele vakken bij het middelbaar onderwijs in Ghana'. Unpublished manuscript.

Dey, J. 1980. 'Women and rice in The Gambia: The impact of irrigated rice development projects on the farming system'. Ph.D thesis. Reading, Agricultural Extension and Rural Development Centre, University of Reading.

Di Domenico, C. 1980. 'Women in development: A case study of their labour force participation in Ibadan and its implications for differential role performance', in *Proceedings of the National Conference on Integrated Rural Development and Women in Development*. Benin, University of Benin.

——1983. 'Male and female factory workers in Ibadan', in Oppong, C. (ed.): *Female and male in West Africa*. London, George Allen and Unwin.

Di Domenico, C.; Asuni, J.B. 1979. 'Breastfeeding practices among urban women in Ibadan Nigeria', in Raphael, D, (ed.): *Breastfeeding and food policy in a hungry world*. Academic Press.

Dinan, C. 1983. 'Sugar daddies and gold diggers' in Oppong, C. (ed.): *Female and male in West Africa*. London, George Allen and Unwin.

Dixon, R. 1982. 'Women in agriculture: Counting the labour force in developing countries', in *Population and Development Review*, Vol. 8, No. 3, pp. 539–566.

Dow, Jr., T.E. 1977. 'Breastfeeding and abstinence among the Yoruba', in *Studies in Family Planning* (New York, The Population Council), Vol. 8, No. 8, pp. 208–214.

Dow Jr. T.E.; Benjamin, E. 1975. 'Demographic trends and implications', in Caldwell, J. et al. (eds.): *Population growth and socio-economic change in West Africa*, pp. 427–454. New York, Columbia University Press for the Population Council.

Dutta-Roy, D.K. 1969. *The Eastern Region household budget survey*, Technical Publication Series No. 6. Legon, ISSER, University of Ghana.

Ekanem, I.I. 1972. *The 1963 Nigerian Census: A critical appraisal*. Benin City, Ethiopia Publishing Corp.

Ekanem, I.I.; Farooq, G.M. 1977. 'The dynamics of population change in Southern Nigeria', in *Genus*, Vol. XXXIII, No. 1–2, 1977.

Eldstrom, K.G. 1981. 'Reproductive health in adolescence: An overview', in Jelliffe, D.B. and Jelliffe, E.F. (eds.): *Advances in international maternal and child health*. Oxford, Oxford University Press.

Ewusi, K. 1978. *Size of labour force and structure of employment in Ghana*. Technical Publications Series No. 37. Legon, ISSER, University of Ghana.

Ezimokhai, M., et al. 1981. 'Response of unmarried adolescents to contraceptive advice and service in Nigeria', in *International Journal of Gynaecology and Obstetrics*, Vol. 19, pp. 481–485.

Fadayomi, T. et al. 1979. *The role of working mothers in early childhood education: A Nigerian case study*. UNESCO/NISER Publication.

Fadipe, N.A. 1970. *The sociology of the Yoruba*. Ibadan, Ibadan University Press.

Fapohunda, E.R. 1983. 'Female and male work profiles', in Oppong, C. (ed.): *Female and male in West Africa*. London, George Allen and Unwin.

Fapohunda, O.J.; Fapohunda, E.R. 1976. *The working mothers of Lagos*. Report of a study submitted to the Interdisciplinary Communications Committee of the Smithsonian Institution, Washington, DC.

Fawcett, J.T. 1977. 'The value and cost of children: Converging theory research', in Ruzicka, L. (ed.): *The economic and social supports for high fertility*. Canberra, Australian National University Press.

Federal Republic of Nigeria. 1981. *Outline of the Fourth National Development Plan*. Lagos, Ministry of Planning.

——1978. *Blueprint 1978–79*. Report submitted to the Hon. Federal Commissioner for Education. Lagos, Implementation Committee for the National Policy on Education.

——1979. *Report of the labour force sample survey, 1974*, Manpower Studies No. 18. Lagos, National Manpower Board.

——1980. *Study of Nigeria's manpower requirements, 1977*. Lagos, National Manpower Board.

——1980. *Guidelines for the Fourth National Development Plan, 1981–85*. Lagos, Ministry of Planning.

——1981. *Fourth National Development Plan, 1981–85*. Lagos, National Planning Office Division, Ministry of Planning.

Field, M.J. 1960. *Search for security: An ethno-psychiatric study of rural Ghana*. London, Faber and Faber.

Fortes, M. 1950. 'Kinship and marriage among the Ashanti' in Radcliffe-Brown, A.R. and Forde, D. (eds.): *African systems of kinship and marriage*, pp. 252–286. London, Oxford University Press.

——1954. 'A demographic field study in Ashanti', in Lorimer, F. (ed.): *Culture and human fertility*, pp. 255–339. Paris, UNESCO.

——1978. 'Family, marriage and fertility in West Africa', in Oppong, C., et al. (eds.): *Marriage, fertility and parenthood in West Africa*. Canberra, Australian National University Press.

Fowler, D.A. 1978. *The informal sector of Freetown (Sierra Leone)*. Geneva, ILO; mimeographed World Employment Programme research working paper; restricted.

Gachuchi, J. Mugo. 1974. *African youth and family planning: Knowledge, attitudes and priorities*. Discussion paper no. 189. Nairobi, Institute for Development Studies, University of Nairobi.

Gaisie, S.K. 1976. *Estimating Ghanaian fertility, mortality and age structure*. University of Ghana Population Studies No. 5. Legon, Population Dynamics Programme, University of Ghana.

——1979. *Fertility levels, trends and differentials in Ghana*. Monrovia, doc. ECA E/CH 14/POP/INF 231.

——1981. 'Child-spacing patterns and fertility differentials in Ghana', in Page, H.J. and Lesthaege, R. (eds.): *Child-spacing in tropical Africa: Traditions and change*, pp. 237–253. London, Academic Press.

Ghana Teaching Service. 1975. *Report on population and family life education survey in schools and colleges*. Accra, Ministry of Education and GNFPP.

Gjertsen, D. 1982. 'Africa's central arithmetic', in *West Africa*, No. 3368, pp. 518–519.

Goddard, A.D. et al. 1971. *A socio-economic study of three villages in the Sokoto close-settled zone*. Samaru Miscellaneous Paper 33. Zaria, Institute for Agricultural Research, Ahmadu Bello University.

Goldschmidt-Clermont, L. 1982. *Unpaid work in the household*. Women, Work and Development series No. 1. Geneva, ILO.

——1987. *Economic evaluations of unpaid household work in Africa, Asia,*

Latin America and Oceania. Women, Work and Development series. Geneva, ILO.

Goody, E. 1978. 'Some theoretical and empirical aspects of parenthood in West Africa', in Oppong, C., et al. (eds.): *Marriage, Fertility and parenthood in West Africa.* Canberra, Australian National University Press.

——1982. *Parenthood and social reproduction: Fostering and occupational roles in West Africa.* Cambridge University Press.

Goody, J. 1972. *Domestic groups.* Reading, Mass., Addison-Wesley Publishing Corp.

Government of Ghana. 1960a. *Population census of Ghana, Vol. I. The gazetteer.* Accra, Census Office.

——1960b. *Population census of Ghana 1960, Vol. II. Statistics of localities and enumeration areas* (sex, age, birthplace, school attendance and economic activity). Accra, Census Office.

——1964a. *Population census of Ghana, 1960, Vol. III. Demographic characteristics of local authorities, regions and total country* (sex, age, school attendance and level of education of total and foreign origin population). Accra, Census Office.

——1964b. *Population census of Ghana, 1960, Vol. IV. Economic characteristics of local authorities, regions and total country* (type of activity, industry, occupation and employment status of total and foreign origin population). Accra, Census Office.

——1964c. *Population census of Ghana, 1960. Advance report of Vol. III and IV.* Accra, Census Office.

——1964d. *Population census of Ghana, 1960, Vol. V. General report.* Accra, Census Office.

——1969a. *Population census, 1970. Enumerator's manual.* Accra, Census Office, Dec.

——1969b. *Population census, 1970. Training guide for census district officers.* Accra, Census Office, Dec.

——1969c. *Population planning for national progress and prosperity: Ghana population policy.* Accra-Tema, Ghana Publishing Corporation.

——1971. *Population census of Ghana, 1960, Vol. VI. The post enumeration survey (PES),* Supplementary Enquiry. Accra, Census Office.

——1972. *Population census of Ghana, 1970, Vol. II. Statistics of localities and enumeration areas,* June. Accra, Census Office.

Government of Ghana, Ministry of Education et al. 1979. *Report on population and family life education survey in schools and colleges.* Accra, University Press.

Government of Nigeria. 1931. *Population census of Nigeria—Vol. I, Nigeria,* Jacob, S.M. Vol. II, *Census of the Northern Provinces,* Brooke, N.J. 1933. London, Crown Agents for the Colonies.

——1953. *Population census of the Northern Region of Nigeria, 1952.* Lagos, Department of Statistics.

——1963. *Population census of Nigeria.* Lagos, Office of Statistics, 10 volumes.

——1973. *1973 Population census enumerator's manual (NCO.8).* Lagos, National Census Office.

Government of Sierra Leone. 1974. *National Development Plan 1974/75-1978/79.* Freetown, Ministry of Development and Economic Planning.

——1981. *National Development Plan, 1981/82–1985/86, in Outline*. Freetown, Ministry of Development and Economic Planning.

Graft Johnson, K.T. de, et al. 1973. 'The determinants of labour force participation rates in Ghana', second progress report, 1 Mar.–28 June. Legon, ISSER, University of Ghana.

——1978. 'Factors affecting labour force participation rates in Ghana, 1970', in Standing, G. and Sheehan, G. (eds.): *Labour force participation in low income countries*. Geneva, ILO.

Grant, B.; Anthonio, Q.B.O. 1973. 'Women's cooperatives in the western state of Nigeria', in *Bulletin of Rural Economics and Sociology*, Vol. 8, No. 1, pp. 7–35.

Greenhalgh, S. 1982. 'Income units: The ethnographic alternative to standardisation in income distribution and family size', in *Population and Development Review*, Supplement to Vol. 8.

Greenstreet, M. 1981. 'When education is unequal. Women and the informal sector', in *Bulletin* (Sussex, IDS), July, Vol. 12.

Gutek, B.A., et al. 1981. 'The interdependence of work and family roles', in *Journal of Occupational Behaviour*, Vol. 2, pp. 1–16.

Gwatkin, D.R. 1975. 'Governmental population policies', in Caldwell, J.C., et al. (eds.): *Population growth and socio-economic change in West Africa*, pp. 169–184. New York and London, Columbia University Press.

Gyepi-Garbrah, B. 1985. *Adolescent fertility in sub-Saharan Africa*. Boston, Mass., The Pathfinder Funder.

Harrington, J. 1978. 'Some micro-economics of female status in Nigeria'. Paper presented at a conference on 'Women in Poverty: What Do We Know?', Washington, DC, International Centre for Research on Women.

Hill, P. 1963. *The migrant cocoa farmers of southern Ghana: A study in rural capitalism*. Cambridge, Cambridge University Press.

——1969. 'Hidden trade in Hausaland', in *Man*, Vol. 4, No. 3, pp. 392–409.

——1972. *Rural Hausa: A village and a setting*. London, Cambridge University Press.

——1977. *Population, prosperity and poverty: Rural Kano 1900 and 1970*. London, Cambridge University Press.

Hirschmann, D. 1985. 'Bureaucracy and rural women: Illustrations from Malawi', in *Rural Africana*. No. 21, Winter, pp. 51–63.

Hofferth, S.L.; Moore, K. 1979. 'Early child-bearing and later economic well-being', in *American Sociological Review*, Oct., Vol. 44, pp. 784–815.

Howell, S. 1979. 'The Chewong of Malaysia', in *Populi*, Vol. 6.

International Labour Office, 1978a. *1978 yearbook of labour statistics*. Geneva, ILO.

——1978b. *Participation of women in economic activities and their working conditions in African countries: Statistical analysis*. Geneva, ILO, doc. no. ILO/W.7/1978.

——1982a. *Revision of the international guidelines on labour statistics,* paper prepared for OECD Working Party on Employment and Unemployment Statistics, 14–16 June 1982.

——1982b. *Amendment draft resolution concerning statistics of the economically active population, employment, unemployment and under-employment,* Thirteenth International Conference of Labour Statisticians; mimeograph.

——1982c. *Labour force, employment and unemployment and under-employ-*

ment. Report prepared for the Thirteenth International Conference of Labour Statisticians, Geneva, 18–29 Oct. Geneva, ILO.

——1983. *Report of the International Labour Organisation on its activities of special interest to women*. Geneva, ILO; doc. no. ILO/W.3/1983.

——1984. *Rural development and women in Africa*. Geneva, ILO.

——1985a. *ILO and women workers' questions in Africa during the UN Decade for Women*. Addis Ababa, ILO.

——1985b. *Assessment of ILO operational activities concerning women*. Governing Body Committee on Operational Programs, 231st Session, November. Geneva, ILO; GB.231/OP/2/5.

——1985c. *Report VII. Equal opportunities and equal treatment for men and women in employment*. International Labour Conference, 71st session. Geneva, ILO.

ILO/JASPA. 1981. *Ensuring equitable growth: A strategy for increasing employment equity and basic needs satisfaction in Sierra Leone*. Addis Ababa.

International Planned Parenthood Federation (IPPF). 1981. *Male involvement in family planning: Some approaches for family planning associations*. London, IPPF, Programme Development Department; working paper.

International Statistical Institute. 1984. *World fertility survey: Major findings and implications*. Voorburg, ISI.

Jackson, S. 1978. 'Hausa women on strike', in *Review of African Political Economy,* May/Aug., No. 13 pp. 21–36.

Jandl-Jager, E. 1982. *Adolescent fertility and family planning: A review of selected research studies*. London, IPPF.

Jegede. M.I. 1981. *Land, law and development*. Lagos, University of Lagos Press.

Johnson, S. 1969. *The history of the Yorubas*. Lagos, CCS Bookshops, first published 1921.

Joshi, H., et al. 1976. *Abidjan urban development and employment in the Ivory Coast*. Geneva, ILO.

Karanja-Diejomaoh, W.M. 1978. 'Disposition of incomes by husbands and wives: An exploratory study of families in Lagos', in Oppong, C., et al. (eds.): *Marriage, parenthood and fertility in West Africa*. Canberra, Australian National University Press.

Ketkar, S.L. 1979–80. 'Socio-economic determinants of family size in Sierra Leone', in *Rural Africana*, Winter, Vol. 6, pp. 25–45.

Kilson, M. 1966. *Political change in a West African state: A study of the modernization process in Sierra Leone*. Harvard University Press.

Kocher, J.E. 1973. *Rural development, income distribution and fertility decline*. New York, Population Council.

Konan, M.M. 1975. *Occupations and family patterns among the Hausa in northern Nigeria*, Samaru Miscellaneous Paper No. 52. Zaria, IAR, Ahmadu Bello University.

Koo, H.P., et al. 1981. 'Long term marital disruption, fertility and socio-economic achievement associated with adolescent child bearing'. Paper presented at the 109th Annual Meeting of the American Public Health Association, Los Angeles, California, 1 Nov.

Kuczynski, R.R. 1948. *Demographic survey of the British colonial empire*, Vol. 1, *West Africa*. London, Oxford University Press.

Ladipo, P. 1981. 'Developing women's cooperatives: An experiment in rural Nigeria', in Nelson, N. (ed.): *African women in the development process*. London, Frank Cass.

Lamptey, P., et al. 1978. 'An evaluation of male contraceptive acceptance in rural Ghana', in *Studies in Family Planning*, Vol. 9, No. 8, pp. 222–226.

Laslett, P. 1972. 'Introduction: The History of the Family', in Laslett, P. and Wall, R. (eds.) *Household and family in past time.* Cambridge, Cambridge University Press.

Lattes, Z.R.; Wainerman, C.H. 1979. *Data from censuses and household surveys for the analysis of female labour force in Latin America and the Caribbean: Appraisals of deficiencies and recommendations* for dealing with them. United Nations Economic and Social Commission, CEPAL; doc. no. E/CEPAL/L.206.

Leibenstein, H. 1977. 'Beyond economic man: Economics, politics and the population problem', in *Population and Development Review*, Vol. 3 No. 3.

Lele, U. 1975. *The design of rural development: Lessons from Africa*, World Bank Research Publication. Baltimore, Johns Hopkins University Press.

Linsenmeyer, D.A. 1976. 'Economic analysis of alternative strategies for the development of Sierra Leone marine fisheries'. Ph.D. thesis. East Lansing, Michigan State University.

Lloyd, P.C. 1955. 'The Yoruba lineage', in *Africa*, Vol. XXV, No. 3, July.

Longhurst, R. 1982. 'Resource allocation and the sexual divisions of labor: A case study of a Moslem Hausa village in Northern Niger', in Beneriá, L. (ed.): *The sexual division of labor in rural societies.* New York, Praeger.

Lucas, D. 1974. *Occupational, marriage and fertility among Nigerian women in Lagos*, Bulletin No. 3/001. Nigeria, University of Lagos.

——1976. 'The participation of women in the Nigerian labour force since the 1950s with particular reference to Lagos'. Ph.D. thesis. London School of Economics and Political Science.

Mabogunje, A.L. 1968. *Urbanization in Nigeria.* London, University of London Press.

MacCormack, C.P. 1982. 'Control of land, labor and capital in rural southern Sierra Leone', in Bay, E. (ed.): *Women and work in Africa.* Colorado, Westview Press.

Marciano, T,D, 1979. 'Male influences on fertility: Needs for research', in *The Family Coordinator*, Oct., Vol. 28, No. 4, pp. 561–568.

Marshall, G. 1970. 'In a world of women: Fieldwork in a Yoruba community', in Golde, P. (ed.): *Women in the field: Anthropological experiences* (Chicago, Aldine).

McGrath, P.L. 1979. *A perspective on adolescent fertility in developing countries: Policy and programme implications.* Arlington Medical Service Consultants Inc. for Office of Population, US Agency for International Development.

McNeil, P., et al. 1983. 'The women's centre in Jamaica: An innovative project for adolescent mothers', in *Studies in Family Planning*, May, Vol 14, No. 5.

McSweeney, B.G. 1979. 'Collection and analysis of data on rural women's time use', in *Studies in Family Planning*, Vol. 10, No. 11/12, pp. 379–383.

Meek, C.K. 1925. *The northern tribes of Nigeria.* London, Oxford University Press.

Mickelwait, D.R. (ed.). 1976. *Women in rural development: A survey of the roles of women in Ghana, Lesotho, Kenya, Nigeria, Paraguay and Peru.* Boulder, Westview Press.

Mondot-Bernard, J. 1981. *Satisfaction of food requirements and agricultural development*, Vol. III. *Results of surveys on workers' activities and calculation of energy expenditure.* Paris, Development Centre of the Organisation for Economic Cooperation and Development.

Mortimore, M.J.; Wilson, J. 1965. *Land and people in the Kano close-settled zone.* Occasional paper no. 1. Zaria, Department of Geography, Ahmadu Bello University.

Nelson, N. (ed.). 1981. *African women in the development process.* London, Frank Cass.

Nicolas, G. 1975. *Dynamique sociale et appréhension du monde au sein d'une société Hausa.* Paris, Institute d'Ethnologie, Muséum National d'Histoire Naturelle.

Norman, D.W. 1974. *An economic study of three villages in Zaria province. 1. Land and labour relationships.* Samaru Miscellaneous Paper No. 19. Zaria, IAR. Ahmadu Bello University; first published 1967.

Okediji, F.O., et al. 1976. 'The changing African family project: A report with special reference to the Nigerian segment', in *Studies in Family Planning*, No. 38, pp. 13–16.

Okonjo, K. 1979. 'Rural women's credit systems: A Nigerian example', in Zeidenstein, S. (ed.): 'Learning about rural women', in *Studies in Family Planning*, Nov./Dec., Vol. 10, No. 11.

Olufokunbi, B. 1981. 'Sources of credit to agricultural food marketers in Southwestern Nigeria', in *Savings and Development*, Nos. 2–3, pp. 189–202. Milan, Centre for Financial Assistance to African countries.

Olusanya, P.O. 1969. 'Rural–urban fertility differentials in Western Nigeria', in *Population Studies*, Nov., Vol. 23, No. 3.

Oppong, C. 1970. 'Conjugal power and resources: An urban African example', in *Journal of Marriage and the Family,* Vol. 32, No. 4.

——1973. *Growing up in Dagbon.* Accra, Ghana Publishing Corporation.

——(ed.). 1974. *Domestic rights and duties in southern Ghana,* Legon Family Research Papers No. 1 Legon, Institute of African Studies.

——(ed.) 1975: *Changing family studies.* Legon Family Research Papers No. 3. Legon, Institute of African Studies.

——1976. *Modernization and aspects of family change in Ghana: With particular reference to the effects of work.* Paper presented at a Conference in Gajereh, Iran.

——1977a. 'A note on chains of change in family systems and family size', in *Journal of Marriage and the Family*, August, pp. 615–621.

——1977b. 'The crumbling of high fertility supports in the persistence of high fertility: Population prospects in the Third World', in J.C. Caldwell (ed.): *The persistence of high fertility.* Canberra, Australian National University.

——1980. *A synopsis of seven roles and status of women: An outline of a conceptual and methodological approach.* Geneva, ILO; mimeographed World Employment Programme research working paper.

——1982a. 'Family structure and women's reproductive and productive roles: Some conceptual and methodological issues', in Anker, R. et al. (eds.): *Interactions between women's roles and population trends in the Third World.* London, Croom Helm.

——1982b. *Middle class African marriage.* London, George Allen and Unwin.

——(ed.). 1983. *Female and male in West Africa.* London, George Allen and Unwin.

——1983a. 'Women's roles, opportunity costs and fertility', in *Determinants of fertility in developing countries: A summary of knowledge*. Academic Press. US National Academy of Sciences. National Research Council Committee on Population and Demography, Panel on Fertility Determinants.

——1983b. *Paternal costs, role strain and fertility regulation: Some Ghanaian evidence*. Geneva, ILO; mimeographed World Employment Programme research working paper; restricted.

——1984. 'Familial roles and fertility: Some labour policy aspects', in *Fertility and family*, Proceedings of the Expert Group on Fertility and Family, New Delhi, 5–11 Jan. 1983. New York, United Nations.

——1985a. 'Some aspects of anthropological contributions to the study of fertility', in Farooq, G. and Simmons, G. (eds.): *Research and policy issues in the analysis of fertility behaviour in developing countries*. London, Macmillan.

——1985b. 'Marriage', in A. and J. Kuper (eds.): *A new social science encyclopedia*. London, Routledge.

Oppong, C.; Abu, K. 1984. *The changing maternal role of Ghanaian women: Impacts of education, migration and employment*. Geneva, ILO; mimeographed World Employment Programme research working paper; restricted. Forthcoming as *Seven roles of women: Impacts of education, migration and employment,* in Women, Work and Development series, Geneva, ILO.

Oppong, C.; Abu, K. 1985. *A handbook for data collection and analysis on seven roles and status of women*. Geneva, ILO.

Oppong, C.; Bleek, W. 1982. 'Economic models and having children: Some evidence from Kwahu, Ghana', in *Africa*, Vol. 52, No. 3.

Oppong, C.; Church, K. 1981. *A field guide to research on seven roles of women: Focussed biographies*. Geneva, ILO; mimeographed World Employment Programme research working paper.

Oppong, C., et al. 1975. 'Womanpower: Retrograde steps in Ghana', in *African Studies Review*, December, Vol. XVIII, No. 3, pp. 71–84.

Oppong, C., et al. (eds.). 1978. *Marriage, fertility and parenthood in West Africa*. Canberra, Australian National University Press.

Organization of African Unity (OAU). 1981. *Lagos Plan of Action for the economic development of Africa.'*

Oronsaye, A.U.; Ogbeide, O., Unuigbe, E. 1982. 'Pregnancy among schoolgirls in Nigeria', in *International Journal of Gynaecology and Obstetrics* (Limerick, Ireland), Vol. 20, pp. 409–12.

Orubuloye, T. 1977. 'High fertility and the rural economy: A study of Yoruba society in Western Nigeria', in Caldwell, J.C. (ed.): *The persistence of high fertility: Population prospects in the Third World*. Canberra, Australian National University Press.

——1981. *Abstinence as a method of birth control: Fertility and child-spacing practices among rural Yoruba women of Nigeria*. Canberra, Australian National University Press.

Osuntogun, A.; Akinbode, A. 1980. *Involvement of women in rural cooperatives in Nigeria and population education*. Nigeria, Faculty of Agriculture, University of Ife for FAO Revue.

Pauls, F. 1974. 'The adolescent and pregnancy in Zaire'. Paper presented at WHO Meeting on Pregnancy and Abortion in Adolescence, Geneva, June.

Pebley, A., et al. 1982. 'Age at first birth in nineteen countries', in *International Family Planning Perspectives*, Mar., Vol. 8, No. 1.

Pellow, D. 1974. 'Woman of Accra. A study of options'. Ph.D. dissertation. Department of Anthropology, Northwestern University.

——1977. *Women in Accra: Options for autonomy*. Algonac, Reference Publications.

Pittin. R. 1976. 'Social status and economic opportunities in urban Hausa society'. Paper presented at the Conference on Nigerian Women and Development in Relation to Changing Family Structure, University of Ibadan; mimeograph.

——1979. 'Marriage and alternative strategies: Career patterns of Hausa women in Katsina City'. Ph.D. thesis. University of London, SOAS.

——1982. *Documentation of women's work in Nigeria: Problems and solutions*. Geneva, ILO; mimeographed World Employment Programme research working paper; restricted.

——1984. 'Documentation and analysis of the invisible work of invisible women: A Nigerian case study', in *International Labour Review* (Geneva, ILO), Vol. 123, No. 4, July–Aug., pp. 473–490.

Pleck, J.H. 1977. 'The work family role system', in *Social Problems*, April, Vol. 24, No. 4, pp. 417–427.

Pool, D.I. 1970a. 'Ghana: The attitudes of urban males towards family size and family limitation', in *Studies in Family Planning,* Dec., Vol. 60, pp. 12–17.

——1970b. 'Social change and interest in family planning in Ghana: An exploratory analysis', in *Canadian Journal of African Studies*, Spring, Vol. 4, No. 2, pp. 207–227.

Porter, A. 1963. *Creoledom: A study of the development of Freetown society*. London, Oxford University Press.

Pradervand, P. 1980. 'People are precious: A critical look at the population control movement' in Bondestam, L. and Bergström, S. (eds.): *Poverty and population control*. London, Academic Press.

Presser, H.B. 1974. 'Early motherhood: Ignorance or bliss?', in *Family Planning Perspectives* (New York), Winter, Vol. 6, No. 1, pp. 8–14.

Prothero, R.M. 1956. 'The population census of Northern Nigeria 1952: Problems and results', in *Population Studies*, Vol. X, No. 2, pp. 166–183.

Rabin, S.A. 1981. *Personal income tax in Nigeria: Procedures and problems*. Ikeja, John West.

Rattray, R.S. 1923. *Ashanti*. Oxford, Clarendon Press.

——1927 *Religion and art in Ashanti*. Oxford, Clarendon Press.

——1929. *Ashanti law and constitution*. Oxford, Clarendon Press.

Reyna, S.P. 1972. 'Family planning, residence rules and preferences and the extended family among the Northwest Barma of Chad'. Paper presented at the Fifteenth Annual Meeting of the African Studies Association, Philadelphia, 8–11 Nov.; mimeograph.

——1975. 'Pronatalism and child labour', in Caldwell, J.C., et al. (eds.): *Population growth and socio-economic change in West Africa*, pp. 582–591. New York, Columbia University Press for the Population Council.

Reyna, S.P.; Bouquet, C. 1975. 'Chad', in Caldwell, J.C. et al. (eds.): *Population growth and socio-economic change in West Africa*, pp. 565–581. New York, Columbia University Press for the Population Council.

Richter, L. 1978. *Labour force information in developing countries*. Geneva, ILO.

Rogers, B. 1979. *The domestication of women*. New York, St Martin's Press.

Rosen, R.H.; Benson, T. 1982. 'The second class partner: The male role in family planning decisions', in Fox, G.L. (ed.): *The Childbearing decision.* Sage Publications.

Safilios-Rothschild, C. 1982a. 'Female power, autonomy and demographic change in the Third World', in Anker, R. et al. (eds.): *Interactions between women's roles and population trends in the Third World.* London, Croom Helm.

——1982b. 'A class and sex stratification model and its relevance for fertility trends in the developing world', in Hohn, C. and Mackensen, R. (eds.): *Determinants of fertility trends: Major theories and new directions for research.* Liège, IUSSP.

Sanday, P.R. 1974. 'Female status in the public domain', in Rosaldo, M. and Lamphere, L. (eds.): *Woman, culture and society.* Stanford, Stanford University Press.

Sarpong, P. 1977. *Girls' nubility rites in Ashanti.* Accra-Tema, Ghana Publishing Corporation.

Schildkrout, E. 1981. 'The employment of children in Kano', in Rodgers, G. and Standing, G. (eds.): *Child work, poverty and underdevelopment.* Geneva, ILO.

Simmons, E.B. 1975. 'The small-scale rural food-processing industry in Northern Nigeria', in *Food Research Institute Studies,* Vol. XIV, No. 2, pp. 147–161.

——1976a. *Calorie and protein intakes in three villages of Zaria Province, May 1970–July 1971.* Samaru Miscellaneous Paper No. 55. Zaria, IAR, Ahmadu Bello University.

——1976b. *Rural household expenditures in three villages of Zaria Province, May 1970–July 1971.* Samaru Miscellaneous Paper No. 56. Zaria, IAR, Ahmadu Bello University.

Singer, H.; Jolly, R. 1973. 'Unemployment in an African setting', in *International Labour Review,* Feb., Vol. 107, No. 2; reprinted in 'The pilot employment missions and lessons of the Kenya missions', IDS Communication III.

Smith, M. 1954. *Baba of Karo: A woman of the Muslim Hausa.* London, Faber and Faber.

Smith, M.G. 1955. *The economy of Hausa communities of Zaria,* Colonial Research Series No. 16. London, HMSO.

Spencer, D. 1974. 'The economics of traditional and semi-traditional systems of rice production in Sierra Leone', in *Proceedings of the WARDA seminar on socio-economic aspects of rice cultivation in West Africa.* Liberia, Monrovia.

——1976. *African women in agricultural development: A case study in Sierra Leone,* OLC Paper No. 4. Washington, DC, American Council on Education.

Spencer, D.; Byerlee, D. 1977. *Small farms in West Africa: A descriptive analysis of employment incomes and productivity in Sierra Leone.* East Lansing, Michigan State University.

Spitzer, L. 1974. *The Creoles of Sierra Leone: Responses to colonialism 1870–1945.* University of Wisconsin Press.

Standing, G. 1978. *Labour force participation and development.* Geneva, ILO.

——1983. 'Fertility and women's work activity', in *Determinants of fertility in developing countries: A summary of knowledge.* Washington, DC, National Research Council.

Starrett, L. 1981. *The National Council of Women's Societies of Nigeria: A brief history 1958–1981,* mimeograph.

Steel, W. 1981. 'Female and small-scale employment under modernisation in Ghana', in *Economic Development and Cultural Change,* Vol. 30, No. 1, Oct.

Stewart, J.B. 1982. 'Some factors determining the work effort of single black women', in *Review of Social Economy*, Apr., Vol. XL, No. 1.

Stokes, B. 1980. *Men and family planning*, Worldwatch Paper No, 41. Washington, DC, Worldwatch Institute.

Stone, L. 1977. *The family, sex and marriage in England 1500-1800*. London, Harper and Row.

Szalai, A. 1975. *The situation of women in the light of contemporary time-budget research*. Background paper, UN Conference of the International Women's. Year, Mexico City, doc. no. E/CONF.66/BP/6.

Umoh, O.E. 1972. 'Demographic statistics in Nigeria', in Ominde, S.H. and Ejiogu, C.N. (eds.): *Population growth and economic development in Africa*. New York, Population Council.

——1979. 'Capital formation', in Olaluku, F.A. et al. (eds.): *The structure of the Nigerian economy*. London, Macmillan.

United Nations. 1975a. *Declaration of Mexico plans of action*. World Conference of the International Women's Year, Dec. New York.

——1981. *Population and economic development in Nigeria in the nineteen-eighties*. New York.

United Nations Economic Commission for Africa (UNECA). 1975. *The role of women in African development*. Addis Ababa; document no. E/CON.66/BP/8, 10 Apr.

——1977. *The new international economic order: What roles for women?*, presented at the Regional Conference on the implementation of National, Regional and World Plans of Action for the Integration of Women in Development, Nouakchott, Mauritania. Addis Ababa; document no. E/CN.14/ATRCW/77/WD3, 31 Aug.

UNESCO, Regional Office for Education in Africa, 1971. *Population education development in Africa south of the Sahara*, Meeting of Experts, 29 Nov.–4 Dec., Dakar, Senegal.

United Nations Fund for Population Activities (UNFPA). 1978a. *Population education*, Population profiles II. New York, UNFPA.

——1978b. *Mali. Report of mission on needs assessment for population assistance*, Report No. 8. New York, UNFPA.

——1979. *Mauritania. Report of mission on needs assessment for population assistance*, Report no. 17. New York, UNFPA.

——1980. *Nigeria. Report of mission on needs assessment for population assistance*, Report No. 38. New York, UNFPA.

——1984. *Sierra Leone. Report of mission on needs assessment for population assistance*, Report No. 66. New York, UNFPA.

USAID. 1975. *Women in national development in Ghana*. Accra; mimeograph.

Uyanga, J. 1980. 'The value of children and child-bearing in rural south-eastern Nigeria', in *Rural Africana*, Spring, No. 7, pp. 37–54.

Vercruijsse, E.V.W., et al. 1974. 'Composition of households in some Fanti communities', in Oppong, C. (ed.): *Domestic rights and duties in Southern Ghana*. Legon Family Research Papers No. 1, pp. 35–56. Legon, Institute of African Studies.

Wallace, C.C. 1978a. *Rural development through irrigation: Studies in a town on the Kano River Project*. Zaria, Centre for Social and Economic Research, Ahmadu Bello University; mimeograph.

——1978b. 'The concept of Gandu: How useful is it in understanding labour relations in rural Hausa society?', in *Savanna*, Vol. 7, No. 2, pp. 137–150.

Ware, H. 1975. 'The limits of acceptable family size in Western Nigeria', in *Journal of Biosocial Science*, Vol. 7, pp. 273–296.

——1983. 'Female and male life cycles', in Oppong, C. (ed.): *Female and male in West Africa*. London, George Allen and Unwin.

Warren, D.M. 1974. 'Disease, medicine, and religion among the Techiman-Bono of Ghana: A study of culture change'. Ph.D. thesis. Indiana, Indiana University.

Waterson, T. 1982. 'What causes kwashiorkor in the older child?', in *Journal of Tropical Pediatrics*, June, Vol. 28, No. 3, pp. 132–34.

Woodford-Berger, P. 1981. 'Women in houses: The organization of residence and work in rural Ghana', in *Antropologiska Studier* (Stockholm), Nos. 30–31, pp. 3–35.

World Health Organisation (WHO). 1980. *Report of a WHO meeting on adolescent sexuality and reproductive health: Educational and service aspects*. Mexico City, 28 Apr.–2 May; doc. no. MCH/RHA/81.1.

Youssef, N.; Hetler, C. 1984. *Rural households headed by women: A priority concern for development*. Geneva, ILO.

Index

Numbers in italics refer to tables